CROSSBILL GUIDES

Southern Portugal

From Lisbon to the Algarve

Crossbill Guides: Southern Portugal – From Lisbon to the Algarve
First print: 2018
Second print: 2024

Initiative, text and research: Dirk Hilbers, Kees Woutersen
Editing: John Cantelo, Brian Clews, Cees Hilbers, Riet Hilbers,
Kim Lotterman, Gino Smeulders, Albert Vliegenthart
Illustrations: Horst Wolter
Maps: Constant Swinkels
Type and image setting: Oscar Lourens
Print: ORO grafic projectmanagement / PNB Letland

ISBN 978-94-91648-30-4

This book is made with FSC-certified paper. The printing process is CO_2-neutral through carbon-offsetting. To compensate for the CO_2-emissions of the printing processes, we've invested in a reafforestation project plus nature conservation in Europe. For more information, scan the qr-code. You can find the certificate of the carbon-offset on our website under 'downloads' on the Southern Portugal guidebook page.

Print product
climate contribution
ClimatePartner.com/20752-2402-1001

The Crossbill Guides Foundation and its authors have done their utmost to provide accurate and current information and describe only routes, trails and tracks that are safe to explore. However, things do change and readers are strongly urged to check locally for current conditions and for any changes in circumstances. Neither the Crossbill Guides Foundation nor its authors or publishers can accept responsibillity for any loss, injury or inconveniences sustained by readers as a result of the information provided in this guide.

Published by Crossbill Guides in association with KNNV Publishing.

KNNV Publishing   SAXIFRAGA foundation

www.crossbillguides.org
www.knnvpublishing.nl
www.saxifraga.nl

CROSSBILL
GUIDES
FOUNDATION

This guidebook is a product of the non-profit foundation Crossbill Guides. By publishing these books we want to introduce more people to the joys of Europe's beautiful natural heritage and to increase the understanding of the ecological values that underlie conservation efforts. Most of this heritage is protected for ecological reasons and we want to provide insight into these reasons to the public at large. By doing so we hope that more people support the ideas behind nature conservation.

For more information about us and our guides you can visit our website at:

WWW.CROSSBILLGUIDES.ORG

4

Highlights of Southern Portugal

1 Go birdwatching in the Alentejo, where steppe birds like bustards and sandgrouse share their home with the shrikes, Hoopoes, Bee-eaters and Azure-winged Magpies of the montado.

2 Go hiking along the shore of the Algarve with its beautiful, honey-coloured cliffs.

3 Explore the bays of Sado and Tejo, where thousands of shorebirds congregate and where you can combine field trips with sightseeing in historic Lisbon and Setúbal.

4 Go hiking in the lovely hills of the Serra da Arrábida or the Algarve, where orchids flower in profusion and butterflies are in abundance.

5 Climb the 'balcony of the Algarve', the Serra de Monchique, with its remnants of old cork oak forests.

6 Enjoy Cabo São Vicente and the Costa Vicentina, where the dune and clifftop flora is rich in endemic wildflowers.

7 Cruise along the hidden inland rivers – little known and little visited, but with a good number of rare dragonflies, butterflies and wildflowers.

8 Visit the Cabos São Vicente and Espichel to watch seabirds like Gannets, terns, skuas, shearwaters, etc. passing offshore. Better still, get closer by adding a whale watching boat trip to your itinerary.

6

 boat trip or ferry crossing

 car route

 bicycle route

 walking route

 beautiful scenery

 interesting history

interesting geology

About this guide

This guide is meant for all those who enjoy being in and learning about nature, whether you already know all about it or not. It is set up a little differently from most guides. We focus on explaining the natural and ecological features of an area rather than merely describing the site. We choose this approach because the nature of an area is more interesting, enjoyable and valuable when seen in the context of its complex relationships. The interplay of different species with each other and with their environment is simply mind-blowing. The clever tricks and gimmicks that are put to use to beat life's challenges are as fascinating as they are countless.

Take our namesake the Crossbill: at first glance it's just a big finch with an awkward bill. But there is more to the Crossbill than meets the eye. This bill is beautifully adapted for life in coniferous forests. It is used like a scissor to cut open pinecones and eat the seeds that are unobtainable for other birds. In the Scandinavian countries where pine and spruce take up the greater part of the forests, several Crossbill species have each managed to answer two of life's most pressing questions: how to get food and how to avoid direct competition. By evolving crossed bills, each differing subtly, they have secured a monopoly of the seeds produced by cones of varying sizes. So complex is this relationship that scientists are still debating exactly how many different species of Crossbill actually exist. Now this should heighten the appreciation of what at first glance was merely a plumb red bird with a beak that doesn't seem to fit properly. Once its interrelationships are seen, nature comes alive, wherever you are.

To some, impressed by the "virtual" familiarity that television has granted to the wilderness of the Amazon, the vastness of the Serengeti or the sublimity of Yellowstone, European nature may seem a puny surrogate, good merely for the casual stroll. In short, the argument seems to be that if you haven't seen some impressive predator, be it a Jaguar, Lion or Grizzly Bear, then you haven't seen the "real thing". Nonsense, of course.

But where to go? And how? What is there to see? That is where this guide comes in. We describe the how, the why, the when, the where and the how come of Europe's most beautiful areas. In clear and accessible language, we explain the nature of southern Portugal and refer extensively to routes where the area's features can be observed best. We try to make southern Portugal come alive. We hope that we succeed.

How to use this guide

This guidebook contains a descriptive and a practical section.
The descriptive part comes first and gives you insight into the most strik-ing and interesting natural features of the area. It provides an understand-ing of what you will see when you go out exploring. The descriptive part consists of a landscape section (marked with a red bar), describing the habitats, the history and the landscape in general, and of a flora and fauna section (marked with a green bar), which discusses the plants and animals that occur in the region.

The second part offers the practical information (marked with a purple bar). A series of routes (walks) is carefully selected to give you a good fla-vour of all the habitats, flora and fauna that southern Portugal has to offer. At the start of each route description, a number of icons give a quick over-view of the characteristics of each route. These icons are explained in the margin of this page. The final part of the book (marked with blue squares) provides some basic tourist information and some tips on finding plants, birds and other animals.

There is no need to read the book from cover to cover. Instead, each small chapter stands on its own and refers to the routes most suitable for view-ing the particular features described in it. Conversely, descriptions of each route refer to the chapters that explain more in depth the most typical features that can be seen along the way.

We have tried to keep the number of technical terms to a minimum. If us-ing one is unavoidable, we explain it in the glossary at the end of the guide. There we have also included a list of all the mentioned plant and animal spe-cies, with their scientific names and translations into German and Dutch.

Some species names have an asterix (*) following them. This indicates that there is no official English name for this species and that we have taken the liberty of coining one. For the sake of readability we have decided to translate the scientific name, or, when this made no sense, we gave a name that best describes the species' appearance or distribution. Please note that we do not want to claim these as the official names. We merely want to make the text easier to follow for those not familiar with scientific names. When a new vernacular name was invented, we've also added the scientific name.

An overview of the area described in this book is given on the map on page 12. For your convenience we have also turned the inner side of the back flap into a map of the area indicating all the described routes. Descriptions in the explanatory text refer to these routes.

interesting flora

interesting invertebrate life

interesting reptile and amphibian life

interesting mammals

interesting birdlife

site for snorkelling

interesting for whales and dolphins

visualising the ecological contexts described in this guide

8

Table of contents

List of Text boxes

LANDSCAPE

The 'Golden Coast' of the Algarve receives (more than) its share of sun-seekers, golfers and pensionados. Further north, the beautiful town of Lisbon deservedly attracts city-trippers. However, the land between the capital and the Algarve is given surprisingly little attention. This is undeserved, as it is a superb region for birders and naturalists.

The huge region of the Alentejo is one of the least developed parts of Europe. This is mainly because of its poor soils, which is also the reason why nature is still so unspoilt. You'll travel through endless *montados*, woodlands of Holm and Cork Oak with pastures and Mediterranean scrub. There are undulating plains with steppes and fields with some of the highest densities of steppe birds in Europe. Beautiful river valleys with rocky outcrops meander through the undulating landscape where hilltops and low sierras stand out. In the ancient villages, the casual visitor may feel himself thrown back in time 50 years or more.

Even in the built-up Algarve, nature isn't far away. There are wildflower-rich limestone hills just a few kilometres inland, while the famous Cape St. Vincent (Cabo São Vicente) is among the great wildflower hotspots of the Iberian Peninsula. While the sun worshippers are sizzling on the beaches in the south, the nearby and still wild Costa Vicentina is largely forgotten. On this impressive coast, small beaches alternate with rock cliffs and dunes at the mouths of crystal clear, clean rivers. Behind the coasts are characteristic lagoons, marshland and estuaries of international significance.

Further north, not far from Lisbon, the little-known Cabo Espichel is almost as impressive as Cape St. Vincent, while the nearby Serra da Arrábida is a scenic hotspot and a highlight for birds and wildflowers. Few naturalists know the two large estuaries near Lisbon, where masses of waders stop on migration two times a year.

This guide will introduce you to all these superb landscapes and help you to discover its flora and fauna.

Springtime in southern Portugal is a guaranteed flower festival. Wild species mix fluently with these Yellow Lupins, which are sown to improve the soil.

12

Geographical overview

This Crossbill Guide covers the regions of Algarve, Baixo Alentejo and Lisbon-Setúbal. These administrative districts (or provinces) were renamed after their main towns: Faro, Beja and Setúbal respectively, but in this book we will use the Algarve, the Alentejo and Setúbal. Together they are roughly 110 x 180 km, which is about the same size as Wales and about half the size of the Netherlands. The area is for the most part very sparsely populated. Baixo Alentejo and Algarve together have no more than 630,000 permanent inhabitants (2022 figures), of which the lion's share live on the south coast. In contrast, the Lisbon and Setúbal area is, with approximately 3.5 million inhabitants, among the most densely populated area in Europe.

From the perspective of a visiting naturalist, southern Portugal as defined in this book, has four distinct regions:

The Setúbal-Lisbon area

The region around these two large cities and the many commuter towns that lie in the area, is the most diverse of the four regions of southern

Portugal. Two huge, shallow bays dominate the landscape – the estuaries of the Tagus and Sado rivers. Both bays and their surrounding wetlands are of unsurpassed importance for (migrating) birds.

In spite of these large bays, the landscape of this region is quite hilly. In particular the coast west of Setúbal is dominated by cliffs and rocky mountains (the Serra da Arrábida) which is one of the country's hotspots for flora and wildlife. Of similar importance are the sand dunes and the deserted beach of the Tróia Peninsula and further south.

There are few places in Europe where it is this easy to combine a city trip, the beach and fine hiking and birdwatching in a small area.

The Baixo Alentejo

Enter the Baixo Alentejo from the west coast and you will encounter rolling fields with wide views. Most of it consists of extensive areas of lightly wooded pastures and cereal fields. With only 152.000 inhabitants, this huge area is thinly populated. With its endless Holm and Cork Oak *montado* woodlands and cistus scrubs, the Alentejo has a special atmosphere. A key landscape feature is the broad Guadiana river which flows in from the east, then abruptly turns south, forming much of the border with Spain before reaching the Atlantic. There are vast steppe-like plains near Castro Verde and cereal fields around Beja.

The Algarve

The pretty, sandstone cliffs and beautiful beaches are what come to mind when one thinks of the Algarve. But the region has a lot more. Between the tourist towns and golf courses, there is plenty to see. The great attraction is the mixture of marshes and the many tidal lagoons, combined with the quiet, rural hinterland with its lovely limestone and granite hills and mountains a bit further inland. The region has a scenically spectacular coastline which is superb for birdwatchers, while the flora inland is, at least in early spring, not to be missed!

Costa Vicentina and Serra da Arrábida – the southwest coast

The southwest coast is different from the rest. The Costa Vicentina is a narrow strip along a coast with impressive sea cliffs, which culminate

The limestone cliffs of Serra da Arrábida.

at its southwestern point, the famous Cape St. Vincent. This is one of the most important areas of Portugal from a botanical perspective. Costa Vicentina's wall of cliffs is interrupted by small beaches and dunes at the estuaries of a series of rivers that originate from the nearby Serra de Monchique.

Together with these cliffs, the river valleys and estuaries are Costa Vicentina's finest characteristics. From the coast it is only 20 km to the Serra de Monchique which, at 902 metres, is the balcony of the Algarve. The unique climate supports a special ecosystem with an attractive flora and fauna.

14

Geology

Even though the relief of southern Portugal is not nearly as extreme as that of northern Portugal or adjacent Andalucía, its geology is highly varied. A walk along the west coast is enough to see the rapid succession of rock types, many of which have impressive, folded strata and beautiful stacks and arches. Some areas are famous for their fossils, including spectacular dinosaur footprints (route 4). The large numbers of old zinc, gold and copper mines in the interior indicate a rich Earth history inland as well.

The geology of southern Portugal consists of three parts: the interior (in the Algarve often referred to as *Serra*) that largely consists of very old, felsic bedrock (felsic meaning rich in feldspar and quartz), then a belt of limestone of varying width, (known in the Algarve as the *Barrocal*) and finally the coastal strip, with a mixture of sandstone and limestone cliffs and sedimentary soils (sand and clay), deposited in the form of dunes with intervening lagunas – the *Littoral*.

The Serra

The interior part of the Algarve consists of a huge area of shales and schists of a mostly felsic nature, which stretches out further north into the Alentejo and beyond. Much of this bedrock is extremely old, dating back to the Variscan or Hercynian orogeny (400-300 million years ago).

At that time, the Earth's landmass was clustered in a single giant continent: Pangea. A massive mountain range ran through Pangea, which broke into two as the mother continent separated into America and Eurasia. Part of the Hercynian range remained in what is now America, forming the Appalachians. Its European counterpart is fragmented and broken, stretching from southern Portugal over western Spain to the Ardennes.

The larger part of southern Portugal is covered by these Variscan mountains, which have eroded into the gentle hills that cover the northern two-thirds of the Algarve and much of the Alentejo. Soils in this region are poor and unproductive, which is reflected in the land use: extensive animal husbandry in open woodlands (*montados*) is the only type of land use possible in this area.

Overall, the topography of the Serra is gentle. Only in the southwest, the land is more hilly – a reflection of age-old erosion of rivers that snaked their way to the sea. In the Serra, solid rock is never very deep underneath the surface. In places, the land is heavily eroded and pointy rocks peak out of the ground. The rockiest parts are in the river valleys, where, over millions of years, the water has carved out wide valleys with rocky slopes.

The Barrocal, Monchique and the interior basins

The separation of the continents was not a clean break. Fracture zones were many and smaller continents or islands drifted on small plates into the new and widening ocean. One such fragment re-joined the Iberian landmass and created what geologists call the *southern Portuguese zone*. Here, the land that collided with the continent pushed up the intervening seabeds, which are now visible as calcareous basins and hills.

In the Algarve, this zone is known as the Barrocal, a fairly thin, unbroken line, roughly north of the A22 motorway. Further northwest, limestone ranges of the same Devonian-Jurassic origin are found near Setúbal and Lisbon, most notably the Serra da Arrábida. Deeper inland, near Beja for

The 'Golden Coast' of the Algarve: heavily eroded sandstone, with arcs, caves, stacks and other typical geological features of cliff coasts. Best enjoyed in the warm evening light outside the tourist season.

example, several smaller basins were pushed up, leaving smaller limestone pockets here as well.

Although the Barrocal hills are no higher than the Serra, the limestone rocks are more precipitous. In this area, there are several steep cliffs and table mountains. The biggest difference between the Serra and the Barrocal is not the topography, though. It is the soil. In the Barrocal and Serra da Arrábida, the soil is basic, instead of acidic, and much richer in nutrients. In more level areas, fruit trees are grown, especially oranges and Carob Trees.

The ecology of the limestone mountains is very different from that of the Serra. For example, the Barrocal and Serra da Arrábida is the hotspot for orchids and butterflies – a direct result of the limestone bedrock.

The tectonic movement did more than just pushing up calcareous marine sediments. The collision increased the pressure underground, reshaping and displacing the bedrock and creating cracks and fault lines. Locally, this resulted in volcanic activity which in turn, for instance near the Serra de Monchique, produced a large outcrop of granite rock. These large, rounded boulders of solidified magma are rich in iron and acidic by nature. This rock type, together with the height and humidity that comes with it, creates yet another landscape; one where cork oak forests and broom scrub are the dominant features. The great Lisbon earthquake of 1755 is testimony that the collision process and the resultant pressures, which cause earthquakes, is not something of the distant past.

The fault lines run deep inland and along these lines, a variety of rock types were able to form, containing important ores, like iron, lead, copper, silver, gold and pyrite. This explains the many old (and still active) mines in the interior Alentejo.

The Littoral

The geologically most diverse region is the Littoral. It is also the part with the most spectacular topography.

Coastal cliffs are the Littoral's main feature, but by no means its only one. Some of the most spectacular tombolos, dunes, beaches and tidal mudflats are to be found here. More about that anon.

The golden, sandstone cliffs of the Algarve are the region's hallmark. They are what sets the region apart from any other sunny beach in Europe. Rock arches and stacks form a major tourist attraction and rightly so. They are beautiful even when they are packed with people (as the tourist resorts are mostly situated on top of the cliff, you can still feel 'away from it all' when you take a walk along the beach below the cliffs).

The cliffs of the Algarve are the classic example of a landscape created by coastal erosion. The continuous and often relentless assault of the waves on the lower cliffs creates shallow caves. The water's erosive force is strongest exploiting the cracks in the rock. In such narrow places, the striking waves compress the air inside, which makes erosion much more forceful. As cracks deepen, the water penetrates and erodes further – this is how the deeper cave systems, the arches and the maze of sea water between the stacks is formed.

Both cliffs and islands are of major ecological importance. Several plant species are only found here, while birds find the islands, isolated as they are from terrestrial predators, important breeding sites. Cormorants, Shags, Yellow-legged Gulls and even White Storks and Cattle Egrets build their colonies on such islands.

Perhaps even more spectacular are the cliffs on the Costa Vicentina, where various types of sandstones, dolomites, marls and clays, often packed on top of each other, create a fascinating series of cliffs. Their origin is the same collision of plates that created the Barrocal with the ocean's weathering forces eroding the hills into seaside cliffs. The cliff coast alternates with flat coastal plains, where sedimentation rather than erosion has the upper hand. The most important beaches and salt marshes are found in the eastern Algarve and the stretch between Vila Nova de Milfontes and Setúbal on the west coast. Elsewhere, there are smaller areas of dunes and saltmarsh where rivers flow into the ocean (e.g. near Aljezur and Odeceixe; routes 22 and 23).

Geological formations are at their most diverse and spectacular on the Costa Vicentina – the wild, deserted southwest coast of Portugal.

Over much of this area, sand dunes dominate the coastline. In places they overlie older, fossilised dunes and low cliffs (e.g. at Aljezur and Cabo Sardão; site H on page 215) resulting in an interesting mix of cliffs and dunes, with the latter often on top of the former.

The strong currents and action of the waves has given southern and western Portugal some of the finest white beaches of the whole of Europe. Interestingly, many of them have hardly been developed. The whole area between the Tróia Peninsula and Sines sees few visitors and has little development.

Geologically, these lowlands have a few curiosities. From north to south, these are the 14 km long tombolo of the Tróia Peninsula, where the joint action of the ocean and the river has thrown up this high and narrow strip of sand. Further south, this process repeats itself in many other estuaries, such as at Villa Nova de Milfontes, Odeceixe, Amoreira, Aljezur and Bordeira. In all of these estuaries, large, natural sand dunes almost entirely clog the mouth of the river leaving only a small outlet. Behind the dunes lies a splendid salt marsh that becomes brackish and eventually fresh as you move inland. Such natural river mouths have become quite rare in Europe, but are still intact in southern Portugal – a geological as well as an ecological delight (see illustration below).

The final geological attraction is the Ria Formosa – a maze of creeks behind a row of sandy islands, which is the result of several small rivers that pour into the ocean parallel to one another. The rivers have deposited clay, while the ocean threw up a row of dunes, which both sea and river punctuated at regular intervals. The Ria Formosa is somewhat like a miniature version of the Wadden Sea in the Netherlands, Germany and Denmark.

The rivers of the southern and western Algarve have a largely intact hydrology. They typically have dunes and a small outlet at sea, followed by a wide saline lagoon with sand and saltmarsh. Further upstream, there is a zone where fresh riverwater and salt sea water mix, recognisable by the lines of tamarisk. Further up, the water is fresh and reeds and alder forest line the banks. This illustration is roughly based on the Aljezur river (route 22).

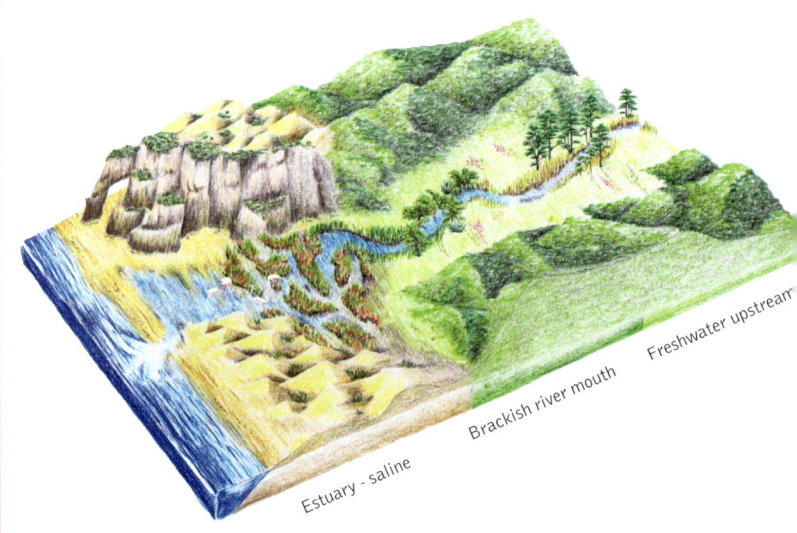

Estuary - saline

Brackish river mouth

Freshwater upstream

Climate

Portugal is the only Mediterranean country that is not a Mediterranean country. Climatically, it is akin to Spain, southern France, Greece and the other countries around the Mediterranean Sea, but Portugal only borders the Atlantic Ocean, not the Mediterranean Sea. It is the climate and affiliated ecology that justifies this Mediterranean classification.

Southern Portugal is characterised by short, mild and wet winters and long, hot and dry summers. Setúbal on the west coast and the Baixo Alentejo inland have a very similar climate. The Algarve on the south coast has higher average temperatures in winter, but the summer maximums are lower. Algarve receives more rain than Setúbal and the Alentejo during the winter months, but less so in spring. The whole area experiences strong winds, especially, of course, the coastal areas, which have only very few wind-free days.

From February onwards temperatures rise steadily until reaching their maximum in July. Average daily maximum temperatures in January, the coldest month, are around 12 °C in Lisbon and Beja and 16 °C in Faro. Summer temperatures peak in July, with 32 °C in Lisbon and Beja and 'only' 28 °C in Faro.

Southern Portugal has more rain and fewer dry days than neighbouring Spain. The rains usually start at the end of October and may last until April in the Algarve and May in Setúbal and Beja. The wettest month is December with 82 mm in Lisbon and Beja and 96 mm in Faro (though precipitation fluctuates strongly between years). The driest month is July with around 5 mm all over the area.

When the rain clouds come in it is always from the ocean, from the south, the west or the northwest. When they come from the northwest, they will not usually reach the Algarve coast. Winter rains can be torrential, especially in the Algarve where heavy rains can fill small rivers in minutes. Snow is extremely rare in southern Portugal. Only the highest mountain, Fóia (902 m), has a bit of snow – once every decade or so.

The sea surface temperature between Lisbon and the Algarve varies from 14–16 °C to 20-23 °C in August.

Average precipitation of southern Portugal. Note how much wetter the Serra de Monchique is compared to its surroundings.

	< 400 mm
	400 - 500 mm
	500 - 600 mm
	600 - 700mm
	700 - 800 mm
	800 - 1000 mm
	1000 - 1200 mm and over 1200 mm

Habitats

What are the ingredients of the perfect wildlife holiday? Whilst this will differ from person to person, beautiful landscapes and a rich flora and fauna are likely to be key ingredients. And in order to get that, an area with a high diversity of intact, outstanding habitats is what you need. And it is what you get in southern Portugal.

Typical of this region is the combination of extensive areas of superb intact steppes and woodlands in the interior, and a swift succession of many small natural areas at the coast that are radically different from one another.

In the following chapters, we describe each of the major habitats of southern Portugal. The steppes are discussed on page 43 and the open oak woodlands (called *montados*) and the scrublands (or *matos*) on page 38. Both these extensive ecosystems are complemented by intact and,

Sea and coastal marshes (p. 22) Cliff coast (p. 29) Limestone hills (p. 41) Volcanic out (Monc

for the most part seasonal river valleys which are the subject of the chapter on page 33.

Closer to the south coast, the landscape changes subtly – the *montados* make way for orchards, the *matos* change in species composition – a sure sign you've arrived at the limestone coastal zone.

The actual coastline is radically different. There are estuaries, salt-marshes and salt pans near Lisbon, Setúbal and in various places on the Algarve's southern coast, which are discussed on page 22. A very different ecosystem is that of the coastal headlands and dunes, which are often situated close to the salt marshes and make the south Portuguese coast so diverse. These are described on page 29.

The final habitat discussed in detail covers only a very small area in the region, yet one that is of vital importance both for nature and for people: freshwater marshes. They are found both at the coast and inland, and are described on page 33.

Cross-section through the habitats of southern Portugal.

Montados (p. 38)   Steppes (p. 43)   Montados (p. 38)   Riverine habitat (p. 36)   Montados (p. 38)

Estuaries, saltmarsh and saltpans

> Routes 1, 2, 3, 6, 13, 14, 15 19, 20 and 22 visit the estuaries, saltmarshes and saltpans of southern Portugal. Sites B, C, D and G on pages 135 to 139 and site C on page 169 are also set in this environment.

There is a large number of river estuaries on the coast of southern Portugal. These shallow bodies of brackish water are hotspots for birds.

Both river and sea chip in to create estuary habitats. Incursions from the sea bring in salt water and nutrients, which the rivers match with fresh water and even more nutrients. No wonder that estuaries are such productive and rich habitats.

The currents of both seawater and river water vary significantly, which makes the estuary ecosystem very dynamic. Seawater pours in when the tide rises; twice a day like clockwork. The height of the tide depends on the position of the moon and the force and direction of the wind. Hence there are times when the sea invades the bays with an unstoppable force, and others when the ocean's incursions are rather modest.

In a dry country like Portugal, rivers carry a steady flow of water only in the winter and spring. During the summer the river water input is negligible on small rivers

On the Tejo and Sado bays and the southern Algarve are large areas of tidal mudflats (bottom). Here, in the salt marsh in spring, the large flowers of the Yellow Cistanche are a conspicuous sight. It is a parasitic plant that taps into the roots of Sea Purslane (top).

and much reduced on larger ones so, in summer and autumn, the water in estuaries is much more saline. However, in winter, especially after periods of steady rainfall, the rivers pour fresh water out into the estuary with force, 'refreshing' it during the winter and early spring. So, all in all, there is a variable gradient from saline to fresh as you proceed deeper upstream, but this transition area lies deeper inland during the summer. Salt is an important ecological player, as it is already in low concentrations toxic to most plants. Along the high tide line there are salt-tolerant plants, like seablites, sea-lavenders, rushes, tamarisks and the Mediterranean bush Limoniastrum (p. 28). These all have thick, leathery leaves and branches to store fresh water and glands that excrete salt – necessary adaptations to survive in this habitat. Interestingly, there are no trees that survive in this saline soil. While in the tropics, mangrove forests would grow in these conditions, no such trees survive in the temperate regions. It is still a puzzle why mangroves are so strictly tropical, but they are and in Europe the saltmarsh is naturally open. Only tamarisks tolerate a fair amount of salt.

The soils of an estuary consist of sand or mud. Sand is blown by the ocean winds and pushed into the estuary. The rivers themselves transport mud that is deposited in the river mouth when the flow stagnates. Intertidal flats of one or both of the materials arise. In normal conditions, these flats slowly grow in extent, but are washed away just as easily during storms or by sudden discharges of the river. Sometimes, the border between sand and mud is a sharp line, such as in the Sado estuary. That of the Tagus in contrast, consists mainly of mud or a mix-

The small Aljezur river has an almost completely natural estuary (route 21).

ture of the two. The Ria Formosa is fed by several small rivers and has again a sandy bed.

So, in short, soil type and salinity is what drives the estuary ecosystem. Salt marshes are the dominant feature around the lower part of the estuaries, while freshwater habitats (mostly rice paddies, fields and a few reedy areas) are found upstream, but there are many 'shades of grey' between these two extremes.

The lower marshes are flooded every high tide and exposed at every low tide. High marshes are only flooded on higher than average tides and can extend well into land. As the soil retains a high level of salt, the typical salt tolerant vegetation still occurs here. Due to the strong currents of the ocean and seasonally feeble flow of fresh water, the tidal flow is pushed far up the Portuguese rivers. In some (e.g. Odeleite River), the effect of salt is visible as far as 70 km inland! As salt water is heavier than fresh water, tidal forces push it inland near the bottom of the river while near the surface the water can be 100% fresh.

Further inland, the salt marshes give way to a 'brackish' vegetation of rushes and bulrushes and finally to freshwater marshes and riverine vegetation. This rather rare habitat in Portugal is described on page 34-36 and illustrated on page 18.

Saltpans

On several places in the saltmarsh, salinas were made to extract salt from seawater. With a long coastline, strong winds and high temperatures during summer, southern Portugal has favourable conditions for the production of salt. In ancient times, salt was a rare and valuable commodity (the term 'salary' comes from salt, as the Roman soldiers were paid their wages in cakes of salt). Today, salt is produced on a more industrial scale, but still in the same place. In salt marshes all along the coast, there are both active and abandoned salinas. The Sado and Tagus

Looking for clams on the mudflats during low tide.

Tidal differences

The process of rising and falling between high and low tide takes several hours and during this time, the water level rises and drops between 2 and 3 metres. The tidal range on the Algarve and Lisbon Coasts is significant. There are also important differences between locations even those that are not far apart.

For both birds and birdwatchers the tide is important. At high tide, birds congregate at high tide roosts, that are found in the higher parts of the bay. Roosting birds can be easier to observe but take care not to disturb them. A rising tide will also drive birds towards an observer on the coast so aim to arrive an hour or two before high tide. The golden coast is best enjoyed during low tide. The height and time the flood peaks, varies from day to day, but is very predictable. So consult a tide time table (e.g. **www.tide-forecast.com** or one of several of the free tide apps) to plan your estuary visits.

The high tide line shows the large ebb and flow fluctuations on the Algarve south coast.

estuaries and Ria Formosa have hundreds of them, although just a few are still in use (e.g. route 15).

Salinas attract massive numbers of waders that feed in the food-rich briny water. The bunds that line the basins are usually constructed from nearby, non-saline soils and form grids of 'fresh' habitat that overlies the salt flats. In many places in the Algarve you can find a great flora on those banks, including many orchids (see page 66).

The Tagus Estuary

The Tagus estuary (routes 1 and 2) is, at 32,000 hectares, the largest wetland of Portugal and one of the largest estuaries in Europe. The upstream limit of the saline water reaches Vila Franca de Xira, 50 km from the estuary mouth. The tidal influence on water levels is felt even further upstream, extending to 80 km inland.

The Tagus bay is almost nowhere deeper than 10 m at low tide. The ebb and flow difference is about 4.5 m. and at low tide, vast areas of mudflats are exposed, which are much appreciated by birds. Towards the edges of the bay, there are lagoons, inlets, salt marshes, saltpans and, towards the north where the river pours into the bay, there are large reedbeds, rice-fields, arable fields and pasturelands.

The value of the Tagus Estuary from an ecological perspective is mostly found in the huge numbers of wintering birds, which peak each year at around 120,000 individuals. It is also an important stopover site for birds on migration. The estuary itself is especially important for wintering Avocet (up to 25% of the European population) and Black-tailed Godwit (thousands) plus Bluethroat in the surrounding wetlands and other habitats. On migration the numbers of waders are in the tens of thousands (although a high turnover rate means far more birds may actually use the site than raw totals reveal) with such highlights as Dunlin, Curlew Sandpiper, Redshank and Grey Plover. Other migrants in important numbers include Greater Flamingo, Spoonbill and Black Tern.

The Sado Estuary

Barely 30 kilometres from the Tagus estuary lies the Sado bay (routes 3 and 6). The river Sado, born in the Alentejo near Beja is only 180 km long but has a huge estuary with an enormous biodiversity. The upper limit of salt intrusion is situated at Alcácer do Sal. Between Alcácer and the ocean lies a shallow bay of 35 km long and up to 16 km wide. Because the Sado is a short river, which catchment lies entirely in the dry lowlands of southern Portugal, the salt water penetrates far inland in dry years. The tidal range varies between 1 and 4 m.

The most striking features of the Sado estuary are the large expanses of intertidal mudflats and the salt marshes, situated on the northern shore east of Setúbal and on the southern shore near Comporta and

Wood stumps serve as a high tide roost for these Turnstones.

Carrasqueira. Large areas of rice paddies dominate the freshwater parts of the bay, while here and there in the saltmarsh, there are abandoned saltpans. Another unique feature of Sado Bay is the large sandbar of Tróia – a nearly pristine 17 km long row of dunes.

As with the Tagus estuary, the birdlife of the Sado estuary is incredible. Birds are especially numerous outside the breeding season. Wildfowl numbers well into the tens of thousands in winter, with significant populations of Black-necked Grebe, Wigeon, Shoveler, Teal and Pintail. Thousands of waders are present throughout the year, with numbers peaking during migration periods. Avocet, Curlew, Grey and Ringed Plover, Curlew Sandpiper, Dunlin, Greenshank and Spotted Redshank are especially well represented. The European Black-tailed Godwit population depends heavily on the rice-paddies (see page 83). Glossy Ibis, White Stork, egrets and herons number in the hundreds and live in rice fields, reeds and agricultural fields.

Flock of Avocets – one of the 21 wader species that are regular on the south Portuguese coast.

Ria Formosa

The Ria Formosa estuary extends for 60 km along the Algarve's southern coast and is completely different from the Tagus and Sado estuaries. A *Ria* should not be confused with *río*, the Spanish and Portuguese word for river. Instead, a *ria* is a series of coastal inlets fed by rivers and subject to flooding from the sea. In case of the Ria Formosa, six small rivers pour out into the site, creating a wide coastal wetland. The rivers however, are small and the water flow is feeble for the most part of the year. Subsequently, the fresh water input is insignificant and salinity of the marshes is high.

The tidal lagoon is protected by five sandy islands and two peninsulas that form a long sand barrier broken by channels that connect the ocean with the bay, which is a 10,500 ha maze of salt marshes, mudflats and intertidal areas.

Near Faro, part of the dunes are full of tourist houses and fishermen's shacks but the rest of the dunes are pristine and undisturbed and have a rich flora and fauna. The dunes are one of the botanical treasure troves of southern Portugal and those of Ria Formosa are no exception. Although most of the Ria Formosa is salt marsh, there are a few freshwater sites, where tamarisks and reeds grow. These sites are teeming with birdlife.

Just like the Sado and Tagus estuaries, the Ria Formosa is a hotspot for migrating waders, especially in autumn. Dunlin, Ringed Plover, Grey Plover and Redshank can be seen everywhere, while Curlew Sandpiper, Green Sandpiper and other species appear in smaller numbers. Many migrating passerines hide in the vegetation in impressive numbers, but raptors pass only in small numbers. Winter population of ducks can exceed 10,000, with species such as Shoveler, Pintail, Wigeon, Teal and

Red-crested Pochard and there is a large number of waders in winter as well. Greater Flamingo, Glossy Ibis and Spoonbill are present most of the year. The freshwater sites harbour Little Bittern, Purple Heron, Little Egret, Collared Pratincole and Purple Gallinule – species that are generally scarce on the Portuguese coast.

Flamingos in the Sado bay (route 6; bottom). Limoniastrum is a colourful bush of the salt marshes (top).

Capes, dunes and beaches

> Impressive capes, including its wildlife, feature on routes 4, 21 and 22, site A on page 135 and site E on page 198 and A, D, F and H on pages 212 to 214.
> Dunes and beaches have a prominent place on routes 6, 7, 14, 20 and 22, plus sites A on page 135 and F and G on pages 214-215.

The southern Portuguese coast is one of steep cliffs, long beaches and broad strips of dunes. Within our area, you can find almost any type of coastline. The popularity of individual locations, and with it the facilities available, varies enormously from place to place. In the touristy southern Algarve the beaches are full of people, but on the west coast they are surprisingly deserted. More resorts appear again near Lisbon, but hotels and tourist facilities are limited to a stretch of about 10 km which were built here for the Expo of 1998. South of Lisbon, empty beaches and fossilised dunes are followed by high sea cliffs, culminating in the magnificent cliffs at Cape Espichel. Between the Tróia tombolo and the harbour of Sines there is no less than 70 km of uninterrupted beach, most of which is devoid of visitors. There are few access points, which have only a few beach restaurants and, with the exception of Tróia itself, no tourist resorts have (yet) been developed. Behind the beaches, dunes protect the interior against the Atlantic Ocean. On the Costa Vicentina, black and reddish sea cliffs rise up to 100 m, and are alternated by a few small and quiet beaches. Most of this stretch of coastline receives few visitors, except for the well-known and spectacular cliffs of Cape St. Vincent, Europe's most southwestern point. There is no place better to watch the sun set in the ocean than here (route 21).

Dune Galingale is just one of the conspicuous wildflowers of the dunes.

Capes and headlands

Ecologically, capes and headlands are strange places. In a way, they are a simple extension from the habitats you find deeper inland – *matos*, grasslands and woodlands with a flora and fauna that match the specific conditions of the soil. But the closer you come to the coast, the more the factor

Shags and White Storks on on the rocks of Cabo Sardão (top; site H on page 214). The spectacular cliffs of Cabo Espichel (bottom; route 4) is a great point for seawatching.

of the wind comes into play. Wind has an enormous impact, and once you are on the windbeaten cape, you appreciate that the landscape is entirely different from the sites five or ten kilometres inland.

Wind does three different things. First, it forces plants to stay close to the ground. Anything tall is blown to bits. Many plant species have special forms or subspecies that represent them on the coast. Others have evolved on the spot into new species. Second, the maritime wind creates a very mild climate. The winter is much milder than at the spots further inland, the summers much cooler, although the hot wind makes the summer conditions even drier at the coast. These unique conditions are another element that gives rise to a special flora. And third, there is the salt spray. During storms, a spray of fine droplets of salt water is blown over the vegetation. This is another ecological 'game changer' and probably the reason why some coastal cliffs support plant species that occur nowhere else but on the cliffs of south-western Portugal.

Cliffs and capes are important breeding sites for birds as well. In particular the stacks that got separated from the

mainland are in demand as nest sites as terrestrial predators can't reach them. Shags, Red-billed Choughs and Yellow-legged Gulls breed and rest on the sea cliffs, the latter especially in colonies. Southern Portugal lacks the great mixed seabird colonies that are such an important feature of the northern Atlantic, but in compensation, there are some very 'un-seabird' like species to be found. Very special is the White Stork colony on a rocky offshore island near Sardão (site H on page 214), and the Cattle Egretry on an offshore cliff near Benagil (site D on page 197). More predictably, the Peregrine Falcon also finds a safe nesting place on the rocks as do Blue Rock Thrush and Rock Bunting.

Dunes

Southern Portugal has some of the finest and ecologically rich dunes in the whole of Europe. Apart from the fact that they are relatively unspoilt, it is the mild climate that is the key to their attraction. The warm summer and very mild winter conditions make them very different from the dunes along the French Atlantic northwards, while the dunes in the gentle Mediterranean Sea are not subject to the immense tidal differences of the Atlantic. As a result, the sand dunes between Setúbal and Tarifa in Spain are an ecological island, with many unique species. This is particularly evident in the many endemic wildflowers of the dunes (see page 65). Also the reptilian world is something special in the dunes, with the Spiny-footed Lizard, Carbonell´s Wall Lizard, Smaller Psammodromus (formerly called Spanish Psammodromus) and Turkish Gecko (or Mediterranean House Gecko) particularly linked to this habitat. European Chameleon and Lataste's Viper are specialities too, although they are rare and have limited distributions.

Submarine canyons

Standing on the cliffs of Cabo Espichel on a calm summer's evening, the ocean is like a mirror. At such times it is hard to imagine that underneath that smooth surface lies a rugged topography. Several submarine canyons are situated not far from the coast. There is a canyon off Cape St. Vincent and several others further north. Near Lisbon lies the Nazaré Canyon, which deepest points are 5 km below sea level! The Lisbon and Setúbal Canyons are submarine continuations of the Tagus and Sado rivers.

The rivers bring down nutrients into these canyons, while deep sea currents from within the gorges well them up again. These water flows support an exceptionally rich submarine ecosystem, which is recognised as a biodiversity hotspot. Off the coast of Sagres lies another canyon.

The Nazaré canyon is well-studied using unmanned, remote-controlled submarines which have uncovered a paradisiacal landscape of cliffs covered by cold-water corals with masses of fish around them. Moreover, due to the rugged terrain, life in the canyons is also protected from human disturbance such as trawling.

Sea mammals are attracted by these food-rich areas in the ocean. The marine biologists who can take you out to find whales, dolphins and seabirds from Sagres (see page 213) know that highest densities are near the submarine canyon west of Cape St. Vincent.

Seabirds are also drawn to these parts of the ocean. Unfortunately, little is known about the species and numbers of birds present in this area, as it is (just) too far out from the coast to see the birds from land and there are no pelagic bird trips organised to these waters.

Large swell waves off the coast of Cabo São Vicente (route 21). The small ways in between the large ripples are wind-induced.

Waves on the ocean

The Portuguese cliffs are an excellent place to observe the behaviour of the waves. This zen-like activity brings you, apart from inner calm and sunstroke, a fascinating insight into the physics of waves.

Waves come in different forms and shapes. Those that are the result of wind blowing over the water are usually superficial. Depending on the wind speed, they can be very small or over 10 m high. Once in motion, the waves are stopped only when they crash on a solid surface. So when the wind ceases, big waves continue to roll along. Such waves are called swell waves and are generated by distant weather. Swell can travel thousands of kilometres, and is not or barely affected by local winds. Swell typically has a long wavelength (from crest to crest). By the length of the waves you can make out the difference between local, short waves generated by the wind you feel blowing in your face and the longer swell waves that travel independently from the wind.

If you stand at the cliffs of Cape St. Vincent, or just anywhere on the Portuguese west coast, look down and observe both wave types. With a little luck you can also see that pelagic birds such as Gannet or shearwaters, and even the local gulls, use the space between two swell waves to glide effortlessly, taking advantage of the calmer winds there.

Freshwater marshes and riverine habitat

> Beautiful river valleys are found on routes 9, 11, 12, 18, 22 and 23, plus sites B and E on pages 159-160. Freshwater marshes are present on routes 2, 6, 7 and 15 and on sites E and F on pages 137 to 139, site A on page 158 and sites A and B on pages 195 and 196. Ecologically rich rice paddies are present on routes 2 and 6.

With a climate of prolonged summer drought in which every plant and animal is aching for a drop of water, rivers play a vital role in the region's ecology. Natural riparian woodlands are shady and damp 'islands' in a 'sea' of dry hillsides. Fertile soil gathers in the valley bottom, feeding a lush vegetation that is in extreme contrast with the surroundings. The presence of water attracts wild animals from afar and thereby river valleys and marshes form an important element in the sustenance of the entire ecosystem. In short, it is hard to underestimate the importance of rivers to the region's wildlife.

Unfortunately, rivers are under tremendous pressure. They are just as important for people and agriculture as they are for nature. Since all rivers spring up within the same area governed by the capricious Mediterranean climate, their water levels fluctuate enormously. The summers are bone-dry and the winters may or may not bring alleviating rains, and the run-off is correspondingly variable, ranging from a small trickle to a roaring stream.

The Odelouca valley – green, diverse, lovely and with a high diversity of flora and fauna (route 18).

The best way to deal with these fluctuations is to save water where and when you can. In the 20th century, large reservoirs were constructed in order to retain water for times of scarcity. The water is used primarily as drinking water and for irrigation, but tourism adds extra demands, such as filling swimming pools and watering golf courses.

Ribbons of Water Crowfoot grace the small brooks in the Alentejo (route 9).

In many cases, these reservoirs destroyed the important riparian environment that sustained the ecology. The shores of the reservoirs are usually steep, lack the rich sediments and their water levels fluctuate enormously from season to season and year to year – conditions that cannot sustain any riverine vegetation. In fact, they cannot sustain any vegetation at all. Most reservoirs are ecologically dead; only few have shores with the right conditions to develop reedbeds or flood forests.

Currently the most important and most beautiful riverine habitat is found in those few places where the river has not been dammed.

Guadiana river

The large Rio Guadiana flows into Portugal from Spain and for a long stretch, it forms the border between the two nations. The river is dammed in several places. There has never been a common policy on water use of the Guadiana river, so Spain, Portugal, their provinces and municipalities have all built reservoirs on their own initiative. In the entire Guadiana river basin (including the Spanish part), there are in total no less than 1,824 dams, many of them in the poorest areas with high unemployment. Building dams and irrigating land for agriculture means jobs. The Alqueva dam is the largest in the Guadiana and was built in 2002, in the face of loud but ultimately fruitless protests of conservationists. Currently, the shores of the Alqueva rerservoirhave little to offer in terms of wildlife. Fortunately, sections of the Guadiana and its adjacent rivers still run freely. In particular, the area within the Vale do Guadiana natural park near Mértola is largely untouched. Here, the river runs through a hilly and rocky landscape, sometimes fast flowing and wild, elsewhere gentle and verdant. There are beautiful unspoilt valleys with stretches of riverine vegetation, of which Rio Ardila and Murtega (routes 8 and 9) are good examples. Willows, poplars, elm and Narrow-leaved Ash trees, Wild Oleander and reeds grow in the river bends and on shallow, slow running stretches. Here you'll still find the ecological idyll of the Iberian rivers: Otter, Kingfisher and Black Stork feed in the water. Bee-eater, Red-rumped Swallow, Crag Martin, Black-eared Wheatear and Rock Sparrow build their nests in sand banks, crags or overhanging rocks near the river and feed nearby. Great Spotted Cuckoo, Woodchat Shrike, Western Subalpine and Melodious Warbler are found in the riverine vegetation. The perky snouts of the Spanish Terrapins peek out between the Water Crow's-foot.

South of Alcoutim (route 12) the Guadiana becomes a broad and slow flowing river which boats can navigate. The riverine vegetation is especially abundant near the mouth of the adjacent streams. Some of those streams dry up in summer, and you can walk upriver over the gravel streambed.

The Sado River

Compared to the Guadiana, the Sado is a short and gentle river. It emerges in the Alentejo, not far west of Castro Verde. The Sado runs north through steppes, agricultural lands, Holm Oak *montados* and widens only the last 20 km before it reaches Alcácer do Sal, where rice is grown

Several streams in the southwestern part of the country are lined with a lush gallery forest of willows and alders – home to Otters, Golden Orioles, Large Tortoiseshells and a superb range of dragonflies. This is the Ceixe River (route 23).

along its shores. In fact rice fields have been constructed as far upriver as technically possible. The Sado and its adjacent rivers hold little gallery forest or reeds. Some good and bird-rich stretches are found west of Beja, at the river Odivelas (site A on page 158).

Rivers in the Algarve and Costa Vincentina

Some of the finest river valleys are found in the southwest. Most of them are rather small and completely unblemished by development. Their lower reaches are fed by water from their small catchments and flushed by tidal seawater creating an intact estuary with sand dunes, salt marsh and grassy meadows and riparian forest further upstream.

The Odelouca, Aljezur and Odeceixe valleys are exemplars of this – they are absolute gems with the latter two being surprisingly lush. You may

Purple Gallinule (top) and Glossy Ibis (bottom), two locally common birds of freshwater marshes.

be mistaken in thinking you are walking along a fine river valley somewhere in central Europe, with the dense river woodlands of Alder and Narrow-leaved Ash, in which Jays, Great Spotted and Iberian Green Woodpeckers, Golden Orioles and masses of Nightingales live along with Turtle Dove, Iberian Chiffchaff, Melodious Warbler, Blackcap and Cetti's Warbler. Large Tortoiseshells (rare butterflies in southern Portugal) rest on the path beside the stream, while various species of demoiselles flutter around the large leaves of Royal Fern and the Yellow Iris. In summer, these sites are very rich in dragonflies (see page 102).

The valleys are little visited, few people live here and they are away from the popular tourist routes.

Freshwater lakes

Apart from the reservoirs, there are only few freshwater lakes in southern Portugal. This guide describes two natural lakes in the Setúbal area, the Santo André and Albufeira lagoons (route 7 and site E on page 137) and only three small but bird-rich sites in the Algarve: Lagoa dos Salgados and Vilamoura wetlands (sites A and B on pages 195-196 and the marshes near Faro airport; route 15). Further up in the Alentejo, there are two lakes that are not of natural origin, but nevertheless sport a well-developed wetland vegetation: the Lagoa dos Patos and Albufeira Odivelas (both described as site A on page 158). These small reservoirs are situated in a shallow depression. The slopes of the reservoirs are very gentle and the soil is rich, which are good conditions for reedbeds and riparian woodland to develop.

As may be expected, these lakes are oases that attract hundreds or thousands of birds. There are concentrations of ducks and coots in winter and swallows, passerines and Spoonbills on migration. Herons, egrets and Purple Gallinules breed in the dense vegetation, Zitting Cisticola, Cetti´s and Great Reed Warblers are found in the reeds. In coastal sites and on rice paddies, two resident escapees from the cagebird trade, Common Waxbill and Black-headed Weaver, thrive.

Rice paddies

To grow rice, one needs fertile soils, a mild climate, flat terrain and large quantities of fresh water. Such conditions are widely available around the bays of the Sado and Tagus estuaries, where rice production is a profitable activity for the Portuguese farmers. A complex water flow system was built that allows the water to flow very gently through one paddy and on to the next. The rice plants grow in water of 10 – 20 cm depth.

Basically, the ideal water regime for rice is also excellent for a range of birds, from waders to herons, Spoonbills, storks and Glossy Ibis. In rice paddies where not too much insecticide is used, the birds find a rich table in these artificial wetlands. Artificial too is the alien American Red-swamp Crayfish whose presence has been linked to the explosive increase in the Iberian Glossy Ibis population.

Rice growing follows a strict annual cycle. The plants are sown in May and harvested in October, after which the fields are ploughed. When wet, the rice fields are very attractive for birds, but in the course of March and April fields are set dry and during this period they are not interesting (see text box on page 83).

About 40% of the world's Black-tailed Godwits spend the winter in the rice paddies of south-western Iberia. The largest concentrations are found in the Sado and Tejo bays.

Woodlands, montados, orchards and matos

> Beautiful montados are a prominent feature on routes 2, 3, 8, 9, 10, 11, 12, 18 and 20, plus site F on page 139, and sites A to E on pages 158 to 160. Pinewoods are present on routes 5, 6, 7, 21 and sites E on page 214. Riparian forest features on routes 12, 18, 22 and 23. Scrublands are found all over, but the unique habitat of the coastal *matos* is present on routes 4, 21 and 22, plus sites A, B, D, E and H on pages 212 to 214.

There is a revealing map on Portuguese woodlands in a book on Mediterranean landscapes (The Nature of Mediterranean Europe; by Grove and Rackham): whereas on the Spanish side of the border, only 3% of the area is wooded, on the Portuguese side, no less than 97% is tree-covered. Yet if you travel in the area, you'd have a hard time figuring out on which side of the border you are. The landscape is exactly the same.

This goes to show how difficult it is to classify the landscape that the Portuguese call *montado* and the Spanish refer to as *dehesa*. The montado (we'll stick to the Portuguese name here) is perhaps best described as lightly wooded pastureland. It is a huge expanse of Cork and Holm Oaks, usually well-spaced, with a mixture of grassland, scrub and even, occasionally, cereal fields. Some montados are dense enough to resemble true forests, while others can be so open that they are more reminiscent of savannahs.

Another great difference between the montado and the forests that we know from temperate Europe is the way they are exploited. In the montado, forestry plays a secondary role. All trees are carefully pollarded to produce wide tree crowns, which shield the soil from sun and rain and produces lots of acorns. The pastures beneath the trees are exploited by sheep, cattle and pigs. Low-intensity husbandry is the main function of the montado, then comes the production of cork, timber (and in bygone days charcoal), cereals and honey. In short, the bounty of the montado is very diverse and its landscape is unique – you can find it only in southwestern Iberia.

The montados are the dominant landscape in much of the Alentejo. It is a wonderful and ecologically very rich area. If you pass through the landscape, you'll find birds everywhere. Hoopoes, Bee-eaters, Iberian Grey and Woodchat Shrikes, Thekla's and Woodlarks, Azure-winged Magpies, Little Owls and lots of Mediterranean songbirds – the diversity is great. It is interesting to see how the montado birdlife gradually changes between different sites. Short-toed Treecreeper, Chaffinch, Great Tit and Nuthatch become increasingly common in denser stands with older trees. A little further on, where the trees are much wider spaced, you may find Stone Curlew. In rocky terrain near rivers, there are Black-eared Wheatear, Blue Rock Thrush, Rock Bunting and Rock Sparrow. Apparently, the montado ecosystem is right at the crossroads of different habitats and offers home to species from all of them. This holds true not just for birds – the reptile, amphibian and mammal world is rich as well. Nearly all species of snake or lizard that occur in southern Portugal are found in the montado. Among the mammals, the Genet and Egyptian Mongoose are particularly frequent. Only the diversity of wildflowers and butterflies lag a little behind – a result of the poor and uniform soils.

Extensive Holm and Cork Oak groves (*montados*) cover much of the surface of the Alentejo (bottom). These savannah-like landscapes have a superb birdlife. One of the common birds is the Woodchat Shrike (top).

The montado is not the only kind of woodland. On sandy soils on the west coast are some large areas with Umbrella Pine forests. This forest is open as well, but there is no animal husbandry here. The trees play an important role in fixing the sand, as well as providing timber.

Along some of the rivers, most notably in the south and southwest, there are fine riparian woodlands. A narrow emerald ribbon of Alder and Ash trees follows the course of the streams down to the coast (see page 36).

On the Costa Vicentina and Serra de Monchique, there are vast areas of Eucalyptus, planted for the paper pulp industry. Whereas the Spanish have abandoned the planting of Eucalyptus, because of the disastrous effects on the ecology, ground water and soil, the Portuguese unfortunately still continue the practice. The Eucalyptus plantations are nothing short of an ecological crime, leaving entire hillsides dead and deserted (see page 55).

Matos

Cork Oak montado with Yellow Lupin on the shores of the Tejo Bay (route 2).

Scrublands in Portuguese are called *matos*. In most places, different species of cistus dominate the scrub. Especially after a wildfire or after a clearcut, the scrubland that returns may appear rather uniform. Especially in the Alentejo and northern half of the Algarve where the soils are poor and acidic, the scrublands are ruled over by a single species: the Gum

Cistus. It is a beautiful plant, though, with large white, delicate petals, each with a typical, dark red dot (present on about 90% of the plants). The top of the plant is sticky and exudes a wonderful, herbal scent. So, there is much to say in favour of the Gum Cistus, except that doesn't allow much other vegetation. All bushes are about the same height and density, so a walk through those matos is a rather dull undertaking. Only the rasping call and short sweet warble of the Sardinian Warbler will be a frequent companion.

The Gum Cistus provides a good litmus test (almost literally) for the acidity of the soil. It grows only on acidic soils and disappears where limestone or other, more basic soil types occur. Here, the Grey-leaved Cistus (with pink flowers), Rosemary, Thyme and other species occur, each with its own height, structure and ecology. These scrublands are much richer and boast a wider variety of insects, reptiles and birds.

Flowery scrubland (*matos*) with Gum Cistus and Purple Viper's-bugloss – possibly the two most common wildflowers of the Alentejo.

Closer to the coast, the wind and drought makes tree growth impossible. This is where you'll find the most special matos, with those on Cape St. Vincent the true champs. The low, wind-beaten coastal scrub has an enormous diversity in wildflowers, which we describe in further detail on page 63 and route 21.

In the dry, Mediterranean landscape of southern Portugal, scrublands appear both as the natural 'climax' vegetation and as a sign of disturbance in places where naturally, a woodland would grow. The natural sites for scrublands are rocky, exposed slopes and cliff-tops, the places where wind, shallow soils and drought doesn't allow trees to develop. The scrubland that grows here is quite diverse, also on acidic soils – patches of dense bushes alternate with grassy parts, some rocky

42

outcrops. Here and there, a tree found a crack in the rock through which the root can reach water.

On better soils, Mediterranean woodland of Holm and Cork Oaks will eventually take over from the shrubs, but even here, the development to forest is a slow process. The cistus scrub that takes over after a forest fire or other kind of disturbance may persist for years before the trees can return.

The world's largest Cork Oak forests are found in southern Portugal.

Cork Oaks in Portugal

Cork is the bark of the Cork Oak (*Quercus suber*), native to the countries of the western Mediterranean. The cork bark protects the trunk and branches against wildfire. Where other trees and plants after a fire recover by growing new individuals from seeds, the Cork Oak renews its bark, makes new shoots and resurrects as an arboreal Phoenix.

Cork as a material is impermeable and elastic and used as a stopper in wine bottles and for other products. Harvesting the cork without damaging the tree

is a tough work that requires a lot of skill. A small axe and specialised tools are used by a team of harvesters that work together on a single tree. The skin of a recently harvested tree first has a pale, sandy colour, but soon develops an impressive, velvety red that disappears gradually as the years go by and a new bark grows.

The cork is separated from the tree for the first time when it is 25-30 years old. After about nine years the tree can again been harvested. On old trees you may see the result of several treatments on one and the same tree. Whereas other trees await a certain death when their bark is removed, the Cork oak survives, although the treatment remains an assault to its health. The lifespan of a Cork Oak is up to about 250 years, but harvesting the bark shortens it by about a 20%.

Portugal accounts for half of the world production of cork. Cork trees are protected and may never be cut without special permission, even if they are old. Local people depend on Cork Oak forest as a part of their economy and therefore look after them well.

Steppes and cereal fields

Steppe habitat is found on routes 8, 11 and above all around Castro Verde, route 10. Sites F and G (pages 161-162) are also steppe sites.

Portugal's largest and most important regions of cereal steppes and steppe grasslands are found around the town of Castro Verde. As early as Roman times, this region was important for both cattle grazing and cereal production.

The steppes of Portugal are not naturally treeless (Some authors therefore insist on calling them pseudo-steppes), but are the result of a rotation of growing cereals followed by several years of fallow land, in which the land is grazed by sheep. The result is a locally changing but overall stable mosaic of cereal fields, fallow land, fields and more or less natural grasslands full of annual and biannual flowers. Especially Purple Viper's-bugloss can flower *en masse* and put up spectacular shows in spring. On these poor soils, there are many rocky areas that function as safe havens for reptiles and rodents as well as for wildflowers that escape the plough and the teeth of grazing sheep. Small streams and ponds add the finishing touch to this diverse ecosystem.

The vast steppes around Castro Verde are a riot of colour in spring, when swathes of annuals are in full bloom, such as these Purple Viper's-buglosses.

Apart from the spectacular empty landscape, birds are the biggest attraction of the steppes. A visit to southern Portugal simply isn't complete without a visit to the steppes of Castro Verde. Large numbers of both Great and Little Bustard plus Black-bellied Sandgrouse, Lesser Kestrel, Black-winged Kite, Montagu's Harrier, Great Spotted Cuckoo, Stone Curlew and Roller form the main attractions. There are many more great birds too including, in recent years, Spanish Imperial Eagle.

Key to this wealth of birds are the large numbers of insects (mainly grass-

hoppers) and rodents, Iberian hares and rabbits that inhabit these steppes. They in turn are drawn to the many seeds and herbs of the grasslands.

Apart from the Castro Verde plains, there are several other areas of cereal steppes, in particular around Beja. These are rather different though. The soils are much more fertile and the cereal fields are larger, more uniform and more intensely farmed. Here too are important populations of steppe birds, but not in the densities found around Castro Verde.

The Great Bustard (top) is one of the delights of the steppes of the Alentejo. It profits from the mixture of herb-rich, grassy fields and areas with cereal steppes (bottom) that together are rich in grains and insects.

History

Early history

Human habitation in what we now refer to as Portugal dates back to about 30,000 years ago, but we know little about the country's early history. Farming, with its inevitable impact on the ecology of the area, arrived around 5,000 BC. The introduction of bronze (an alloy of copper and tin) around 2,000 BC stimulated agriculture, the exploitation of Portugal's tin resources and th e development of trade routes to Britain. Around 800 BC, the Phoenicians, partly attracted by these mineral resources, started to trade with the inhabitants of the Iberian Peninsula and established the first settlements on the Portuguese south coast where they mixed with Iberians. A little later, Greek traders arrived and introduced coinage, olive cultivation and writing. Celtic tribes entered Portugal from the north about 700 BC, but they did not become established in the south. However, the new iron technology they brought with them would have allowed a greater exploitation of natural resources throughout the region.

The Romans and the Moors

When the Romans invaded the Iberian Peninsula in 210 BC, the conquest of southern Portugal was easy. The Romans ruled and organized most of the country for more than five centuries. Most of Portugal became part of the province south of the river Duero, *Lusitania* (including the Spanish Extremadura and western Andalucia). The Roman language, its customs and culture were fully adopted in the Iberian provinces. Trade increased, roads and cities were built. Roman ruins can still be found in the Algarve, e.g. near Vilamoura (Algarve; see site B on page 196) and on the Guadiana river near Alcoutim (route 12).

With the fall of the Roman Empire in the beginning of the 5th century, people of German origin invaded the Iberian Peninsula. The Visigoths, who became the dominant group, adopted the Christian religion and mixed with local people but their rule was plagued by internal divisions.

The arrival of the Moors on the Peninsula from North Africa in 711 resulted in a rapid conquest of southern Portugal, leading to greater stability and thus many centuries of prosperity. Agriculture became more important thanks to greater productivity and new crops such as citrus and rice. The Moors made Silves the capital of the Algarve (from the Arabic *al-Gharb* meaning 'the west'). Silves became more important than Lisbon, the old Roman capital. Another important town was Mértola in the Alentejo which the Moors ruled for more than 500 years. Mértola had

Traditional husbandry is what sustains the nature-rich landscape of the montado. The poor soils of the Alentejo are the reason why more intensive forms of agriculture are impossible.

a port that connected with the sea, exporting agricultural products and minerals. The town was well protected by old Roman walls supplemented by new fortifications. It was one of the last Moorish towns to be recaptured (in 1238) and is one of the few with many buildings from this period today. Therefore it is often called 'the most Arabic town of Portugal' (which has far fewer such relics than nearby Spain). The mosque, which is the only largely intact medieval mosque in Portugal, is now used as a Christian church.

The Moorish control never extended beyond Oporto and its hold on lands north of the Tagus was weak and relatively brief compared to elsewhere in Iberia which explains why Portuguese has far fewer words from Arabic than Spanish. The origins of the invading Christian forces from the north also explain why the Portuguese language has close ties with Galician. The major turning point came in 1139 when Afonso Henriques (Afonso I) won an overwhelming victory at the Battle of Ourique (in central Portugal, not Ourique in the Alentejo) after which he was proclaimed King of Portugal. The new king took Lisbon in 1167 and other Moorish lands at the border of the river Tagus.

Succeeding monarchs chiselled away at Moorish possessions until King Afonso III captured Faro in 1249, incorporating the Algarve into his kingdom, to complete the 'Reconquista', some 250 years earlier than in Spain. Portugal's Arabic inheritance, although less than Spain's, can still be detected in the language, in place names (especially those starting with 'Al'), in the decorative tiles, the latticework designs and the flat roofed, small windowed buildings. Traditionally, the Portuguese monarchs were styled 'King of Portugal and of the Algarves'. Apart from the disputed region of Olivença, the current border with Spain dates from this time.

The imperial era and decline

The history of Portugal from the 13th century onwards is one of 'political' marriages with the royal families of neighbouring mini-states which gained some short term stability but in the long run often caused dynastic struggles thanks to disputed inheritance. For example, in 1369 Ferdinand I of Portugal claimed the throne of León and Castile causing a long running dispute which was ultimately settled by the establishment of a new dynasty in 1385, founded by João (John) of Aviz, the illegitimate half-brother of Ferdinand. Inevitably, this sparked an abortive counter invasion by his dynastic rival. However, his great victory at the Battle of Aljubarrota both firmly asserted Portuguese independence and, by the treaty of Windsor (1386), established an alliance with England that still persists.

It was Prince Henry, the third surviving son of João, who primarily initiated Portugal's overseas explorations although his popular title 'Henry the Navigator' only came into use in the 19th century and he never personally embarked on voyages himself. At his instigation, important African discoveries were made and the Azores were colonized. Lagos in the Algarve was the most important starting point for these voyages. This development explains why Portuguese, the language of what is now regarded as a small, relatively poor country at the periphery of Europe, is the sixth most widely spoken language in the world today.

Meanwhile Spain, under the rule of Ferdinand and Isabella, had also initiated a rival bout of maritime exploration. The Treaty of Tordecillas (1494) divided the world between these two Iberian powers with all new land east of an arbitrary line drawn about halfway between the Cape Verde islands and those discovered by Columbus awarded to Portugal and those to the west to Spain. By this time, Portugal had become a powerful nation with a navy that ruled over much of the world's oceans thanks to a succession of famous explorers such as Bartolomé Díaz, Vasco da Gama and culminating in Ferdinand Magellan's expedition (1519-1522) circumnavigating the world for the first time (although Magellan himself died in 1521). More discoveries were made and Portugal became a very rich country thanks to the trade resulting from their domination of the seas. It established colonies in Brazil, Mozambique and Angola and numerous settlements along the African and Asian coasts. At one time the Portuguese navy controlled the Atlantic between Portugal, South America and the whole of the African coast, the Persian Gulf and the Indian Ocean from South Africa to India, Malaysia and up the coast up to Japan. Portugal ruled the very profitable spice trade with Asia.

In another dynastic twist, the death of the childless Sebastian I (Sebastião I) in 1578 ultimately led to his uncle King Philip II of Spain adding the King of Portugal to his many titles (confusingly, though, he was King Philip I of Portugal). On one hand this was an advantage because Portugal could exploit Spanish trade routes and networks but on the other hand Portugal was dragged into wars with England, France and the Dutch Republic. English and Dutch privateers captured many Spanish and Portuguese ships carrying wealth from the colonies (bullion, spices, silks, gems and other valuables). The Dutch attacked Portuguese Brazilian colonies, but enjoyed greater and more permanent success in the Far East. The Dutch Portuguese War, which was fought largely at sea, lasted for more than sixty years (1602 - 1663) only coming to an end when Portugal regained its independence from Spain. This was restored when Philip IV of Spain antagonised the Portuguese by attempting to make their country a Spanish province. Seizing a moment when Spain was overstretched, the Duke of Braganza, a great-great grandson of Manuel I of Portugal, was proclaimed John IV in December 1640. The subsequent hostilities, dragged on for decades, although mainly as a matter of local skirmishes rather than formal campaigns. Peace was finally concluded in 1668, but this long period of instability and widespread poverty resulted in many Portuguese emigrating to Brazil during the 17th century and later. Portugal was not only losing its people but also its colonies. The country lost the lucrative spice trade to the Dutch and the British who also gradually took over and monopolised the trade with India. Despite all the setbacks, the Portuguese economy did not collapse thanks to the discovery of gold and diamonds in Brazil.

In the 18th century efforts were made to modernise Portugal economically and financially but this

An earthquake and subsequent Tsunami ravaged Lisbon in 1755. In the capital alone, between 10,000 and 100,000 people died. The disaster had an immense effect on the economy but also on the (religious) worldview in the whole of Europe.

was disrupted by a natural disaster, the Lisbon earthquake of 1755. The earthquake, and subsequent tsunami, not only destroyed most of Lisbon, killing tens of thousands of people, but also wrought huge damage on the Algarve, along the Atlantic coast and even on Madeira, the Azores and the Brazilian coast. This event had a terrible effect on the economy in the short term but in the longer run it helped to usher in reforms and reduced over-reliance on Britain. The earthquake also had an extraordinary impact on European culture and philosophy influencing luminaries like Voltaire (who was inspired to write 'Candide') and Rousseau as well as stimulating the study of seismology and the design of anti-seismic building techniques.

The French Wine Blight (*Phylloxera*; a small fly) destroyed wine stocks all over Portugal in the 1870s. Vineyards were abandoned or transformed to cereal fields (bottom).

Napoleon and the Republic

The 19th century was marked by a struggle between liberals and autocratic factions. The critical factor in this was the Napoleonic invasion in 1807 which resulted in the king and the royal family fleeing to Brazil. In the political vacuum thus created, the liberals were able to push through some political reforms. When the royal family returned in 1821

(just before Brazil declared itself indepent from Portugal), conflicts started with the royal family over the liberal reforms, provoking two civil wars: the War of the Two Brothers (1829-1834) and the 8 month *Guerra da Patuleia* (1846-1847). Both wars further disrupted and impoverished Portugal. The country subsequently also lost its colonies in the Far East to the Dutch and British (retaining only a handful of small enclaves). Portugal shifted its imperial focus on Africa, gaining Angola and Mozambique. However, further expansion was prevented by Britain.

With territorial ambitions thwarted and increasing financial ruin (the country was declared bankrupt in 1892 and 1902), the long running tension between monarchists and republicans grew, culminating in the murder of King Carlos I and his heir. and then the declaration of a Republic.

During World War I Portugal aligned with the allies and fought several battles in Africa. Many ships were destroyed by German U-boats in African harbours and Madeira.

Internal problems and chronic political instability continued, resulting in several attempted military coups which finally succeeded in 1926. By 1933 this had

Carob from the Carob or Black Locust Tree has long been an important crop in the lower Algarve. Locally it is still grown, but many of the groves are now abandoned and gradually transform into scrub and woodland.

evolved into the authoritarian second republic known as the *Estado Novo* (New State). Under the leadership of the brilliant, but authoritarian, António de Oliveira Salazar (who ruled until 1968) Portugal was a dictatorship. Salazar maintained Portuguese neutrality during World War II and, although internal tensions increased, he was able to divide the opposition and remain in power. In the post-war world Salazar's regime was increasingly anachronistic and little by little, Portugal became isolated particularly due to its long running colonial wars in Africa. These strained the economy, created a manpower shortage and increasingly caused dissatisfaction. In April 1974 an army coup, the *Revolução dos Cravos* (Carnation Revolution), took place but this time to restore, not destroy, democracy.

Modern Portugal

With the new constitution, approved in 1976, democratic Portugal was subdivided in 18 districts and two autonomous regions (Madeira and Azores).

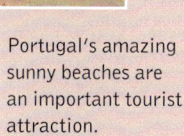

From this moment onwards, Portugal may be considered a modern European state, however with a backward economy. There had been less industrial development in Portugal than in other European countries so agriculture and fishing remained very important. Setúbal, Portimão and Olhão were some of the most important fishing ports with canning industries that employed thousands of workers. Tourism, mainly based on the Algarve, became a growing industry from the 1960s onwards. Initially popular with British tourists, the area rapidly became popular with other European countries.

Portugal's amazing sunny beaches are an important tourist attraction.

In 1986 Portugal joined the EU, improving its economic prospects with European funds and opening new markets. With this came a sense of new prosperity and optimism about the future. New industries were founded and the infrastructure improved, stimulating tourism which had become more important with ever increasing numbers of foreign tourists. However, when Portugal joined the euro in 1999, things were not so positive. Economic development lagged behind, inflation and unemployment rates were high and wages were low. Many people looked for work abroad, particularly in Spain which was doing better. Accordingly, efforts were made to increase the agricultural productivity and provide cheap energy. Having been discussed since the 1950s, a dam across the River Guadiana near Alqueva in the Alentejo was completed in 2002. It was constructed to provide both water for irrigation and hydro-electric power. This was aimed at improving conditions for people living in a countryside that still exploited pine plantations established in the 14th Century and centuries old, scarcely profitable, Cork Oak woodlands. The economic crises of 2008 was a heavy blow to Portugal, but, after years of austerity, the economy is recovering and people are becoming more optimistic again. Today the population in Portugal is 10.3 million (2022).

Nature conservation

Nature conservation did not appear on the Portuguese political agenda until fairly recently and is still not a major concern. Despite the early foundation of the LPN (*Liga para a Protecção da Natureza*) in 1948, in general the conservation movement started much later than in Spain and other western European countries. The Portuguese BirdLife partner, for instance, was founded only in 1993. Until 2008 the red lists of endangered flora and fauna in Portugal still had no legal framework for protection. The European Habitat and Birds Directives and Portugal's participation in the Natura 2000 network have given species and habitats a legal protection. Nevertheless, only few conservation measures are carried out and only the very minimum of protective legislation required by the EU is actually implemented.

The Eucalyptus plantations for the pulp and paper industry (here near Monchique) are among the greatest environmental disasters of Portugal. This industry has turned large areas in the Algarve and Alentejo into ecological deserts. Currently, new legislation is drawn up to restrict the Eucalyptus industry.

The Portuguese red list of endangered species

A first red list of endangered species was published in 1990 as *Livro Vermelho dos Vertebrados de Portugal*. A more definitive list was published in 2005, but for many species there is still a lack of data to justify their inclusion or exclusion on the list. In 2017, Portugal is one of the four countries with no Red List available on the IUCN website **www.nationalredlist.org**.

The Iberian Lynx is the most famous red list species. European funds support a reintroduction program carried out together with Spain, which resulted in the reintroduction of this beautiful feline in 2013. The Mediterranean and Mehely´s Horse-shoe Bats are also listed as Critically Endangered. The work that is carried out on bat conservation has received a lot less press attention than the lynx. Among the birds, Spanish Imperial Eagle is the most famous endangered species. Although rare, their numbers are increasing now. The small Alentejo population is at the edge of the range of this eagle but is expected to grow over the years. Protection of their territories and education projects also help other endangered raptors as Egyptian Vulture, Black Vulture and Bonelli´s Eagle that breed in the same areas. In the same way, conservation projects on red list species like Great and Little Bustards also help endangered Black-bellied Sandgrouse and Montagu´s Harrier.

In Portugal no less than 17 species of fish are considered endangered or critically endangered. One of them is the 10 cm long endemic Spanish minnowcarp or Jarabugo (*Anaecypris hispanica*), the only living member of its genus that lives exclusively in the Portuguese/Spanish river Guadiana and its tributaries. It needs slow flowing water and its population is seriously affected by the reservoirs that block the water flow as well as by predatory species introduced for sport fishing. In addition, there are a number of plants, reptiles and invertebrates on the Red List of Portugal.

The existence of swathes of splendid habitat in Portugal has more to do with lack of threat than with conservation. Not only is the conservation legislation very new, the environmental issues are also relatively recent. Even the built-up Algarve coast, where habitat destruction and land mismanagement is so painfully visible, was until recently a quiet rural land with some fishing villages. In many places in the Alentejo, this ancient atmosphere with the accompanying rich flora and fauna, is still intact. But as soon as economically more attractive alternatives are available, they are carried out without concern for the landscape, history or ecology of the region. Many wonderful sites in the Algarve and Monchique cannot be reached without a sobering trip through an ecological desert of golf courses or hillsides raped by Eucalyptus plantations.

But just as you think Portugal is Europe's poor relative in terms of conservation, its NGOs surprise with a state of the art conservation project that serves as an example to the whole of Europe. The conservation measures of steppe birds near Castro Verde is one such shining example.

Habitat destruction, water consumption and desertification

The destruction of habitats is the major threat to nature and wildlife in southern Portugal. The wonderful Cork and Holm Oak montado woodlands, the steppes in the Baixo Alentejo, the traditional orchards of Olive, Carob, Fig and Almond in the Algarve – they are all the product of a centuries-old traditional land use. Slowly, modern, industrial scale agriculture is getting a foothold in the Portuguese countryside and where it does, the ecologically rich rural habitats disappear. The construction of the huge Alqueva reservoir in 2002 produced one such sudden change in the traditional Alentejo landscape. Not only were over a million trees drowned, it also paved the way to exploiting the pockets of fertile soil in the region, pushing out traditional methods that go so well together with nature conservation. At the time of writing, irrigation systems are still being set up in the Beja area that are causing habitat loss for species that depend on natural vegetation.

The tourism industry in the Algarve and at the Lisbon coast started to create conservation problems from its inception in the 1970s. Ever growing numbers of tourist attracted by the sun and the beautiful beaches of the Algarve resulted in the construction of large tourist facilities, flats, apartments and resorts, with in their wake a dense infrastructure network and massive water consumption. This process has not ended yet. Much of the fragile coastal habitats are affected or simply disappear under concrete. For many areas that were saved, it was a close call. The fossil cliffs of Costa de Caparica (site A on page 135) and the Albufeira lagoon at the Setúbal coast south of Lisbon (site E on page 137) are sandwiched between urban areas developed for tourism. In many places in the Algarve (e.g. Castro Marim; route 13), the tourist flats reach right to the border of the protected site, like a tidal wave frozen in mid air just before it engulfs the beach.

The pretty Hottentot Fig is an agressive invasive species of the Portuguese coast. Especially in sandy open areas, it can cover large areas where originally rare and endemic coastal flowers bloom.

It is not just the use of space. Water demand has skyrocketed to serve hotels and golf courses precisely during the summer, when an already scarce resource is at its lowest point. A single 18-hole golf course in the Algarve (and there are about 40 of these in total), uses the same amount of water annually as 10,000 homes! As a result, nearby wetlands are drying up. Incredibly, there are still new golf courses built, mostly funded by foreign investors. Further inland, dams are built across ecologically valuable river valleys to ensure the water supply in the summer months but they deny critical water flow in winter to wetlands downstream.

The growth of Eucalyptus plantations introduced large scale habitat destruction in some areas in inland Algarve. This tree was introduced from Australia for the pulp and paper industry. In the 1960s Scandinavian timber companies established vast plantations of the Blue Gum Tree (*Eucalyptus globulus*) in Portugal. This helped local economies in the countryside in a moment Portugal was fighting its wars in Africa, so the income was badly needed.

Eucalyptus is the forestry equivalent of asbestos. It seemed right at the time, but now we're stuck with some very nasty problems. These arose fairly soon after the first plantations were created. Villagers noted that their wells dried up and started to complain. Eucalyptus sucks moisture out of the soil, preventing all other vegetation from growing. The plantations are exceptionally poor in insect life as native insects can't consume the leaves, cutting off the food chain and leaving noting for local fauna. Hence there are hardly any birds in eucalyptus plantations. Eucalyptus is nicknamed the Gasoline Tree for its propensity to burn. In spring 2017, 62 people died of a Eucalyptus forest fire in central Portugal.

Portugal shares its history of Eucalyptus plantations with its neighbour Spain, but there, the planting and harvesting of the tree has stopped and a lot of money and effort has been put into the eradication of this harmful tree. It is therefore all the more surprising to see that the exploitation of Eucalyptus is still very much alive in Portugal. Portugal is the country with the largest area of Eucalyptus in Europe, covering more than 20% of its forested area.

A third environmental problem facing Portugal, particularly in the south, is desertification. Climate change, forest fires and extraction of water are to blame. Portugal shows the strongest decline in average yearly rainfall in Europe. Add this to the growing water demand we already mentioned and you see a huge problem emerging.

Natural Parks, reserves and NGOs

So far about the challenges. The solutions come in the form of formally protected areas and a lot of private and NGO initiatives.

Within the area of this book, fourteen areas are legally protected as a Nature Park, Nature Reserve or Protected Landscape. A quick look on the map tells us that they are all near the coast or, in the case of the Guadiana Valley Natural Park, near the Spanish border. The routes we describe in this book reflect their location. Together, they cover and help to preserve the most ecologically valuable areas of southern Portugal, although Monchique continues to be heavily threatened by the Eucalyptus plantations. This and other sites, such as the Castro Verde steppes, are protected under the European Natura 2000 network, which covers a much larger area than the collective sites under national protection.

Aside from the official protected areas, there are various environmental organisations, doing important conservation work. The League for the Protection of Nature (LPN; **www.lpn.pt**) was founded in 1948 and is in fact the oldest Environmental NGO of the Iberian Peninsula. It runs the nature reserve *Reserva Biologica Herdade de São Marcos* on the steppes near Castro Verde and works on a diversity of conservation projects in southern Portugal, including the reintroduction of the Iberian Lynx. Almargem in the Algarve (**www.almargem.org**) is active in the field of nature education, study and conservation projects. Likewise, the Christian conservation organisation A Rocha (**www.arocha.pt**) is doing important work in the Algarve. You'll find them when you're visiting the Alvor lagoon (route 20), where they run their core project. Quercus (**www.quercus.pt**) is the biggest environmental NGO of Portugal, with numerous activities, eight-

Gate to the *Reserva Biologica Herdade de São Marco,* run by the non-governmental organisation LPN (*Liga para a Protecção da Natureza*).

een local groups and the journal Quercus Ambiente (in Portuguese) that can be downloaded for free from its website (**www.quercus.pt/jornal**). The Society for the Study of Birds (SPEA, **www.spea.pt**) is the Portuguese BirdLife partner.

Will the legal framework, complemented by NGO work be enough to preserve southern Portugal's natural heritage? That's a hard question to answer. Much will depend on relieving the pressures of mass tourism and water consumption.

Raising environmental awareness among (tourist) enterprises and local governments is key in steering the country towards a more sustainable land use, particularly in the Algarve, where companies seem to act in a completely demand-driven, free market. In other words, it is up to the customer – you, us and all the other tourists – to influence developments into a more sustainable direction. We do this through the choices we make. Consume wisely, is the motto here. Further, by giving wildlife an economic value we raise the political likelihood of action to conserve what we value. On pages 221 and 222 we give some tips on how to do this.

Protected areas of southern Portugal. The dark green areas are protected on a national level as well as being Natura 2000 sites and Important Bird Areas. The light green areas are only designated Important Bird Areas.

Natura 2000

There are two major European laws for nature conservation, the Habitats Directive and the Birds Directive. A result of these laws is the designation of two types of protected areas, the Special Protection Areas for Birds (largely coinciding with the Important Bird Areas (IBA's) used by Birdlife International) and the Special Areas for Conservation. A third network of protected marine sites is in the making, but not yet complete. Together these sites form the Natura 2000 network, the backbone of European nature conservation.

Natura 2000 sites

1 Ponta da Erva (page 136)
2 Serra da Arrábida (routes 3, 4, 5)
3 Sado Bay (routes 4, 6, site F)
4 Lagoa de Santo André (route 7)
5 Costa Vicentina NP (routes 21 to 23)
6 Vale do Guadiana NP (route 11)
7 Rocha da Pena (route 17)
8 Fonte de Benémola (route 16)
9 Ria Formosa (routes 14 and 15)
10 Castro Marim (route 13)

Important Bird Areas

A Tejo estuary
B Lagoa Pequena
C Cabrela
D Cuba (Beja)
E Mourão, Moura and Barrancos
F Castro Verde
G Luzianes (Beja)
H Serra de Monchique

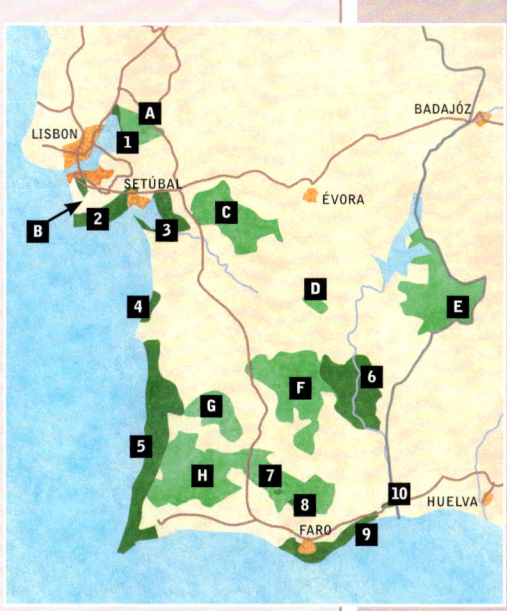

FLORA AND FAUNA

Dolphins and shearwaters cruise the breezy ocean off the coast and sandgrouse hide on the baking inland plateaux. Hundreds of thousands of birds gather in bays near Lisbon and Setubal, while equal numbers of daffodils and orchids flower on the nearby coastal headlands. The matos of Cape St. Vincent and the mountain pastures of the Serra de Monchique support a unique flora. Indeed, the flora and fauna of southern Portugal is remarkably rich and diverse. Whether you visit the Algarve, Costa Vicentina, the Alentejo or the bays near the capital, there is a massive variety of flora and fauna to discover.

Each of these areas is different. In particular you'll find great differences in the flora and fauna at the coast and that further inland.

The plants and animals that inhabit the inland areas, the Alentejo, are all adapted to the peculiar environmental conditions here: very mild and fairly wet winters, extremely hot and dry summers and a soil that is both poor in nutrients and incapable of retaining water. Without mountains nearby to feed the lowlands with water, the wildlife of the Alentejo must be capable of coping with drought.

The vegetation of the interior of southern Portugal is rather uniform, consisting of a number of grasses and herbs on the steppes, scrublands of cistus bushes and Holm and Cork Oaks that form the montado-ecosystem. Over vast areas, you'll encounter these in an unscathed and undisturbed landscape, ideal for a good number of birds. The Alentejo is, above all, an area for birdwatchers.

The coastal strip, both in the south and in the west, is very different. The soils are much more diverse, the slopes much steeper and

The beautiful Azure-winged Magpie is a common sight in the montados and pinewoods.

therefore, nature manifests itself in different ways. There are nutrient-rich wetlands with masses of shorebirds, limestone and acidic soils, woodlands, cliffs and sand dunes each of which have their own flora and fauna.

The climate is more benign too. The winters are even milder, fog brings in moisture and several streams from the Serra de Monchique provide some water even in the dry season. This climate type, which essentially holds sway along the coast between Lisbon and Tarifa (Spain), gives rise to a unique flora and fauna, known as the *Lusitanian ecoregion* (after the ancient Roman province *Lusitania* that covered the western part of the Iberian Peninsula). It is Mediterranean with a twist, combining widespread Mediterranean species with a large number that you'll only find in this particular region, as they rely on the mild winter conditions. The species name *lusitanica*, which you'll find frequently when you flip through a flora of the region, refers to these species.

The largest number of Lusitanian species (again particularly the wild-flowers) are found in the area of Cape St. Vincent, the sand dunes on the west coast and the upland heathlands of the Serra de Monchique.

Cape St. Vincent, the far southwestern tip of Portugal, sports many rare and endemic wildflowers, such as this Saint Vincent Cistus* (*Cistus palhinhae*).

Main biogeographical regions in southern Portugal

Lusitanian region
e.g. Portuguese Squill
(Scilla peruviana)

Ibero-African region
e.g. Aetherie Fritillary
(Melitaea aetherie)

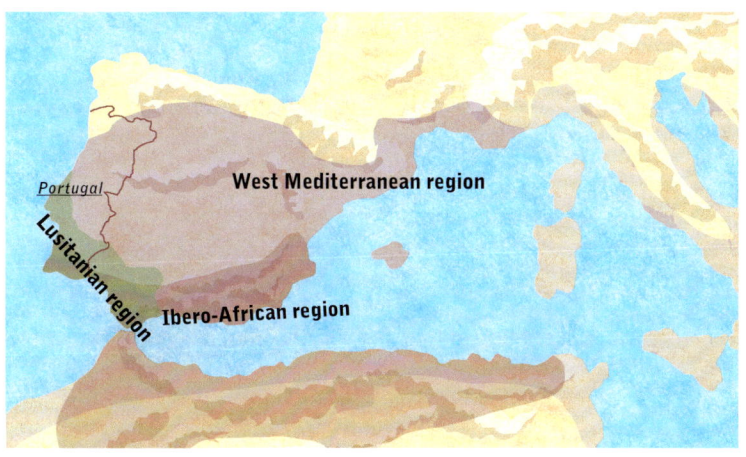

(West) Mediterranean region
e.g. Short-toed Eagle
(Circaetus gallicus)

Temperate region
e.g. Alder
(Alnus glutinosa)

Flora

The richest areas for wildflowers in southern Portugal:
1 Limestone hills of Serra Arrábida and Cabo Espichel, with lots of bulbs and orchids.
2 Dune flora of the west coast, with a specific set of coastal species, many of which are endemic.
3 Cape St. Vincent, which is species rich, with many rare and endemic species.
4 Monchique, which has a different flora from the surroundings due to high precipitation and acidic soils.
5 Barrocal, a limestone zone very rich in orchids.

> Rich cliff flora is found on routes 4, 21 and sites A and D on pages 212-213. The dune flora of southern Portugal is very special and can be enjoyed on routes 6, 7, 14, 15, 21, 22 and sites D on page 213 and E on page 214. The saltmarsh flora is easily observed on routes 6, 14, 15 and 20. The limestone flora is impressive on routes 3, 4, 5, 9, 16, 17 and sites A and B on page 212. A very attractive flora of granite hills can be enjoyed near Monchique, route 18.

Come in spring and the flora of southern Portugal is a vivid spectacle of colour. Brooms, rockroses, lavenders and thymes paint the landscape in all imaginable hues of purple, yellow, white and blue. There are stout and impressive plants like the bright blue Portuguese Squill (p. 68), the thick yellow spikes of the Cistanche (p. 22), the pink dots of the Naked-man Orchids (p. 123) and the large, paper-thin sheets of the Gum Cistus (p. 41). Other wildflowers are more subtle, graceful and delicate, such as the narcissi, orchids and toadflaxes in a dazzling variety. In the Alentejo the ground turns purple with Purple Viper's-bugloss, is white-washed by daisies and chamomiles and subsequently carpeted with all sorts of yellow crucifers and composites.

The right time is rather short though and the peak comes early in the year. From late February to early May, southern Portugal is a riot of colour, but as soon as it gets hot and dry, the flowers disappear.

The short season is the result of the special climatic conditions of the far south: the winters are very mild and the summer heat and drought sets in early. This shifts the flowering season to earlier in the year. Since there are no cooler high mountains in the area and very little permanent water, there is no refuge from the summer heat for late bloomers – hence the concentration of the flowering period in early spring.

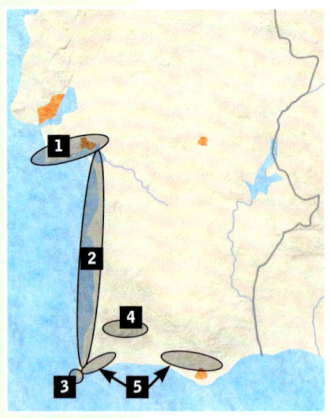

The spring flora is not only impressive in its profusion but also by the presence of some attractive species. Southern Portugal, more precisely the Algarve and south-west coast, is home to a fair number of highly localised or even endemic wildflowers.

The flora of the Algarve is well studied. Usually, it is divided into three different regions that coincide with the geological zone (page 14): the coast or

Littoral, a strip of limestone hills known as the *Barrocal* and the interior *Serra* with mostly acidic soils. The area described in this book is much larger but, with some modifications, these distinctions are useful in getting to grips with the flora.

Flora of the coast

The coastal region is the most diverse and attractive from a botanical perspective. There are dunes, salt marshes, cliffs and wind-beaten headlands, often in close proximity to one another. Each have a rich and attractive flora of their own. It is in this region that you'll find a large number of endemic wildflowers – species that occur nowhere else than here on this coast. The pearl in the crown is the magnificent Cape St. Vincent, which even has a number of wildflowers unique to it alone, plus a large number of species that are typical of the Iberian southwest coast.

The *matos* in spring boast a very high number of flowering herbs and shrubs.

If you look at a flora of Portugal (the online flora **www.flora-on.pt** is excellent for this) you'll find many wildflowers that occur on the coast roughly from Lisbon, round Cape St. Vincent, across the border into Spain and even on to Tarifa. Like the local micro-climate, this ecological region is called, in botanical jargon, *Lusitanian* – warm in summer, extremely mild in winter and strongly influenced by the ocean. The conditions for growth here are so different from the climatically harsh interior, that one could see this ecologically as an island, bordered by a 'sea' of different environmental conditions. On such 'islands', plants may evolve into new species and that is exactly what happened here. That's why there are so many endemic species (see box).

Apart from Cape St. Vincent, the dunes and capes of the entire western coast are very rich in wildflowers, with the Cabo Espichel and Serra da Arrábida being further hotspots.

A wildflower walk around one of the capes (Cape St. Vincent or any other) typically means going back and forth between the most exposed headlands, where hardy species like Goldcoin, Saint Vincent Cistus*

64

(*Cistus palhinhae*; p. 60) and the invasive, South-African Hottentot Fig can be found, to several hundred metres inland, where the diversity of species is much higher. Here, sheltered between the shrubs, there are Spanish Fritillaries, Two-leaved Gennarias, Hoop-petticoat Daffodils, Snapdragons and Sawfly Orchids. A common shrub on Cape St. Vincent is the afore-mentioned Saint Vincent Cistus*, which has shiny, sticky leaves and large white flowers. It is closely related to the Gum Cistus which is widespread on acidic soils in the interior, but the Cape St. Vincent version is much lower and has more rounded (and glossier) leaves.

The coast of the Algarve, in particular the southwestern parts and the lime-stone hills just inland, are superb wildflower haunts. The rare Cadiz Daffodil* (*Narcissus gaditanus*) is one of the spring delights here.

> **Endemic wildflowers of the south-west coast**
> Saint Vincent Bucklar-mustard* (*Biscutella vicentina*), Rothmaler's Catchfly* (*Silene rothmaleri*), *Astragalus tragacantha*, Shrubby Violet (*Viola arbores-cens*), Saint Vincent Cistus* (*Cistus palhinhae*), Algarve Toadflax (*Linaria al-garviana*), Ficalho's Toadflax (*Linaria ficalhoana*), Saint Vincent Germander* (*Teucrium vicentinum*), *Thymus camphoratus*, Hackel's Bellevalia (*Bellevalia hackelii*)

On many headlands, low dune complexes have formed, which have a very different set of wild-flowers. Notable species here are Portuguese Crowberry, Spiny Thrift, Yellow Rockrose, Wrinkle-leaved Cistus and Creeping Gromwell* (*Lithodora prostrata*). Between these shrubs grows a wealth of wildflowers, many of which have only small, Lusitanian ranges.

The environment of cliff slopes is one of ex-tremes – intense solar radiation (on southfacing cliffs), drought exacerbated by strong gales, salt spray and unstable soils which make for a set-ting that is both severe and unique. It is here that some of the special wildflowers are found. One of them is the Shrubby violet, among the few European species of pansy to form a shrub and also extremely rare: it only grows at Cape St. Vincent and Cape Trafalgar in Andalucia. Other rarities include the sea-lavender *Limonium vir-gatum* and the Cape St. Vincent endemic pink *Silene rothmaleri*.

One group of wildflowers that occur on many headlands (as well as in the interior) are daffodils. The hundreds of thousands of Hoop-petticoat Daffodils on Cabo Espichel (no exaggeration!) are a positive assault on the retina. The cliffs of the Costa Vicentina also host a number of rare species.

The daffodils are something special in Iberia anyway. The genus of Narcissi evolved on the Peninsula and it is here that the diversity of species is the highest. In fact, within the area of this book, no less than 8 species occur, and in Portugal as a whole there are 17 species, plus numerous subspecies.

Once you've trotted around for a little while grappling with the cliff flora, you'll notice that one of the attractions of Portugal's coastal flora is that dunes and salt marshes are usually close by. This adds a second string to your bow on a day out, since the dune flora is both distinct and particularly attractive.

Below the dunes lies a subterranean reservoir of freshwater. It is there, but to reach it plants need to invest in deep roots. The perennial, deep-rooted species are Spiny Thrift, which forms tussocks with pink flowers, Dune Galingale, Coastal Crucianella, Cottonweed, the yellow Branched Restharrow* (*Ononis ramosissima*), Yellow Rockrose, Shrubby Figwort and the familiar Marram Grass.

Other dune plants follow a different strategy: germinating, flowering and setting seed in the short favourable season when it rains. The Stitchwort-leaved Allseeds* (*Polycarpon alsinifolium*), the white-flowering Nice Catchfly* (*Silene nicaeensis*), the pink, sticky Seaside Catchfly* (*Silene littorea*) and various toadflaxes are among these species.

In the dunes you'll see a similar change as on the headlands when you walk inland: more and different plants appear as you walk further from the sea. The harshest growing conditions on the coast are nearest to the sea where the wind is strongest and the air most salt laden. These conditions can be tolerated by only a few plants, like Sea Holly, Sea Bindweed, Sea Spurge and Sea Daffodil. Their names reflect that they grow in close proximity to the sea, something which requires such a level of adaptation that only they can thrive. Further inland, the aforementioned species, together with Stinking Broomrape (despite its name a pretty species), the endemic toadflax *Linaria ficalhoana*, Sage-leaved

Shrubby Violet (top) and Ficalho's Toadflax* (*Linaria ficalhoana*; bottom) are two endemic wildflowers of the Lusitanian coast.

Cistus, Pale Stonecrop, Snapdragon (p. 63), Shrubby Pimpernel (p. 134), Sand-crocus (p. 202), Yellow Rockrose (p. 129) and many others.

In comparison to the headlands and dunes, the saltmarshes are less diverse, but they nevertheless are worth exploring. In spring the first plant to catch the attention is the parasitic Cistanche (p. 22). It taps the roots of Sea Purslane, which grows in profusion in the saltmarshes. Broomrapes, to which the Cistanche is related, are often much less common than their host plants but this case is a fortunate exception (fortunate for us observers of beautiful wildflowers; less so for the host plants). Cistanches may occur by the hundreds on the edges of saltmarshes and saltpans.

Another typical wildflower that blooms in spring is the pink-flowered bush Limoniastrum, which only grows in the saltmarshes of the southern Algarve. It is related to the sea-lavenders, of which there are many species in the saltmarsh. These, in contrast to the vast majority of the southern Portuguese flora, flower in summer.

Saltmarshes are rarely free of human meddling – dikes and tracks are everywhere and they are often constructed from sand and limestone soil from the nearby hills. The edges of these banks (which provide your route into the habitat) can, depending on the material they are made of, be very rich in wildflowers. In early spring (February-March) there are in certain places, masses of orchids. Bumblebee, Yellow Bee, Common Bee and Mirror Orchids are the most frequently found. Ecologically, this has little to do with saltmarsh of course, but that's easily forgotten when you stand back and admire a patch of several thousand of these little gems.

Portuguese Crowberry (top) grows on low sand dunes. It is a species of south-western Iberia, a taller shrub than the familiar Crowberry of the north, and with berries like pearls. The stout Stinking Broomrape is a common species on the southwestern coast (bottom).

Flora of the limestone hills

Just behind the coastal plain of the Algarve lies a narrow belt of limestone that is known as the barrocal.

Conspicuous wildflowers of the coast

Cape flora Spanish Fritillary (*Fritillaria lusitanica*), Hoop-petticoat Daffodil (*Narcissus bulbocodium*), Cadiz Daffodil* (*Narcissus gaditanus*), Sea Carrot (*Daucus halophilus*), Tree Mallow (*Lavatera arborea*), Camphor Thyme (*Thymus camphoratus*)

Flora of primary dunes Linaria pedunculata, Seaside Catchfly* (*Silene littorea*), Sea Holly (*Euphorbia paralias*), Sea Daffodil (*Pancratium maritimum*), Chalk Alkanet* (*Anchusa calcarea*), Branched Restharrow (*Ononis ramosissima*), Spiny Thrift (*Armeria pungens*), Yellow Rockrose (*Halimium calycinum*), Ficalho's Toadflax* (*Linaria ficalhoana*), Shrubby Figwort (*Scrophularia frutescens*), Dune Galingale (*Cyperus capitatus*), Coastal Crucianella (*Crucianella maritima*), Stitchwort-leaved Allseeds* (*Polycarpon alsinifolium*)

Flora of secondary dunes (a bit further inland) Prostrate Candytuft* (*Iberis procumbens*), Yellow Centaury (*Centaurium maritimum*), Two-leaved Gennaria (*Gennaria diphylla*), Heart-flowered Tongue Orchid (*Serapias cordigera*), Sharp-lipped Tongue Orchid (*Serapias strictiflora*), Round-headed Knapweed (*Centaurea sphaerocephala*), Spiny Thrift (*Armeria pungens*), Yellow Rockrose (*Halimium calycinum*), Snapdragon (*Antirrhinum majus*), Stinking Broomrape (*Orobanche foetida*), Sand-crocus (*Romulea bulbocodium*), Three-leaved Snowflake (*Leucojum trichophyllum*), Spotted Rockrose (*Tuberaria guttata*), Shrubby Pimpernel (*Anagallis monelli*), Capeweed (*Arctotheca calendula*)

Saltmarsh Tree Purslane (*Atriplex halimus*), Limoniastrum (*Limoniastrum monopetalum*), Yellow Cistanche (*Cistanche pelyphaea*), the sea-lavenders *Limonium ferulaceum* and *Limonium ovalifolium*

A rarity of the hills with acidic schists and granites: the Portuguese Sundew. It is a beautiful carnivorous plant that catches insects with the sticky glands on the leaves.

Bulbs are common in spring in the Algarve. The grape-hyacinth-like Bellevalia (top) grows on limestone and sandstone close to the coast, as does the Portuguese Squill (centre). Both are native to the southwest coast of the Iberian Peninsula.
The Barbary Nut (bottom), a handsome dwarf iris, is very common throughout southern Portugal.

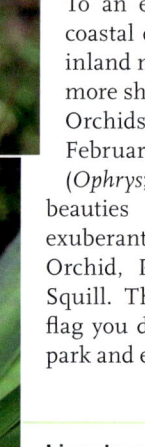

Similar coastal limestone hills are found further north all along the west coast, with important outcrops around Setúbal (the Serra da Arrábida). This zone offers many wildflower hotspots. Orchards, scrubland and roadsides (especially roadsides!) offer a great number of beautiful wildflowers. To an extent, the flora is similar to the coastal cliff flora, but the position further inland means a more benign climate, with more shelter, no salt spray and taller scrub. Orchids are a key attraction here between February to May, especially bee orchids (*Ophrys*; see page 71). These discrete beauties often grow close to the more exuberantly coloured plants like Naked-man Orchid, Pyramidal Orchid or Portuguese Squill. These are the plants that seem to flag you down, urging you to find a spot to park and explore the roadside – when you do,

Limestone flora Andalusian Birthwort (*Aristolochia baetica*), Lusitanian Milkvetch (*Erophaca baetica*), Purple Jerusalem-sage (*Phlomis purpurea*), Spanish Fritillary (*Frittilaria lusitanica*), Hoop-petticoat Daffodil (*Narcissus bulbocodium*), Cadiz Daffodil* (*N. gaditanus*), Rosy Garlic (*Allium roseum*), Portuguese Squill (*Scilla peruviana*), Illyrian Gladiole (*Gladiolus communis*), Wild Gladiole (*G. italicus*), Spanish Iris (*Iris xiphium*), *Barbary Nut (Gyrandriris sisyrinchium),* Hackel's Bellevalia (Bellevalia hackelii), Tassel Hyacinth (*Muscari comosum*), Grape-hyacinth (*Muscari neglectum*), Yellow Bee Orchid (*Ophrys lutea*), Woodcock Orchid (*O. scolopax*), Bumblebee Orchid (*O. bombilyflora*), Bee Orchid (*O. apifera*), Mirror Orchid (*O. speculum*), Lusitanian Mirror Orchid (*O. lusitanica*), Spanish Omega Orchid* (*O. dyris*), Sombre Bee Orchid (*O. fusca*), Naked-man Orchid (*Orchis italica*), Man Orchid (*O. anthropophora*), Southern Early Purple Orchid (*O. olbiensis*), Pyramidal Orchid (*A. pyramidalis*)

you're likely to find many other species of wildflowers, including many orchids.

Other eyecatchers are the shrubs. Masses of pink-flowered Grey-leaved Cistus grow here alongside Sage-leaved Cistus, Etruscan Honeysuckle, Wild Olive, Rosemary and Strawberry Tree. In grassy spots, there are Wild Gladiolus, the baby-blue Spanish Iris and various birthwort species, including the pretty pink Andalusian Birthwort* (*Aristolochia baetica*). There are three common parasitic species that take nutrients and minerals from grasses although, in contrast to broomrapes, they have green leaves. These are Yellow Bartsia, the white-and-pink *Bartsia trixago* and the much smaller, deep-pink Southern Red Bartsia, all of which can form large drifts.

Flora of the interior

Visit the Alentejo between February and mid-May and you'll find the fields and montados full of wildflowers. Swathes of Purple Viper's-bugloss, patches of Pink Catchflies, splashes of blue from the bellflowers and seas of Yellow Lupin. The bushes of Gum Cistus dot the hillsides with their large white flowers.

The wildflower show is so exuberant that it even exceeds that on the coast and in the Algarve. The diversity however, is fairly low and the species that occur are common and widespread, both within Portugal and beyond. The flora of the interior is above all scenic, and not one for connoisseurs. Generally speaking, that is – there are of course exceptions.

The fairly uniform, poor acidic soil is the main reason for the limited number of species. Another reason is the periodic ploughing, which

The poor and overall acidic bedrock of the Alentejo supports few wildflowers, but those that do occur, are beautiful and present in overwhelming numbers. One of them is the French Lavender, which spreads a wonderful, herbal scent.

The Andalusian Birthwort* (*Aristolochia baetica*) is a pretty climbing plant that is found in scrub and waste places all over the southern part of the region. In the Alentejo it is replaced by other birthwort species. They are the host plant of the impressive Spanish Festoon butterfly (p. 100).

favours annual and biannual species – plants that do well in disturbed soils because they produce lots of seeds that spread widely. These include various species of chamomiles, hawkbeards, cudweeds, daisies, the yellow crucifer *Diplotaxis catholica* and Purple Viper's-bugloss. These are the ones that put up the spectacular display of colour that greets you on hillside after hillside in late winter and spring. Another plant that grows here in jaw-dropping profusion is Yellow Lupin (p. 146). Though native to the Portuguese Flora, this plant is often planted as a 'green fertilizer' – bacteria in the roots fix nitrogen which improves the quality of the soil. Meanwhile, the flowers do the same for the scenery.

The more interesting wildflowers are found on the rocky hillsides, often right beside the road. Although most species here are widespread within the Alentejo and northern Algarve, the plants are quite typical for this region,

Shrubs French Lavender (*Lavendula stoechas*), Spiny Greenweed (*Genista hirsuta*), Sage-leaved Cistus (*Cistus salvifolius*), Narrow-leaved Cistus (*Cistus monspeliensis*), Gum Cistus (*Cistus ladanifer*), Mediterranean Mezereon (*Daphne gnidium*)

Herbs Steppe Edelweiss* (*Paronychia capitata*), Pink Catchfly (*Silene colorata*), Small-flowered Catchfly (*Silene gallica*), Narrow-leaved Lupin (*Lupinus angustifolius*), Yellow Lupin (*Lupinus luteus*), Spotted Rockrose (*Tuberaria guttata*), Purple Viper's-bugloss (*Echium plantagineum*), Large Blue Alkanet (*Anchusa azurea*), Iberian Jerusalem-sage (*Phlomis lychnitis*), Ballast Toadflax* (*Linaria spartea*), Lusitanian Spreading Bellflower* (*Campanula lusitanica*), Rampion Bellflower (*Campanula rapunculus*), Golden Thistle (*Scolymus hispanicus*), Corn Marigold (*Glebionis segetum*), Tolpis (*Tolpis barbata*), Galactitis (*Galactitis tomentosum*), Friar's Cowl (*Arisarum vulgare*), Barbary Nut (*Gyrandriris sysirynchium*), Large-flowered Sand-crocus* (*Romulea bulbocodium*), Autumn Narcissus (*Narcissus serotinus*), Autumn Snowflake (*Leucojum autumnale*), Brown Bluebell (*Dipcadi serotinum*), Italian Gladiole (*Gladiolus segetum*), Autumn Squill (*Scilla autumnalis*), Tassel Hyacinth (*Muscari comosum*), Sea Squill (*Drimia maritima*), White Asphodel (*Asphodelus albus*), Sawfly Orchid (*Ophrys tenthredinifera*), Champagne Orchid (*Anacamptis champagneuxii*), Small-flowered Tongue Orchid (*Serapias parviflora*), Tongue Orchid (*Serapias lingua*) (plus adjacent Extremadura and northern Andalucia in Spain). Typically, you'll encounter shrubs like Gum, Narrow-leaved and Sage-leaved Cistus, French Lavender (p. 69) and Spiny Greenweed (p. 155). In winter, you'll find Friar's Cowl to be a common wildflower – in spring the leaves of this small relative of Lords-and-Ladies are still a common sight.

On the better spots – particularly those with a deeper and slightly moister soil, Barbary Nut (a small, pretty and light blue iris; p. 68) can be very common, and, with a little luck, you may see some orchids, particularly Champagne and Tongue Orchids. You'll find these most often near streams.

The uniformity of the Alentejo flora is a direct result of the poor schist and granite soils. Hence the limestone pockets in the vicinity of Beja are a welcome change from the rest of the region. The landscape may not be that different from the rest of the Alentejo, the flora is. Perhaps, in contrast to the ubiquitous montados, the higher frequency of agricultural land and olive groves indicate (at least to the careful observer) that the soils are more fertile here. If you search the pastures and groves, you'll find a great number of orchids of limestone soils, such as Mirror, Sombre Bee and Yellow Bee Orchid, and lots more. These are the botanical treasures of the Alentejo.

Two of the more uncommon orchids of southern Portugal: the Fragrant Bug Orchid (top) and the Black Spider Orchid (bottom).

Orchids

Southern Portugal is a very fine region for orchids. With around 38 species, the diversity is, by European standards fairly high. Although there are areas with a higher diversity of species in parts of Greece, Italy and France, the sheer number that flower in parts of southern Portugal is astonishing. Many of the species found in the region are widespread Mediterranean species, but there is also a good number that have only a small range. Spanish Omega Orchid* (*Ophrys dyris*) for example, is limited to the Iberian Peninsula and northern Morrocco. Southern Early Purple-orchid* (*Orchis olbiensis*) is restricted to the Iberian Peninsula and a very small area in France. The odd, green-flowered Two-leaved

Gennaria is only common in southwestern Portugal, Madeira and a few Canary Islands and has only a handful of other populations in the Mediterranean. The small Bumblebee Orchid is rare almost throughout its Mediterranean range, except for the Portuguese and western Andalusian coast. The Lusitanian Mirror Orchid (*Ophrys lusitanica*) is rarer still, being endemic only to southern Portugal and Andalucia.

To appreciate this wealth of orchids, you have to be here early in the year. The first start to bloom in January and during the course of February, numbers start to swell until they peak around the middle of March. By mid-April, most species are past their prime and a more modest set of 'late bloomers' appear to hold out until mid-May. A few helleborines and the Summer Lady's-tresses flower between mid-May and late June.

This being said, there is a clear difference between the coastal regions and the interior. A Yellow Bee Orchid on the Algarve coast may already be flowering in the first week of February and may have withered a month later, when its relative in the Alentejo is yet to open its first flower.

Orchids of the genus *Ophrys* are particularly numerous in the region. The flowers are famous for mimicking insects – each orchid species attracts its own species of wasp of which the males attempt to copulate with the flower. Pollination occurs as the wasp flies from one flower to the next.

The most common species in southern Portugal are Sombre Bee Orchid (top), Sawfly Orchid (centre) and Yellow Bee and Mirror Orchid (bottom).

The limestone regions of the *Barrocal* (a little inland from Cape St. Vincent), the Serra da Arrábida and the limestone pockets in the Alentejo are the richest orchid haunts. The pink Naked-man Orchids (p. 123) and Pyramidal Orchids are the most eye-catching wildflowers here in March-April and April-May respectively. They flower here together with large numbers of orchids of the bee orchid genus (*Ophrys*). Most numerous are Yellow Bee, Mirror, Sawfly, Sombre Bee (both of the forms *fusca* and *bilunulata*; the latter with a thin yellow margin along the lip) and Woodcock Orchid (in the forms *scolopax* and *apiformis*). Close to the coast, the tiny Bumblebee Orchid may form large drifts. This species is very rare inland. The late Black Spider Orchid is a feature of the Serra da Arrábida and is not found further south. Bee Orchid is rather local, but where present, it is often found in large numbers.

Much less common is the Spanish Omega Orchid* (*Ophrys dyris*) and Lusitanian Mirror Orchid* (*O. lusitanica*) – the latter species is very much a feature of the south.

There are more differences between the various regions. Two-leaved Gennaria for example, occurs only on the coast, roughly from Lisbon down to Lagos. Within this limited range, it can be very common though. The beautiful and early-flowering Fan-lipped Orchid grows only in a few sites inland, close to the Spanish border. Another winter-flowering species, the Giant Orchid, is not found in the Algarve either, but is, within our region, exclusive to the Serra Arrábida and a few limestone areas in the Alentejo. The striking Pink Butterfly Orchid grows, in large numbers, exclusively in the Serra da Arrábida.

Tongue Orchids form another common group, but one that grows both on limestone and acidic soils. On limestone, Long-lipped (*Serapias vomeracea*), Sharp-lipped (*S. strictiflora*), Heart-flowered (*S. cordigera*) and Small-flowered Tongue Orchids (*S. parviflora*) are often found, whereas on acidic ground, Small-flowered and Common Tongue Orchids are particularly numerous. The latter often grow together with Champagne and sometimes Green-winged Orchids.

A final orchid region is the Serra de Monchique. It is not nearly as rich as the limestone regions, but the acidic soils, the moisture and shade allow for a number of orchids that are rare or absent elsewhere: Tremols and Portuguese Helleborine, Violet Bird's-nest and Green-winged Orchid are the more frequent species.

Apart from the above-mentioned species, there are still others. A full list of orchids can be downloaded from our website.

Mammals

On the small backroads in the Alentejo (e.g. routes 8 to 12), you have a chance on spotting Mongoose or, more rarely, the other predators. For Otters, try route 8, 9 and 11. Dolphins may be spotted from the Setúbal Ferry and with luck from the headlands (route 4 and 21), but better on a whalewatching trip in summer from Sagres (site C on page 213).

The Genet is a nocturnal, cat-like mammal that is quite common in the woodlands and montados, though hardly ever seen. This is a young animal.

Southern Portugal is not the first European destination you'd have in mind when searching for mammals. With the exception of a few species, they are very hard to find, even if you go out actively to look for them with the use of specialised equipment like live traps and bat detector. In this section, we'll focus on mammals that are fairly commonly seen or are of special interest.

Predators

As in much of Europe, large predators are lacking in southern Portugal, but there is a good range of medium-sized carnivores, like Red Fox, Genet and Egyptian Mongoose.

The Red Fox is fairly common and widespread. It is largely nocturnal, but every now and then, it shows itself in daytime too. The same goes for Otters, which are widespread along the larger rivers. Occasionally, they are present during the day, playing in the water or lazing on the bank.

Perhaps the most graceful of all the predators is the Genet. It is still not clear how this essentially African animal reached Europe, except that it was a long time ago. This tree dwelling carnivore finds a perfect climate in southern

Portugal where it is common in forested areas and probably more abundant here than anywhere else in Europe. However, it is strictly nocturnal and extremely difficult to see.

Another carnivore considered to have been introduced a long time ago into Europe from Africa is the Egyptian Mongoose. About the size of a cat and with an elongated, dark grey-brown body, short legs and a long broad tail, it is easy to recognise. Although it prefers humid areas, the Mongoose is common and widespread in most of the region, especially the interior. The Egyptian Mongoose avoids areas with intensive agriculture and busy, built-up areas. As this animal is active by day, it is seen fairly often crossing the road or path. Interestingly, hunters consider it a pest for its presumed impact on Rabbits and Hares, while the Moors (who probably introduced it to the Iberian Peninsula) considered it a useful pest controller as Mongoose are active snake hunters.

The Wildcat is similar to the domestic cat (with which it interbreeds) but it has a broad, ringed tail and longer legs. It is common in wooded areas. With a highly secretive and nocturnal life the Wildcat is very difficult to spot.

The rarest predator of southern Portugal is the Iberian Lynx. Its distribution in Portugal at the end of the 20th Century was reduced to the foothills of the Algarve and by the turn of the century no animals survived. Its preferred habitat is scrubland and open woodlands with an abundance of Rabbits. Habitat fragmentation, decline in the Rabbit population, road casualties and hunting are the main causes of its local extinction and nowadays the elusive Iberian Lynx is considered the most threatened feline in the world.

Following the re-introduction program in Spain, for the first time in Portugal, a pair of Iberian Lynx was introduced into the Guadiana Valley Natural Park near Mértola in December 2014. More Iberian Lynxes are being released from the breeding centre near Silves in the Algarve or from any of the four Spanish breeding centres. At the time of writing, several animals have been spotted in different parts of southern

Otters live in all the larger rivers of southern Portugal, because they are still clean and full of fish.

Portugal and there seems a well-founded hope for its return. The goal of this European conservation (Life+) project is to re-establish the historical distribution and a stable population on the Iberian Peninsula.

Other predatory mammals in southern Portugal are the Weasel, the European Polecat, the Badger and the Beech Marten.

Grazing animals

Once, southern Portugal must have had many deer and other grazing animals. They have largely disappeared. The Red Deer is extinct in the wild, but animals are kept in fenced estates where they are kept for the hunt. Fallow Deer (not a native species in Portugal) are also kept in some estates, particularly in the Guadiana area. These animals can survive for some time in the wild and even breed. The small Roe Deer occurs in central Portugal, where it has reached the very southwestern edge of its distribution range. However, the population is increasing on the Iberian Peninsula, so perhaps it may expand to the wooded areas of the southern Guadiana valley.

In contrast to the above, the Wild Boar is common and widespread in the rural areas of the region. It is heavily hunted, though, and has therefore become a shy and largely nocturnal animal.

Bats

The lives of bats always have an air of mystery about them and, unless you've come equipped with a bat detector, their identity is likely to remain a secret. Suffice to say that there are lots of them in southern Portugal, both in numbers of individuals and in diversity of species.

No less than four species of horse-shoe bats are known to live in the area. The Greater and Lesser are widespread, the Mediterranean Horse-shoe Bat mainly lives in caves in the Guadiana region, while the endangered Mehely´s Horse-shoe Bat has several colonies in cliffs in the central Algarve and near Setúbal.

Eight other bat species are widely present in the area: the Lesser and Greater Mouse-eared Bats, Natterer´s Bat, Kuhl´s, Common and Soprano Pipistrelles, Serotine and Grey Long-eared Bat. Another

Due to its typical broad ears that touch on top of its head, the Barbastrelle is easily recognised. Many of them have bright orange mites on the outer fringes of the ears.

seven species have a more restricted distribution. There are several colonies of the migrating Schreiber's Bat in the central Algarve sea cliffs. Daubenton's, Geoffroy's, Brown Long-eared, the high and fast flying European Free-tailed Bat, Barbastelle and Lesser Noctule are present, but in low numbers (or their distribution is insufficiently known).

Mice, voles, shrews, hedgehog and rabbits

This is another group of secretive animals that are widespread and present in large numbers. Only the Common Hedgehog is seen fairly often as it scurries through the underbrush at dawn or dusk. It is widespread and lives in lowlands and hills, in woodlands, pastures, wetlands and gardens near resorts at the coast. The small Iberian Shrew is rare in the Lisbon area, the tiny Etruscan (Pygmy) Shrew is scarce in extensively used lands and the Greater White-toothed Shrew is widespread and common all over. The Iberian Mole, living underground, is a common and widespread endemic whose presence can be confirmed by the molehills it produces.

With some luck you may find a Southwestern Water Vole, as it is common and may be seen at daytime on riverbanks and in marshy areas. Cabrera's Vole with a fragmented distribution in grasslands, fields and clearings in woodlands has also been recorded on the coast (e.g. routes 7 and 14). This vulnerable endemic from the Iberian Peninsula is under pressure from agricultural intensification. The Mediterranean Pine Vole produces complex systems of galleries and burrows in grasslands and pastures while the less abundant Lusitanian Pine Vole prefers

The familiar Red Fox is common all over Portugal and one of the predators that is most easily seen.

orchards and vegetable crops and can be such a pest locally that control measures are taken. The smaller Wood and the Western House Mouse are common all over the area. The distribution of the beautiful Garden Dormouse extends from Portugal to the Urals but the species is not common in the woodlands and orchards of our area.

The Rabbit can be found almost everywhere and is locally common. The Iberian Hare is abundant in the steppes and agricultural areas of Setúbal and the Alentejo.

Sea mammals

The Atlantic Ocean off the southern Portuguese coast is frequented by a large variety of dolphins and whales (cetaceans in jargon). Around twenty species have been reported so far. Most of them follow deep chasms and edges of submerged banks and plateaux where they find their prey.

Sometimes, dolphins can be seen from the headlands of Cabo Espichel and Cape St. Vincent but be aware that a telescope, patience and luck are important ingredients for success. Big whales have been reported, but most of the sea mammals remain far from the coast. There are accounts of trawlers being 'surrounded' by dolphins. Whether they are true or the proverbial fisherman's tale remains questionable, but it is clear that your best chance of seeing them is on a boat trip. Fortunately, whale-watching trips are organised from Sagres or Portimão which take you some 15 kms offshore where the cetaceans gather to hunt (see page 213). Sea mammals to be expected on such trips are Common Dolphin (on rare occasions, up to a hundred animals are seen on a single trip), family group of Bottlenose Dolphins and Harbour Porpoise. Your chances of encountering larger whales are decidedly slimmer but from time to time, Minke Whale, Orca, False Killer Whale and Long-finned Pilot Whale are reported.

Common Dolphins are frequent in the waters off Cape St. Vincent and Cape Espichel.

Birds

Waders, flamingos, spoonbills and other birds of saltmarshes are found on routes 1, 2, 3, 6, 13, 14, 15, 19 and 20. For herons, ducks, Purple Gallinules and other birds of freshwater marshes, visit routes 6, 7, 14 and 15 plus site C and E on page 136-137, A on page 158 and A and B on pages 195-196. For birds of the montados (like shrikes, bee-eaters and Azure-winged Magpies), spend time on routes 2, 6, 8, 9, 10, 11, 12 and 18. Steppe birds are best on route 10, but also on route 8 and sites F and G on pages 161-162. The best raptor routes are 9, 10 and 11 and for seabird watching, try routes 4 and 21. Cape St. Vincent (route 21) is the best for witnessing migration.

Do you want to try the White-rumped Swifts today or have a crack at the sandgrouse? Take some frame-filling photos of Purple Gallinules or spend some pleasurable hours solving what-is-that-wader-puzzles? Whichever way you turn, southern Portugal is a paradise for birdwatchers. Pretty birds like Bee-eater, Hoopoe and Azure-winged Magpie come by the dozens, while the likes of Bonelli's Eagle and Rufous Bush-chat are real possibilities when you set out to search for them.

Southern Portugal is one of the best places in Europe to see steppe birds like this Great Bustard.

The attraction of southern Portugal as a destination for birders (and other naturalists) is in its variety of Mediterranean species and its Iberian specialities in combination with an unpredictable but rich number of migrating birds in spring and autumn. Seabirds form an attractive distraction, as do the many exotic escapees that have established feral populations.

An added bonus is that coastal and inland birding sites are not too far from one another, making it possible to see a lot of different species without having to drive too much. The steppes of the Alentejo are just over an hour's drive from the Algarve and provide some of the best birding in Europe. Rather unknown and undervalued are the extensive estuaries near Lisbon, which are rich in migrating birds set in rugged surroundings.

Waders and other birds of the estuaries

The estuaries and coastal lagoons are the birding hotspots of southern Portugal. Hundreds of thousands of waders, gulls, terns and ducks

are present in the estuaries of the Tejo, Sado, Ria Formosa and Castro Marim (the Guadiana estuary). Waders on the East Atlantic Flyway pass through the Portuguese marshes as they move between their breeding grounds in the Arctic and the wintering grounds on the African west coast. Their numbers and the exact composition of species vary through the year, but at any time, there will be wading birds present. Four species dominate: Avocet, Grey Plover, Black-tailed Godwit and Dunlin account for 90% of the waders present in winter on the Tagus. Of these, Dunlin is the most abundant species.

For Dunlin and other waders that breed in the 'far north', this is roughly the over-

The dainty Black-winged Stilt is a common sight in estuaries, rice paddies and saltpans.

all pattern: numbers are lowest in Portugal from late May to July, when the birds are on the breeding grounds. By late July numbers start to increase, first by failed breeders, and then in August onwards, successful adults and young birds follow. For some species, such as Lapwings and Black-tailed Godwits, this autumn migration may have already started at the end of June, thereby almost overlapping with the last spring migrants heading north. During autumn, more and more birds pour in from the north whilst earlier arrivals push on further south. Late winter, when the last of the groups migrate south, the first are returning again, their numbers building up during spring.

Although this is the general pattern, the exact dates differ from species to species and according to the weather conditions. The Black-tailed Godwit inhabits the estuaries from June to February, while the Redshank peaks in August. Bar-tailed Godwit builds up the largest numbers in September but for the Red Knot the peak is in November. Many Avocets from the north spend the winter in southern Portugal and highest numbers are found from November to February. Other non-breeding species, with maxima of several hundreds of individuals, are Oystercatcher, Lapwing, Turnstone, Sanderling, Curlew Sandpiper, Little Stint, Ruff,

Curlew, Whimbrel, Spotted Redshank, Greenshank, with other species in lower numbers. In fact, any wader can show up, including American and Asian vagrants.

Far fewer species breed on the Portuguese estuaries. These are primarily Avocet, Black-winged Stilt, Kentish, Ringed and Little Ringed Plover. They are most numerous in spring and early summer.

All these waders occur in roughly the same habitat

and often in mixed groups, making any flock (and there are quite a few of them), a tempting reason to stop and scan. It's not only waders that use the tidal areas; other birds are at least as conspicuous. Outside the breeding season, thousands of Black-headed, Yellow-legged and Lesser Black-backed Gulls and many hundreds of Mediterranean Gulls forage during low tide.

As the name implies, Cattle Egrets prefer the company of cattle. They often ride along the backs of sheep, cows or horses, using the animals both as a vantage point and hunting tool – Cattle Egrets feed on large insects that jump or fly off in front of the animal hooves.

Until recently, both Slender-billed and Audouin's Gull were listed as rarities in Portugal but both have increased in recent decades with two small colonies of the latter being established at Castro Marim and Ria Formosa. Little Terns breed whilst Common Terns appear on passage and Sandwich and (far fewer) Caspians Terns winter. The hundreds of Little Egrets and Grey Herons (increasingly joined in winter by Great White Egrets) can be seen from afar but the most conspicuous of all is the Greater Flamingo. Hundreds of them can be found in the estuary of the Tejo all year round. In the Sado bay they are most common in autumn and at Castro Marim it is even the most abundant bird during most of the year. Flocks of 10 or 20 Spoonbills can regularly be seen feeding during low tide, or resting during high tide.

The birds of the coastal lagoons and estuaries are easy to observe on the south coast of the Algarve and the bays of the Sado and Tejo, but using a telescope is highly recommended. During low tide, the birds are feeding far from the shore. The best strategy is to find a viewpoint at rising tide (see **www.tide-forecast.com**) and watch the birds as they move towards you.

Birds of freshwater wetlands

As sizeable as the saline mudflats are in southern Portugal, freshwater wetlands are surprisingly small and few. Nevertheless, this habitat is the home of many attractive birds so the few small freshwater wetlands are chock-a-block with goodies, making these sites among the most attractive (and fragile!) birdwatching sites. The birds to look for are Little Grebe, Purple Heron, Little Bittern, Purple Gallinule, Red-crested Pochard, Coot, Great Reed and Savi´s Warbler. Wintering Teal, Pintail, Shoveler and Wigeon also prefer freshwater wetlands, and Kingfisher is present as well. In the reedbeds of the Sado and Tejo estuaries, you should also be able to find Bluethroats and a number of feral tropical birds (see page 89).

Birds of the Montados

What the Portuguese call montados (and the Spanish know as dehesas) is a type of open oak woodlands with pasture that has a very rich birdlife. In the extensive montados, Mediterranean birds are abundant: Bee-eater, Woodchat and Iberian Grey Shrikes, Hoopoe, Red-legged Partridge, Thekla's Lark, Rock Sparrow, Sardinian Warbler and Cirl Bunting – you should be able to see dozens of them on a day in the Alentejo. The Azure-winged Magpie is abundant in the Portuguese montados. Black-winged Kite is quite common in montados in the vicinity of more open areas with cereal fields.

You can see Little Bitterns (top) flying in in out of the reedbeds in some places, such as the Sado Bay (route 6).
Frequent, conspicuously coloured yet remarkably difficult to see in the dense foliage, the Golden Oriole lives in woodlands close to rivers (bottom).

In contrast, Western Subalpine and Sardinian Warbler are fond of montados with dense scrub. Small colonies of Spanish Sparrow can be found particularly in the nests of White Stork. The Red-rumped Swallows build their nest under bridges and are often seen near rivers. Their nests also provide a home for the very local and the rare White-rumped Swift

Rice paddy birds: Glossy Ibis and Black-tailed Godwit

The area of wetland habitat in Portugal is greatly enhanced by an artificial version of freshwater marsh: rice paddies. Although rice paddies with their constant shallow water and low vegetation appears superficially very suitable for birds, the diversity is not as high as in the natural lagoons.

Freshly ploughed rice fields, with the tractors still roaring, are most attractive for birds. The fields can literally be black and white by masses of White Storks and Glossy Ibises. As ploughing takes place in autumn and winter, many migrants take advantage of this feast as well. You can see hundreds and hundreds of Lapwings, Black-headed and Lesser Black-backed Gulls and Cattle Egrets. A more thorough search will produce numbers of Water Pipit and Bluethroat. Groups of thousands of Black-tailed Godwits and Glossy Ibises can be seen moving from one field to another in continuous streams, causing impressive sights and good opportunities for photographers.

The most important bird using rice plantations around the Tejo and Sado estuaries in winter is the Black-tailed Godwit. Peak counts reach 45,000 birds each year. Birds use the fields as a stop-over between their winter quarters in Africa and their breeding grounds in central and north Europe from the end of December to the beginning of March. The main food of the Black-tailed Godwit is rice. With their bill as chopsticks, they select the rice that is flooded, especially shortly after the paddy has been ploughed. Most birds are of the European subspecies *limosa*, of which 40% of the total population fourages on the rice paddies of Portugal. This bird is drastically declining, and the Portuguese rice is of utmost importance for its conservation. Despite this, most of the rice paddies are outside the Special Protected Areas (IBA´s).

The soft *Pooh-pooh-pooh* of the Hoopoe is heard all over the countryside, wherever there are crevices in trees for it to build a nest.

which evicts the hapless swallows. In the river beds Black Storks search for food. You will also find some species in the montados that you probably will associate more with central Europe. Great Spotted Woodpecker, Woodlark, Chaffinch, Hawfinch, Nuthatch and Short-toed Treecreeper are resident breeders.

This habitat is also wonderful for raptors, although, for reasons that are poorly understood, they are not nearly as frequent as in the dehesa of neighbouring Spain. The birds to

look out for are Black Kite, Griffon, Black and Egyptian Vultures, Golden, Bonelli's, Booted, Short-toed and Spanish Imperial Eagles. They are all most often found in the areas adjacent to the Spanish border, the Vale do Guadiana nature park and the steppes of Castro Verde.

The winter birding in the montados is almost as pleasant as spring. Many of the above-mentioned birds are present in winter as well. Those that migrated south are replaced by wintering Little Bustards and Cranes. Family groups of Cranes, typically consisting of two parents and one young, stride under the trees in search of acorns and bulbs. Large groups of Wood Pigeons, Stock Doves, Chiffchaffs and Chaffinches also spend the winter in the montados.

The montados of the Alentejo are, together with the adjacent Extremadura in Spain, the prime wintering ground for Cranes in Europe (top).
From late March onwards, the Red-rumped Swallow is frequent in the Alentejo, especially in rocky areas near water (bottom).

Birds of the steppes

The rather small area of pastures around Castro Verde is superb for steppe birds. Comparisons with the more famous steppe regions of Extremadura and northern Spain are inescapable. And you'll find that the Castro Verde steppes are at least as rich.

Aside from Castro Verde there are other, smaller areas of dry fields and steppe-like habitat. In fact, the dividing line between steppes and the Montados is not always clear. The transition zone between steppe and

Visitors from Africa

From the end of the 19th century, at least, southern Europe has seen a surge in the natural colonisation of birds from Africa; a process that is accelerating in the last few decades due to climate change. Southern Portugal has many examples. Some representatives of African bird families (including introduced species) do better in southern Portugal then in other Mediterranean countries. The benign winter temperatures seem to play an important part in this.

A good example is the Black-winged Kite. Its status in Portugal was obscure even into the 1950s but it has since expanded its range explosively across the country and into Spain. A more recent arrival is White-rumped Swift whose spread has been inadvertently aided by Red-rumped Swallow whose nests it usurps. It first bred in Portugal in the 1990s having first been found in Spain in the 1960s. Interestingly, the Red-rumped Swallow, which most view as a native bird of Mediterranean Europe, was initially only a rare visitor here in the 19th century. It was proved to breed in Spain in the 1920s and in Portugal only in the 1950s. Further back in time, the history of these colonists, even obvious ones, is less well known. Cattle Egret, for example, is often cited as a recent arrival but its presence in Iberia possibly goes back at least as far as the 16th century. What is clear, though, is that the population subsequently contracted only to expand again in the 19th century.

The tropical appearance of the Bee-eater never ceases to impress.

Delving further back in time throws up more possibilities, such as Bee-eater and Roller which belong to largely African groups. In a sense the Bee-eaters are ambassadors we have on loan in the summer and return to the mother continent in winter.

It is quite likely that we'll see new birds arriving from Africa to Portugal, indeed some have already arrived in Spain (e.g. Little Swift). The latest wave of exotic immigrants, though, are of our own making. The large number of naturalised species like Red Avadavat, Common Waxbill, Black-headed Weaver, Yellow-crowned Bishop, Monk and Ring-necked Parakeet were introduced, by accident or design, by humans and survive here due to the mild climate.

montado has an attractive birdlife. Species such as Roller, Bee-eater, Great Spotted Cuckoo, Quail and Black-eared Wheatear can be found here.

The most outstanding bird (literally) on the open steppes is the Great Bustard. A healthy population of these impressive birds live around Castro Verde and you should have little difficulties in finding them. Smaller populations inhabit the cereal fields near Beja. The Little Bustard is still fairly common, but, in keeping with the alarming European decline of this species, the Portuguese population has lost half of its calling males in just over a decade (2005-2016). Calandra Lark and Corn Bunting can be heard and seen everywhere and Red-legged Partridge, Iberian Grey Shrike and Thekla's Lark are also widely distributed. In a single morning you should find lots of these birds. Black-bellied Sandgrouse, Short-toed Lark and Stone Curlew are also abundant but more difficult to find and you will have to make an effort to find them (see 'finding birds in the steppe', page 230).

The steppes are important hunting grounds for raptors. Lesser Kestrel and Montagu´s Harrier breed there while Black Vulture, Black-winged Kite and Spanish Imperial Eagle (in the process of recolonising Portugal) are regular visitors.

A winter visit to the Portuguese steppes is a different experience. The fields are wet and green, the air is perfectly clear and the temperature is pleasant. Resident species such as Great Bustard show well, numbers of sandgrouse and Little Bustard are higher than in spring and Calandra Larks form huge groups. In winter, such birds as Hen Harrier have arrived and you will be surprised by the presence of large numbers of Red Kites, Lapwings, Golden Plovers, Iberian Grey Shrikes and Meadow Pipits.

Stone Curlews are extremely well camouflaged and very shy. This bird is cautiously following a Montagu's Harrier that is scouting the steppes for prey.

Seabirds

The geographical location of southern Portugal suggests that seabirds in the pelagic zone should provide some surprises. The prevailing southwestern winds bring birds from more tropical regions to the waters of Portugal. In fact, the first regular sightings of Wilson´s Storm-petrel in Europe have been made in the waters off the Sagres coast. The sea bottom off the coast of

The Iberian Azure-winged Magpie

When, in 1831, Captain S. E. Cook found an attractive magpie in central Spain, he could have had no idea that his discovery would spark an ornithological controversy that would rumble on for over 150 years. Astonishingly, his birds were quickly identified as Azure-winged Magpie, a species described fifty-five years earlier and known only from the Far East (Siberia, China and Japan). Initially, it was assumed that populations would be discovered to bridge at least some

of the 9,000 km gap. Then, as no such populations were found, it was widely assumed that the Iberian birds were a result of an unrecorded introduction by Portuguese sailors in the 16th or 17th century when Portuguese trade with the Far East was booming. How else, it was argued, could such an attractive and distinctive bird have gone unnoticed for so long? When naturalist Charles Lucien Bonaparte (nephew of Napoleon) described minor plumage differences in Iberian birds in 1849, proponents of this theory claimed that this was simply the result of the 'founder effect'. This theorises that when lifeforms originate from a small genetic pool then divergence

Iberian Azure-winged Magpie.

from the original template will be more rapid. This and environmental factors, they claimed, could account for the differences. Yet others argued with equal certainty that the two populations had once been united but that some ancient cataclysmic environmental change had forced them apart thousands of years previously. This not only better explained the minor differences in plumage but also found support in our growing understanding of past climates. Each side had its adherents who fiercely defended their thesis well into the 1970s and 1980s with the 'accidental introduction' theory perhaps having the edge.

The problem remained unresolved until archaeological excavations in Gibraltar in 1997 turned up remains of Azure-winged Magpie dated to 44,000 BP thus destroying the idea of a recent introduction. Any lingering doubts were set to rest with DNA analysis, which showed that the two populations were sufficiently genetically distinct to represent two separate species whose last common ancestor lived many millennia earlier. Although conclusive evidence regarding the species' former range remains lacking, we now know that glaciation or the growth of deserts in central Asia could provide the mechanism for isolation of the two forms. As noted above, the Iberian bird, *Cyanopica cooki*, is now considered a different species from its similar looking relatives in the Far East. Confusingly, the name originally given to Chinese birds, Azure-winged Magpie, is still widely used for both birds without any qualifier although the western species is sometimes called 'Iberian Magpie' or, less often, 'Cook's Magpie'.

southern Portugal is a shallow continental shelf interrupted by ridges and canyons. In these interruptions sea life flourishes and a concentration of pelagic birds can be expected (see also page 31). The biggest canyon is just a few kilometres from the Setúbal coast near Cabo Espichel. A smaller canyon is west of Cape St. Vincent and there is a small ridge south of the Algarve that gets close to Faro.

Seabird numbers and species out at sea and near the coast are especially good during migration periods and in winter. Many species take advantage of the fishing vessels that are around and of shoals of Sardines and Mackerel that live near the water surface. Around the fishing boats concentrations of birds can be large and some get very close to the observer.

The most numerous species are Cory's Shearwaters, Gannet, Lesser Black-backed and Yellow-legged Gull. Great, Sooty and Balearic Shearwater, (European) Storm-petrel and Great Skua are frequently seen too. These are all birds that breed elsewhere, but visit the Portuguese coast to feed. Shag, Yellow-legged Gull and Little Tern are the only breeding seabirds in southern Portugal. Cormorant is a winter bird, which mixes with Shag on the coastal rocks.

Griffon Vultures are mostly seen in the eastern part of the Alentejo and on the plains of Castro Verde (routes 8-11).

The Gannet, (with sometimes hundreds of birds per day) and the Sandwich Tern are the most obvious species outside the breeding season, because they often pass by very close to the shore.

Raptors

Southern Portugal doesn't have the reputation for raptors enjoyed by its neighbours Extremadura and Andalucía. As the habitat on either side of the border is similar, the lack of raptors on the Portuguese side has long been a puzzle. A recent study (2017) sheds light on the issue: politics is to blame. Whereas carcasses in Spain are left in the field, they are collected by the Portuguese authorities.

However, the valley of the Guadiana, the montados next to the border with Extremadura and the steppes of Castro Verde do have a lot to offer.

The Egyptian Vulture is rare, but many Griffon Vultures breeding in nearby Spain cross into the Alentejo where the Black Vulture is also seen regularly. Short-toed Eagle and Booted Eagle are widely distributed. Increasingly, a small number do not migrate to Africa but remain in winter. Only a few pairs of Golden Eagle breed at the border near the Guadiana. Although increasing, the shy Bonelli´s Eagle remains scarce and endangered but it can be surprisingly easy to find. The rare Spanish Imperial Eagle became extinct in Portugal, but since 2003 has been re-colonising the south. They breed in the Guadiana valley and the mountains of the Algarve, and juvenile birds are regularly seen, especially in the Castro Verde area. Montagu´s Harrier is more numerous. It breeds in open lands and is especially common in the steppes. The Black-winged Kite is a relatively recent addition to the European avifauna (see box on page 85). It

The Short-toed Eagle is the most common eagle in southern Portugal.

is a widespread, but not abundant bird in the Alentejo and the Setúbal-Lisbon area in agricultural lands with trees and woodlands with open fields. After breeding, there is some dispersal when Black-winged Kites can be seen in the Algarve as well. The Lesser Kestrel almost became extinct in Portugal at the end of the 20th century. Nest boxes and even purpose built 'kestrel towers' in Mértola and near Castro Verde have helped the population to bounce back and now about 450 pairs breed. Lesser Kestrel is easy to see in these areas.

Naturalised exotics

It is surprising how easily some exotic and brightly coloured birds have established populations in southern Portugal. Whether they escaped from captivity or were released deliberately is uncertain, but what is clear is that the warm climate and very mild winters are one important factor of their success in Portugal. Here we present four photographs of the most often seen species, as they are not included in most of the European bird identification guides.

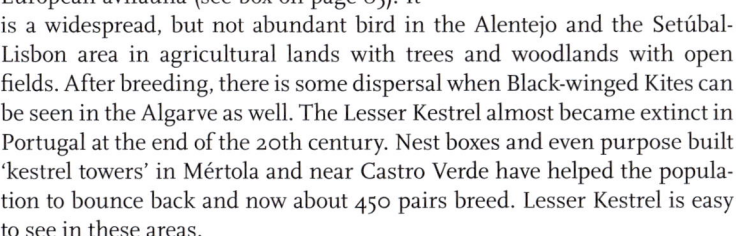

Crested Myna (top)
Common Waxbill (2nd
from top)
Black-headed Weaver
(3rd from top) and
Yellow-crowned
Bishop (bottom)

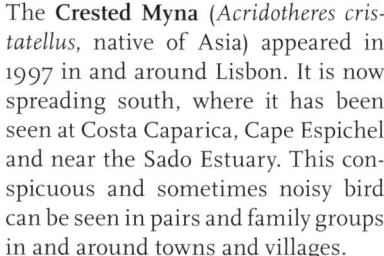

The **Crested Myna** (*Acridotheres cristatellus*, native of Asia) appeared in 1997 in and around Lisbon. It is now spreading south, where it has been seen at Costa Caparica, Cape Espichel and near the Sado Estuary. This conspicuous and sometimes noisy bird can be seen in pairs and family groups in and around towns and villages.

After releases in 1967, the tiny **Common Waxbill** (*Estrilda astrild*, native of Africa) is widespread in the Algarve, at the west coast and around the Tagus and Sado estuaries. It habitually flies in flocks and can be identified by its soft twittering, buzzing and nasal sounds. It feeds on grass seeds and during spring also on insects.

The **Black-headed Weaver** (*Ploceus melanocephalus*, native of Africa), a bird of reed beds, is common when enough of its favourite habitat is available. It behaves semi-colonially and several pairs can be present in only 20 or 30 metres of reeds. The bright yellow-black colours of the males are wonderful during their courtship, which takes place from spring to autumn.

The **Yellow-crowned Bishop** (*Euplectes afer*, native of Africa) colonised Portugal more recently. Its status is not well known, but it seems to become widespread in coastal wetlands as the Tagus estuary.

The actual status of the **Red Avadavat** (*Amandava amandava*, native of Asia), is also little known. The Tricoloured Munia (*Lonchura malacca*, native of Asia) has been found breeding south of the Tagus and north of the Sado estuary, but its present status is not clear. In addition, Monk and Ring-necked Parakeet are found in Lisbon. Around another ten species of exotics have been regularly seen but breeding has not (yet) been confirmed.

Bird migration at the Sagres Peninsula

The southwestern tip of Europe is especially good for observing autumn migration between the end of August and November. More than 4,000 raptors of more than 20 species pass over the Sagres Peninsula during this time. Griffon and Egyptian Vultures, Booted and Short-toed Eagles, Honey Buzzard, Black Kite and Sparrowhawk are the more frequent ones. Buzzard, Montagu´s, Marsh and Hen Harrier, Red Kite, Osprey and Hobby pass by in lower numbers. Other species are scarce, but Spanish Imperial Eagle, Black Vulture, Lesser Kestrel, Eleonora´s Falcon and Black Stork are all recorded regularly, so it is important to check accurately every bird.

Lots of migrating songbirds rest in the vegetation or on the ground. Ironically, the best conditions for migrant birds are often not the best for birdwatchers as, with clear skies and favourable winds, most birds will press on overhead and largely out of sight. However, if they suddenly meet adverse conditions after setting out (e.g. rain and cloud), then large numbers will drop down to seek cover, to rest or to feed. In such conditions, the bushes and pine forests may be full of Nightingales, Whitethroats, Willow Warblers or Pied Flycatchers. The open fields may hold many Tawny Pipit, Short-toed Lark, Common Wheatear or Yellow Wagtail. In this period, rarities show up regularly so searching through the many commoner species to find that hidden gem can be great sport.

The Sagres Peninsula is such a good spot as it juts out into the Atlantic so any bird following the Portuguese coast southwards inevitably ends up at Sagres. This being said, the main stream of birds on this east Atlantic flyway lies much further inland. In comparison to migration hotspot Tarifa in Andalucía, far fewer migrants reach the west coast of the Iberian Peninsula, passerines as well as raptors. Compared to Tarifa, where each autumn about 200,000 raptors and storks are counted, numbers near Cape St. Vincent are rather low.

Spring migration on the Sagres Peninsula is less intense compared to autumn. This is not so strange as migrants head north with greater urgency in spring to be as early as possible on the breeding grounds. Again, the geographical location plays a part, coming from Africa the Sagres Peninsula is far from the desired route of most birds.

The Sagres Birdwatching Festival, celebrated each year at the beginning of October is based on migration (**www.birdwatchingsagres.com**).

Black Kites pass by in large numbers during migration in autumn. The Sagres Peninsula is located strategically to see the migration spectacle.

Reptiles and amphibians

Reptiles and amphibians can be found, at the right time and weather conditions, on nearly all routes. The best habitat for amphibians is found on routes 11, 14, 16, 18, 23 and site B on page 159. These are also the routes to look for Spanish Terrapins and aquatic snakes. Mediterranean Chameleon occurs on routes 12 and 14; Schreiber's Green Lizard on route 18 and coastal species like Spiny-footed Lizard and Mediterranean House Gecko are best observed on routes 6, 12, 14, 19, 21 and 22.

Europe's largest lizard, the Ocellated Lizard, is spread all over southern Portugal.

There are no less than 35 different species of reptiles and amphibians in southern Portugal, including ten species of frogs and toads, fourteen lizard species, eight different snakes, three terrapins (one of which is not native), plus at least two sea turtles that regularly occur in oceanic waters.

Reptiles and amphibians are usually mentioned in one breath and draw the same audience of naturalists. In life style, though, they are radically different. The amphibians, with their obligatory aquatic larval stage and their drought-and-salt-sensitive skin, find the conditions in the southern Portuguese summers daunting. Most species are only active during the winter season – roughly between October and April. During the dry summer months, they hide deep in the ground. Those that don't, are restricted to those pools and rivers that never dry out.

For reptiles, the situation is reversed. They need the warmth of the sun and are unconcerned by drought. Hence they are only active during the warmer months, roughly between March and October.

Amphibians

The Iberian (Spanish) Ribbed Newt is, together with the Olm, the largest European newt. It reaches a length of up to and sometimes over 20 cm. It is an endemic of Portugal, Spain and northern Morocco. It has a big head and sharp ribs that form part of a unique defence mechanism in which the venom-coated ribs can puncture the skin through special tubercles to deter would-be predators. This gives the newt a typical and easily distinguishable appearance, although its brownish colour also camouflages the animal well. The Iberian Ribbed Newt lives in and near ponds, pools, streams, riversides and livestock watering places. In the dry season, it hides under stones or underground, sometimes far away from water. It is widely distributed in the area of this book, but it seems not to be very abundant.

The small and aquatic Bosca´s Newt can be identified by its bright, orange underparts. It lives in (temporary) pools and streams and is most abundant in the Algarve hills, the Guadiana Nature Park and other areas with traditional forms of agriculture.

The Southern (Pygmy) Marbled Newt is only found in southern Portugal and south-western Spain. It lives in similar habitat as the Bosca's Newt but is thinly distributed in the area. It is threatened by the expanding towns and villages and intensification of agriculture.

The brightly coloured Fire Salamander is fairly abundant in the cooler areas with woods and streams. It only comes out at night in the cool season, which makes it a difficult animal to track down. Damp evenings after rainy spells between November and April will offer you the best chances of finding it.

The Iberian Midwife Toad is another endemic amphibian with a distribution restricted to western parts of Spain and the southern half of Portugal. It is an interesting animal because the male takes care of the eggs after they are laid. They arrange the eggs around their hind legs, and keep them moist until they are ready to hatch. Then they are brought to shallow ponds and pools near (temporary) streams. The Iberian Midwife Toad is widely distributed in southern Portugal, preferring open areas away from the coast.

The gregarious Iberian Water Frog is the most common and visible amphibian of southern Portugal. It is the default frog of Portugal, looking like a 'normal green frog'. It occurs, often abundantly, in any kind of pond, pool or ditch, as long as it doesn't dry out in summer.

The Fire Salamander is a relict of the fauna of temperate climates, that survives in river valleys with a permanent presence of moisture and shade.

The small Iberian Painted Frog has a rounded pupil, not a horizontal one as in the Iberian Water Frog. The distribution of the Iberian Painted Frog is limited to the western part of the Iberian Peninsula and it is widely distributed in southern Portugal, though not so easy to find. It prefers to live in streams and ponds in rocky areas.

The plump-faced and smooth-skinned Iberian (Western) Spadefoot is restricted to parts of Iberia and France. It has a black 'spade' (a tubercle) on its hind foot, which permits it to dig itself in sandy ground at amazing pace. It is most active at night and occurs, often in abundance, in places with soft, moist soils. The Iberian Spadefoot is one of the few amphibians able to live in (slightly) brackish water and is widely distributed in southern Portugal although its habit of hiding in the ground makes it hard to find.

The Common Parsley Frog is very small, growing no taller than 4.5 cm. It is a slender animal with long hind legs and a flat head with a sulking, drooping mouth. The Iberian Parsley Frog is very similar but not quite so small and with shorter limbs. Both live in southern Portugal and occupy similar habitats, but the Common Parsley Frog is found in the West, from Lisbon down to Sagres, whereas the Iberian Parsley Frog occurs close to the Guadiana river, from the Alentejo down to the coast. Both are species of temporary pools and streams. They may be found in rather dry terrain

Two tree frogs occur in southern Portugal. The Stripeless Tree Frog (on photo) has no or very little black between front and hind legs. If there is a black line (such as here) it has no upward tip near the hind leg.

and, like the Western Spadefoot, tolerate a high level of salinity.

The Spiny Toad (formerly a subspecies of the Common Toad) can be found anywhere in southern Portugal. If you've never seen one before, your first encounter will be memorable – this is a huge beast! The Natterjack Toad, with its yellow line along the centre of its back, is much smaller, but still larger than the specimens of northern Europe. It is also widely distributed and common in open areas with little vegetation, but spends most of the daytime hidden in the ground.

Finally, the bright green tree frogs can be found among vegetation and in low trees. Two species occur: the Iberian Tree Frog (formerly considered the Common Tree Frog) in the north of our area and the Stripeless Tree Frog, which is more common and widely distributed.

Characteristic calls of toads and frogs in southern Portugal

Iberian Midwife Toad　　　Calls September to May
A clear and repeated brief tone. May be confused with the song of the Scops Owl
(but Midwife Toads call from the ground and usually there are more than one).

Iberian Painted Frog　　　Calls January to June
Deep, harsh and weak notes audible to only a few centimetres.

Western Spadefoot　　　Calls October to June
Short notes, "*crop-crop-crop ...*", the speed varies with excitement. The alarm
call is a mewing sound.

Common Parsley Frog　　　Calls September to May
Loud choirs. Two squeaky notes separated by half a second, the last note may be
repeated. Singing frogs may be submerged in the water.

Iberian Parsley Frog　　　Calls October to April
Call like Common Parsley Frog.

Common Toad　　　Calls November to June
Soft series of hoarse and rough notes.

Natterjack Toad　　　Calls December to June
Loud choirs. Long sequences of notes without a break, "*ra-ra-ra-ra-ra-ra-...*".

Iberian Tree Frog　　　Calls March to July
Loud choirs. A melodious and very fast "*guec-guec-guec-guec ...*", between 6
and 8 notes a second.

Stripeless Tree Frog　　　Calls December to July
A set of low, monotonous and somewhat nasal sounds, which last half a second.
Unlike Iberian Tree Frog, the Stripeless does not form choirs.

Iberian Water Frog　　　Calls April to September
Loud choirs. Up and down going shrill tones, like a common water frog.

Reptiles

The rustling scramble of lizards in the *matos*, the sight of geckos on the
village walls on a balmy evening or the ripple of a snake cutting through
the water – all serve to remind you that reptiles are everywhere in southern
Portugal. Other than in winter, it is hard to visit this region without seeing
at least a couple of lizards.

Most of the reptiles you'll see will belong to just a few species: Large
Psammodromuses, Geniez's Wall Lizards and Moorish Geckos are likely
to constitute the bulk of the lizards and the Spanish Terrapin is the com-
monest water turtle in the streams. Snakes tend to be more elusive. The
reptilian diversity, however, is considerably larger than casual sightings
may suggest. The following species are present in the area.

Lizards

One of the star species is the European Chameleon, which occurs locally along the coastal littoral of the eastern Algarve. It is originally a north African species that was introduced by the Moors and currently has colonies along the coast of Andalucía and the Algarve. Chameleons usually ramble around in a small tree or a bush and are most active in summer and autumn. If you find one, it is better not to spread the news because collectors are still illegally catching these animals.

In contrast to the seemingly slow and clumsy Chameleons, the skinks are agile and fast as quicksilver. Bedriaga's Skink with its smooth cylindrical body and short limbs lives in sandy coastal areas and a variety of sites inland. It is active during the day but is secretive and heads for cover when disturbed, usually long before you're able to spot it. Iberian Three-toed Skink has only rudimentary legs and is found in a wide range of grassy habitats.

Much easier to find is the Moorish Gecko. This robust gecko is widespread and abundant all over the region. On warm evenings, you'll find it on the walls of houses (often close to lamps), but it is equally common in rocky areas. The Turkish or Mediterranean House Gecko, more slender, paler and with obvious claws, is most common near the coast, where it occupies similar habitat as the Moorish Gecko. Both species occur together here, but the Turkish Gecko is much scarcer. Geckos can be seen between February and November.

Large Psammodromus, probably the most common of the lizards of southern Portugal.

The legless Worm Lizard in southern Portugal and adjacent Spain is now recognised as a different species from the one that is found elsewhere in the Iberian Peninsula. This is Maria's Worm Lizard and like its widespread Iberian cousin, it looks like a large earthworm. It lives underground and is widespread but because of its secretive habits is usually only accidentally seen. Little is known about its abundance as worm lizards are so secretive, but the numbers found during excavation works indicate that they are quite numerous, especially in areas with loose soil.

There are seven species of 'typical' lizards. Two of these are large and bright green. The Ocellated Lizard is the biggest of all lizards in southern Portugal and occurs in any type of open, dry habitat, including cultivated areas. The males reach over 80 cm in length and sport, in the mating season, a series of bright blue spots. The second large green lizard is, at 12-13 cm, clearly smaller, but still an impressive animal. This is the Schreiber's Green Lizard – a rare lizard that is restricted to the mountains of western Spain and Portugal that has a small population in the Serra de Monchique.

Among the smaller lizards, the Spiny-footed Lizard stands out because of its bold pattern. The juveniles and females sport a red tail, which is over half the length of its body. It prefers hot, sandy areas and can run over sand dunes where the temperature rises to over 50 °C.

Molecular and morphological studies have recently split 'Iberian Wall Lizard' into seven very similar species, two of which are found in southern Portugal: Geniez's and Carbonell Wall Lizard. They are about the same size as the Spiny-footed, but much duller in colour. Geniez's Wall Lizard is the most widespread; Carbonell's lives, within our area only in sandy dunes and oak forests on the coast.

The heat-loving Large Psammodromus is the most abundant, widespread and visible lizard of southern Portugal. With a plain olive back with long pale stripes it is easily identified. It occurs in almost any habitat. Although it is mostly seen on the ground, it can climb up in the vegetation as well. The smaller and more secretive Western Psammodromus (split from Spanish Psammodromus in 2012) is a lowland species that prefers dry, rocky or sandy soils.

Terrapins and turtles

Two species of terrapins are native to southern Portugal – one common and another one rare and localised. The Spanish Terrapin is the 'default species' and can be found in any permanent water body. It is often seen sunbathing on flat stones, or heard as it jumps into the water with a loud splash. The European Pond Terrapin with its diagnostic yellow spots is much scarcer. In a few places in the Algarve the Red-eared Slider, an introduced species from the USA, can be found.

On rare occasions, sea turtles are seen off-shore on sea trips (see page 213). The Loggerhead Turtle migrates into the Mediterranean each year and is the most regularly observed species, especially near Cape St. Vincent.

Snakes

Of the eight snake species that occur in southern Portugal, two are found in dry bushy terrain and can, at least theoretically, turn up anywhere. Snakes are without exception shy and hard to find. The Horseshoe Whip

Snake grows up to 1.5 m in length and has a striking horseshoe shaped pattern on its back, which makes it easy to identify. The Ladder Snake has a very recognisable pattern too: in juveniles two long, fine lateral lines linked by blotchy 'steps' give the species its very descriptive name but in adults only the lateral lines remain.

The Southern and False Smooth Snakes are much smaller and even more secretive. Both are greyish-brown with darker blotches along the back (more marked in the former) and the latter has a distinct dark collar. Both share broadly similar lowland habitats. The largest Portuguese snake is the Montpellier Snake. Animals of over 2 m are recorded regularly. It is common and widespread and the most frequently seen snake of the scrublands. That large snake that rapidly dashes across the road in front of your vehicle is often a Montpellier Snake.

By far the most frequently seen snake though, is the Viperine Snake. This aquatic animal is usually found in or very close to rivers and reservoirs. The zigzag pattern of this small animal resembles that of vipers, but the Viperine Snake is not poisonous. Another aquatic snake, the Grass Snake, is much rarer in Portugal. They look very different from their northern cousins, being more uniformly coloured with adults lacking the characteristic collars (present on juveniles) so it is not surprising that the Portuguese and Spanish animals are often 'split' as Iberian Grass Snake. The only viper of the area is the Lataste´s Viper. It has the characteristic viper pattern, a triangular head and an upturned nose. It lives in dry habitats, both sandy and rocky, but is scarce, declining and tends to avoid human settlements.

The Montpellier Snake is the largest snake of the region. It can grow over two metres in length!

Insects and other invertebrates

The richest routes for butterflies are routes 4, 5, 9, 17, 18, 21, 22, and 23, plus site F on page 198, and B and E on page 212. For dragonflies, we advise to follow routes 11, 12, 13, 16, 18, 22 and 23, plus sites B and E on pages 159-160 and B on page 196.

Butterflies

If you are seeking out a destination to go butterfly watching in Europe, southern Portugal is not the first that comes to mind. The region does not abound in butterflies, neither in numbers nor in species. However, there is a range of attractive butterflies that form an excellent 'by-catch' for naturalists.

The reason for the relative paucity of butterflies in the region is not easy to deduce. The lack of high mountains and upland valleys with their excellent butterfly habitat may be one of the reasons. The montados of the Alentejo with their uniform soil and lack of larval food plants might be another. The extreme summer drought could play a part as well. All that is easily forgotten though, when you see a Monarch butterfly graciously floating by, or when the spectacular Spanish Festoons fly around by the dozen in spring.

The richest butterfly haunts are in the limestone areas of the Algarve and Serra da Arrábida. This is where you'll find good numbers of blues, like Lorquin's, Panoptes, False Baton, Baton, Lang's Short-tailed, Short-tailed, Black-eyed and Adonis Blues (in addition to the other, more widespread species). A hotspot is the southwestern tip – the Sagres Peninsula, from the tip to some 10 kms inland. Here you can search for Ilex and False Ilex Hairstreak (the latter being more widespread), Provençal Fritillary and Chapman's Green Hairstreak. The tiny African Grass Blue is a typical species of the Algarve, where it is often found on golf courses and brackish

The spectacular Two-tailed Pasha flies in open cork oak montados with lots of Strawberry Trees, the host plant of the caterpillar.

If you visit the region in spring, you are very likely to come across the Spanish Festoon with its typical zigzag marking on the hind wing (top). To see the Monarch (bottom) you need more luck. It is mostly found in the Algarve and the numbers increase during the year until they peak in the end of the summer.

grasslands. Not far from this area, Monarchs may also be found. It remains a rare butterfly in southern Portugal, with highest numbers in autumn. It may turn up anywhere, but the area around Silves (see route 18) is where it is most often recorded. A very common species in summer and autumn on the coast is the Geranium Bronze, a tiny butterfly from the blue family that originates from South Africa having been accidentally introduced.

Heading up to the Serra de Monchique, there are two more local beauties to add to the list: the splendid and highly localised Spanish Fritillary (easily confused with Marsh Fritillary; see site E on page 198) and Two-tailed Pasha. The Spanish Fritillary's host plant is the tassel *Dipsacus comosus*, an Iberian endemic plant that grows in streamside meadows on the flanks of the Serra de Monchique. The Pasha (as well as Chapman's Green Hairstreak) depends on Strawberry trees and is usually found where good stands of these trees are present.

Another wildflower hotspot and hence a good locality for butterflies is, as already noted, the Serra da Arrábida, with its beautiful, flower-rich limestone grasslands and open woodlands. This is the haunt of Provence Hairstreak, the look-alikes Little and Lorquin's Blue, both Baton and False Baton Blues, Adonis Blue, Two-tailed Pasha, Cleopatra, Spanish Gatekeeper and lots of Spanish Festoons (but they are common all over). The Serra da Arrábida is also one of the few spots in the area where Portuguese Dappled White and Western Marbled White occur, alongside the widespread Spanish and Iberian Marbled Whites.

Most interesting butterflies of southern Portugal

Widespread species Red-underwing Skipper (*Spialia sertorius*), Sage Skipper (*Muschampia proto*), Cleopatra (*Genopteryx cleopatra*), Western Dappled White (*Euchloe crameri*), Green-striped white (*Euchloe belemia*), Green Hairstreak (*Callophrys rubi*), Black-eyed Blue (*Glaucopsyche melanops*), Panoptes Blue (*Pseudophilotes panoptes*), Lang's Short-tailed Blue (*Leptotes pirithous*), Short-tailed Blue (*Lampides boeticus*), Spanish Festoon (*Zerinthia rumina*), Swallowtail (*Papilio machaon*), Iberian Scarce Swallowtail (*Iphiclides feisthameli*), American Painted Lady (*Vanessa virginiensis*), Knapweed Fritillary (*Melitaea phoebe*), High Brown Fritillary (*Argynnis adippe*), Marsh Fritillary (*Euphydryas aurinia*), Striped Grayling (*Hipparchia fidia*), Spanish Marbled White (*Melanargia ines*), Iberian Marbled White (*Melanargia lachesis*), Spanish Gatekeeper (*Pyronia bathseba*)

Algarve False Mallow Skipper (*Carcharodes tripolinus*), Mediterranean Skipper (*Gegenes nostrodamus*), False Ilex Hairstreak (*Satyrium esculi*), Blue-spot Hairstreak (*Satyrium spini*), Chapman's Green Hairstreak (*Callophrys avis*), Provence Hairstreak (*Tomares ballus*), Lorquin's Blue (*Cupido lorquini*), False Baton Blue (*Pseudophilotus abencerragus*), African Grass Blue (*Zizeeria knysna*), Monarch (*Danaus plexippus*), Two-tailed Pasha (*Charaxes jasius*), Large Tortoiseshell (*Nymphalis polychloros*), Spanish Fritillary (*Euphydryas desfontainii*), Provençal Fritillary (*Melicta dejone*), Aetherie Fritillary (*Melitaea aetherie*), Cardinal (*Argynnis pandora*), Tree Grayling (*Hipparchia statilinus*)

Serra Arrábida False Mallow Skipper (*Carcharodes tripolinus*), Provence Hairstreak (*Tomares ballus*), Lorquin's Blue (*Cupido lorquini*), Little Blue (*Cupido minimus*), False Baton Blue (*Pseudophilotus abencerragus*), Two-tailed Pasha (*Charaxes jasius*), Large Tortoiseshell (*Nymphalis polychloros*), Cardinal (*Argynnis pandora*), Western Marbled White (*Melanargia occitanica*)

The Spanish Gatekeeper is another spring species, recognisable by the bold white stripe in the hindwing.

Heading into the Alentejo, the butterfly diversity decreases, but interesting species remain. The typical butterflies in a springtime montado landscape are Black-eyed Blue, Small Heath, Western Marbled White and Spanish Festoon, but locally on limestone soils you may be treated to the very rare Aetherie Fritillary.

Dragonflies

It is only very recently that dragonflies started to receive the attention they deserve in Portugal. Reports of dragonflies were few and far between, and mostly written by foreign naturalists on holiday in the country. Not until 2005, was the first overview of the existing literature on the dragonflies published. Hence, the dragonfly fauna remains little known and the known distribution ranges of many species are strongly biased towards easily accessible sites visited by casual observers. The upside of this lack of knowledge is that new discoveries are bound to be made by anyone who is dedicated to the exploration of Portugal's dragonflies.

All sightings combined draw a picture of southern Portugal as being a region that is quite blessed when it comes to dragonflies.

The highest diversity is found in the edges of our region: the river mouths on the west coast, the few rivers in the interior Algarve and the banks of the Guadiana river. Come here in the right time (which is June-July) and you'll encounter a large number of attractive species. Of greatest interest to the visitor from northern Europe are of course the species of African origin that, within Europe, are limited to the southern half of the Iberian Peninsula. Examples are Black Pennant, Black Percher, Northern Banded Groundling and Violet Dropwing, the latter two being recent colonists from Africa. Another African species, the beautiful Orange Dropwing has spread with spectacular speed in Andalucia. However, the expansion is in north-eastern direction so up until now, there have been only a few records from southern Portugal although this may change in the near future. Finally, another African species, the Ringed Cascader, was first found in Portugal in 1985 when three males were collected in Serra de Monchique. Over twenty years later, the first skins of larvae (the surest sign of breeding Ringed Cascader), were discovered in the Algarve in 2017.

The Black Percher is essentially an African dragonfly that occurs very locally in southern Portugal and Spain. Where it occurs (usually in estuaries), it flies in large numbers.

Apart from southern species, there are also a number of species of temperate Europe (e.g. Broad-bodied and Four-spotted Chaser) that occur here on the very southern limit of their ranges.

The most attractive dragonfly habitats are the larger, slow-flowing rivers whose current drops to zero at the height of summer. The Guadiana and its tributaries on the eastern border is one such a dragonfly hotspot, as is the Sado in the west. The small, southern rivers of

A typical image of a Western Spectre – its habit of lazing in the shade of branches of shaded streams, makes this dragonfly not so easy to find.

Most interesting dragonfly species

Dark Spreadwing (*Lestes macrostigma*; Castro Marim mostly), Copper Demoiselle (*Calopteryx heamorrhoidalis*), Western Demoiselle (*Calopteryx xanthostoma*), Orange Featherleg (*Platycnemis acutipennis*), Vagrant Emperor (*Anax ephippiger*; Algarve), Lesser Emperor (*Anax parthenope*), Western Spectre (*Boyeria irene*; Algarve), Pronged Clubtail (*Gomphus graslinii*; Guadiana), Western Clubtail (*Gomphus pulchellus*), Green Hooktail (*Paragomphus genei*), Orange-spotted Emerald (*Oxygastra curtisii*), Northern Banded Groundling (*Bracythemis impartita*), Black Percher (*Diplacodes lefebvrii*), Epaulet Skimmer (*Orthetrum chrysostigma*), Yellow-veined skimmer (*Orthetrum nitidinerve*; very rare), Long Skimmer (*Orthetrum trinacria*), Violet Dropwing (*Thrithemis annulata*), Ringed Cascader (*Zygonyx torridus*; very rare)

Widespread White Featherleg (*Platycnemis latipes*), Iberian Bluetail (*Ischnura graelsii*), Western Willow Spreadwing (*Chalcolestes viridis*), Small Red Damselfly (*Enallagma cyathigerum*), Blue-eye, (*Erythromma lindenii*), Blue Emperor (*Anax imperator*), Small Pincertail (*Onychogomphus forcipatus*), Large Pincertail (*Onychogomphus uncatus*), Broad Scarlet (*Crocothemis erythraea*), Red-veined Darter (*Sympetrum fonscolombii*)

Mira, Ceixe, Arade, Odelouca, Odeleite, Aljezur and Gilão all have their attractive dragonfly spots. Some of them (e.g. Odelouca, and Guadiana) run through rocky, more or less open terrain. Their margins consist in summer of a series of desiccating pools. Look here for species like Violet Dropwing, Northern Banded Groundling and Green Hooktail. Others, such as the Ceixe, the Aljezur and the Mira river are shaded by alder woods and support a different set, including Small and Large Pincertail,

Orange-spotted Emerald, Western Spectre and various species of demoiselles. The Splendid Cruiser is another dragonfly to look out for in this habitat.

Estuaries with fresh and brackish waters, plus the broad rivers that sluggishly poor into them, form another dragonfly hotspot. Often, brackish or freshwater ditches on the edges of such habitats are the best. It is the place for Iberian Bluetail, Broad Scarlet and Red-veined Darter which occur by the hundreds, if not thousands. This is also the habitat of southern attractions like Long and Epaulet Skimmers, Black Percher and Northern Banded Groundling.

Other invertebrates

In this large, catch-all category of 'other invertebrates', we'll limit ourselves to a few conspicuous and easily recognisable species you are likely to encounter on a trip to southern Portugal if visiting at the right time of year.

In dry grasslands your attention is easily drawn by fast-flying, boldly marked insects: Owlflies or Ascalaphids. Two species are rather common, *Libeloides longicornis* (with much yellow in the wing) and *L. ictericus* (with clear dark hindwings).

The Iberian Spoonwing* (*Nemoptera bipennis*; top) and the Hooded Praying Mantis* (*Empusa pennata*; bottom) are both conspicuous insects of dry, flowery grasslands.

With some luck you may encounter, in the summertime, the fragile and graceful Iberian Spoonwing* (*Nemoptera bipennis*) whose name derives from its peculiar rear wings which are in the form of long spoon-shaped pennants. Both Owlflies and the Spoonwing are relatives of the ant-lions. Some insects impress by their size or oddly shaped bodies. The Hairy Flower Wasp* (*Scolia hirta*) with its large, orange-marked abdomen is often seen on flowers as is the glossy, purple-black Violet Carpenter Bee, one of Europe's largest bee species. The latter lays its eggs in dead but solid wood, such as poles on the edge of fields.

There are no less than 14 praying mantis species in southern Portugal. With oddly jerking movements they creep towards their pray, which they catch in a sudden, fast blow with their forelegs. Common species are European Dwarf Mantis, Common Praying Mantis, Hooded Praying Mantis* (*Empusa pennata*) and the small, ground-dwelling *Geomantis larvoides*. Also of note are the large, fast and somewhat scary Megarian Banded Centipede and the slow Spanish Scorpion – both animals you are likely to encounter when you start turning stones. Both should be treated with respect – the first has a nasty bite and the second a painful sting.

Also ground-dwelling is the Red-striped Oil Beetle – a thumb-sized 'blister' beetle with a long bloated abdomen (usually) with obvious red warning stripes. It is locally common in grassy terrain and easily seen as its ability to squirt caustic liquid makes it quite brazen. Finally, southern Portugal is home to a large variety of beetles, among which the darkling beetles (*Tenebrionidae*; glossy, black) and leaf beetles (*Lachnia ssp*; somewhat reminiscent of Lady Bugs) are eye-catchers.

You'll find both of these owlfies frequently hunting over grassy patches: *Libelloides ictericus* (top) and *Libelloides longicornis* (bottom).

PRACTICAL PART

In this section we describe 23 routes and 29 sites in southern Portugal, by which you can explore the landscape and discover the flora and fauna of the region. We've ordered them in four distinct regions and each of these can be explored from a single base. These are the Lisbon-Setúbal area (routes 1 to 7; pages 108 to 140), the southern Alentejo (routes 8 to 11; pages 141 to 162), the southern Algarve (routes 12 to 20; pages 163 to 198) and the western Algarve (routes 21 to 23; pages 199 to 214). At the beginning of each of these sections, you'll find a map with the location of the routes and sites and a brief overview of the area.

Every region has its own specific characteristics. The Lisbon-Setúbal is dominated by two large shallow bays and several low mountain ranges and capes, which makes it enormously diverse, both in landscape and in flora and fauna. Huge numbers of shorebirds are just as much a feature of this region as are the butterfly and orchid rich dry grasslands and extensive areas of dunes, with its reptiles and endemic wildflowers. Not all of this area is attractive though as some parts are rather built-up, busy and in places messy too, but the presence of several historic cities (above all the capital Lisbon) and the beach makes this an area perfect to combine nature rambles with urban sightseeing and beach tourism in a relatively small area.

The southern Alentejo is very much the opposite: a huge, empty land with small, isolated, traditional villages. Fields, steppes and montados (see page 38) dominate this landscape. It is superbly flowery in spring and has a stunning birdlife and many reptiles and amphibians.

The southern Algarve is again busy. Here it is all about beach and golf tourism of which the vast majority is situated is situated on the thin strip between the A22 motorway and the coast. North of the motorway, the countryside is lovely and the limestone geology explains the presence of orchids and butterflies in the interior. The coast has its own attractions, such as tidal and freshwater marshes that attract large numbers of birds.

The Western Algarve is again rather quiet. Wild cliffs and capes, secluded beaches and pretty river valleys a little inland, is what makes this region. The birdlife is less rich than in the other areas, but the flora, insect and reptilian life is splendid and your hiking options are much wider than in the rest of the region. The Cabo São Vicente is a great draw, as is the laid-back atmosphere in the small, original villages and towns.

The rough coast of the Costa Vicentina, southern Portugal's finest area for walking. This is Praia do Cordoama, site D on page 214.

108

Routes in the Lisbon – Setúbal area

The Lisbon – Setúbal area is little visited by birdwatchers and naturalists

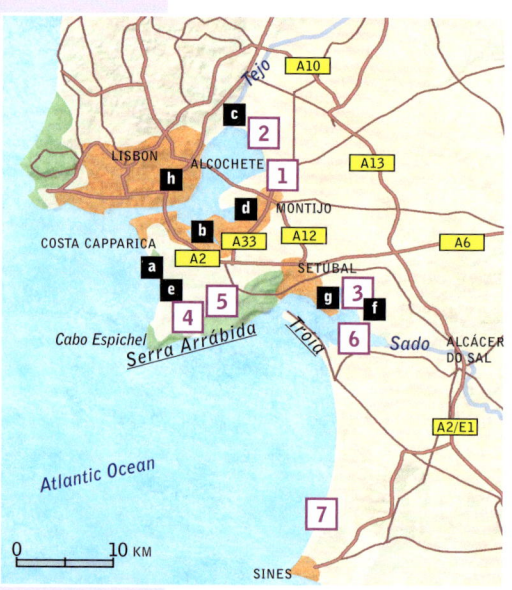

from outside Portugal, so this is an insider tip: go there! Its anonymity as a destination for naturalists is completely undeserved. Although this part of Portugal is rather busy and the attractive sites are separated by unattractive areas, this small area has an enormous diversity of habitats and wildlife – one that equals or perhaps even surpasses that of the famous Algarve. Combine the presence of masses of birds and orchids with easy access to Lisbon and other historical towns such as Setúbal and Palmela plus some of the most beautiful and quiet beaches of Portugal, and its attraction as a comprehensive destination is clear.

The Lisbon – Setúbal area is south Portugal writ small. All important habitats can be found in a compact region: there are extensive fresh and saline marshes,

Overview of the Setúbal region. The letters refer to the sites on page 135-140.

rice paddies and saltpans around two large bays which are the defining elements of the area: the Tejo (Tagus) estuary in the north (routes 1 and 2) and the Sado in the south (route 3 and 6). Birds are the main attraction here as both estuaries collectively form Portugal's most important wetland area. More freshwater marshes are found around two natural lagoons, that of Albufeira (site E on page 137) and of that Santo André (route 7).

Cork oak montados and open pinewoods cover large areas in the east and southeast (e.g. route 6 and 7), while beautiful dunes are found on the Tróia Peninsula and further down (route 6 and 7). Scenically beautiful is the Serra da Arrábida – a limestone range (up to 499 metres), clad in scrubland, pastures, oak and pinewoods that holds a rich flora and butterfly fauna. It is a hotspot for wild orchids (route 3, 4 and 5) and also offers some options for walking. The Lisbon area even has its own 'end of the world headland' in the form of Cabo Espichel (route 4), which has splendid views over the ocean making it a good vantage point for watching seabirds and for scenic walks along the cliffs as you explore the attractive flora and fascinating fossils.

Route 1: The Tagus Estuary near Alcochete

HALF A DAY, 13 KM

Best season
Autumn to spring

Observing thousands of waders.
Pay a visit to the same spot at low and at high tide to see the differences.

Habitats: estuary, salt marsh, salt pans
Selected species: Shelduck, Flamingo, Osprey, Avocet, Dunlin, Greenshank, Grey Plover, Kentish Plover, Little Tern, Caspian Tern

On both sides of the scenic village of Alcochete, on the south bank of the river Tagus and close to Lisbon, you'll find bird-rich saltpans and tidal areas with masses of wildfowl, waders, gulls, flamingos and other birds. At low tide, thousands of them feed on the mud of the broad river, which largely falls dry at low tide. Up to 20 species of waders may be seen in a single day during the migration seasons. Winter flocks of Avocet can be impressive, Kentish Plover breeds in several places and Osprey is a regular visitor outside the breeding season. A good telescope and a position on a strategic viewpoint are certainly a good help as birds can be quite distant. This route follows the banks of the Tagus estuary, bringing you to some of the best saline habitat of the region.

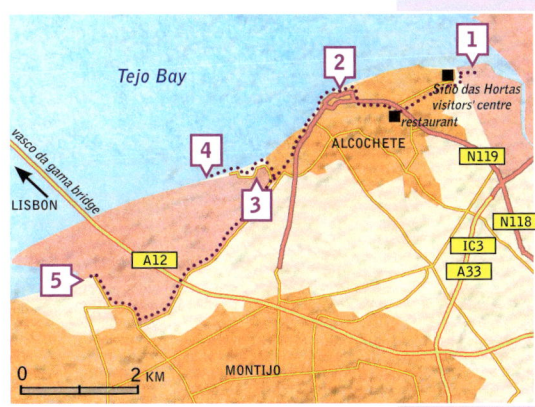

Starting point
Sitio das Hortas

Getting there From Lisbon, follow the A12 over the Vasco da Gama bridge. Take exit 3 onto the A33/IC3 towards Alcochete. After a short stretch on the IC3, exit onto the N119 to Alcochete. At the roundabout, go straight (signposted Alcochete). After 2 km, in front of a small restaurant turn right towards *Sitio das Hortas* (signposted), which you reach after another 1.3 km.

1 You can enjoy some superb views over the Tagus as you walk along the coast from here to look for waders and wildfowl. Small fishing boats lie on the beach and at low tide the outgoing water has drawn fascinating figures in the mud, where the birds are scattered in small groups. At high tide you have to search for them roosting on the other side of the small river flowing into the estuary. In winter and on passage Ringed Plover, Dunlin, Little Stint, Knot, Sanderling, Black-tailed and Bar-tailed Godwit, numerous Grey Plover, some Greenshank, hundreds of Redshank and Whimbrel as well as Turnstone join the resident Kentish Plovers. Little Egret and Grey Heron may wade in the shallows and Shelducks swim in the creeks. Further out there are lots of gulls, especially in winter when Lesser Black-backed and Black-headed Gull are abundant. Numbers of wintering Avocet vary from year to year, while Flamingo can number in the hundreds. Terns are mostly seen on migration, with Black, Sandwich and Caspian Tern the most noteworthy.

Drive back to the small restaurant, turn right and enter the fishing town of Alcochete. Find a place to park your car on the boulevard.

2 Check the shoreline for waders at low tide and walk the 250 m long pier, where birds can be seen from up close. You can expect the same species as at Hortas and enjoy better views over the Tagus River Estuary Natural Reserve with Lisbon beyond.

The quay of Alcochete.

Continue along the boulevard of Alcochete in western direction. Continue all the way until you arrive at a roundabout. Go right and follow the street as it bends to the left. At the next roundabout go right. The tarmac makes way for a cobbled road. At the next one roundabout (following shortly after the previous) go left and continue to the *Salinas do Samouco* (GPS 38.743592, -8.981271).

3 The Samouco saltpans (360 ha.) were expropriated and given to a foundation with the objective to conserve its birdlife as compensation to the building of the Vasco da Gama bridge (almost 14 km from end to end). About 5% of the wintering birds of the Tagus estuary use this relatively small area, either to feed or as a high tide roost. There are several places where you can stop along the road and enjoy views over the fenced saltpans. Similar birds as at the previous sites can be seen. In addition, Black-winged Stilt breeds here (up to 314 nests), as does Little Tern (up to 134 nests) and Kentish Plover. On the lagoon edges, look for Great Cormorant, Grey Heron and Sandwich Tern as well as small numbers of Pied Wagtails (alongside White Wagtail) on migration.

The tidal marshes near Alcochete are full of birds, especially during migration. Dunlin (top) and Caspian and Common Terns (centre) are just three of the species to be found.
At low tide, clam-diggers cross the mudflats to search for shellfish.

4 The road ends at the nearby beach (GPS: 38.744829, -8.982070), which is another good area to search for waders, plus Shelduck, Shoveler, Wigeon and other wildfowl and gulls (including Mediterranean Gull in autumn and winter). There are a few low dunes where Hoopoe, Black Sardinian Warbler and passage migrants can be found.

Go back to the second roundabout and turn right onto the M501 that runs along the southern edge of the salt pans. Unfortunately, it is difficult to park along this road, so continue and follow the road underneath the A12 motorway to the village of Samouco. At the round-about in the village, turn right on (direction *base aérea no 6*) and at the next, right again (*Praia Fluvial*) to reach the coast again.

5 Views from here over the muddy Tagus estuary are again superb. There is a wide creek to your right where birding is interesting. At low tide you'll see the clam fishers out on the mudflats.

From autumn to early spring, you can see thousands of Glossy Ibis in the marshes and rice paddies along the Sado River.

Clam fishing

Clam fishing or clam digging is a generic term for harvesting molluscs that live in or on the mud. The most important species that are caught in the Tagus estuary are Clam (*Ruditapes decussatus*) and Oyster (*Crassostrea angulate*). Clam fishers go out at low tide, equipped with spade or fork to dig out the shellfish, which are cleaned and put in a bag. Clam fishing is laborious work but worth the effort as the clams are considered a delicacy in Lisbon and restaurants are willing to pay a good price for them. Thousands of people earn some money digging clams. Clam fishers are very active at the Tejo and Sado estuaries, but also in the Algarve, such as at Alvor.

Route 2: The Tagus Estuary near Barroca d´Alva and Pancas

FULL DAY, 37 KM

Great birdwatching.
Possibly the best site for naturalized exotic birds.

Best season
Autumn to spring

Habitats: marshland, reedbeds, Cork Oak woodlands, rice fields, grassland
Selected species: Waxbill, Black-headed Weaver, Yellow-crowned Bishop, Black-headed Munia, Booted Eagle, Bee-eater, Red-necked Nightjar, Iberian Chiffchaff, Iberian Hare

A little inland from the Tagus Estuary, you'll encounter a very different landscape than that of the shores you visited on route 1. Here it is reedbeds, rice paddies and cork oak montados that form the key ingredients. This route combines two very different sites that are some 20 kms apart. First, you'll explore the surroundings of the hamlet Barroca d´Alva (also called Paul da Barroca) which is one of the best sites to see Portugal´s naturalised exotic birds – Common Waxbill, Black-headed Weaver, Yellow-crowned Bishop and Black-headed Munia. Some of them even form large roosts, taking advantage of the seeds of reedbeds and the dense herbal vegetation along the watercourses.

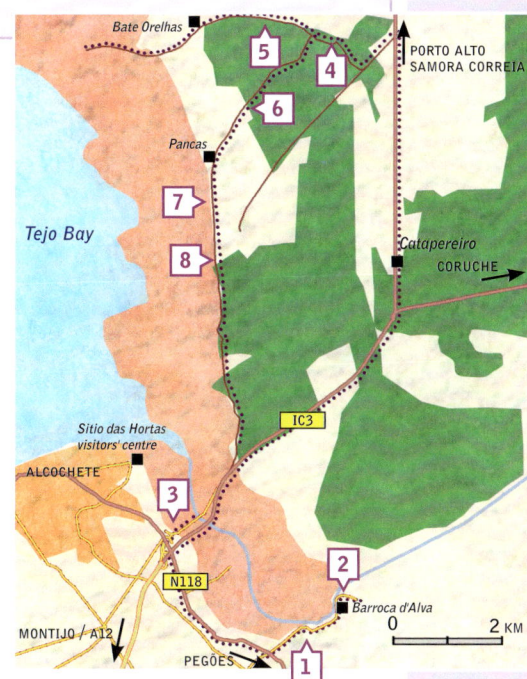

The second part of the route explores the dry fields and cork oak montados in the eastern section of the area. Both sites are predominantly interesting for their birdlife.

Starting point Barroca d'Alva

Getting there From Lisbon, follow the A12 over the Vasco da Gama bridge. Take exit 3 onto the IC3 towards Alcochete. After a short stretch on the IC3, exit onto the N118 to Pegões. Once you are on th N118 to Pegões, turn left at the next roundabout to Barroca. For your first stop, park near the second bridge.

1 Look for exotics on either side of the reedy river and channels. Common Waxbill, Black-headed Weaver and Yellow-crowned Bishop have a roost by the bridge and breed in the reeds and riverine vegetation. Presumably, this area is blessed (or cursed, depending on your point of view) with these invasive birds due to a combination of gentle climate (mild winters in particular) and plenty of food (see page 85). In addition to naturalised species, native reedbed specialists occur as well, being represented by Savi´s, Reed and Great Reed Warblers in summer and Bluethroat and Reed Bunting in winter). Cetti´s Warbler and Zitting Cisticola are residents.

Walk the road and the track adjacent to the channel to scan the rice and agricultural fields and look for Marsh Harrier, Grey Heron, Little, Cattle and Great White Egret, Glossy Ibis, Black-winged Stilt, Common Snipe and Green Sandpiper. Purple and Night Heron are present but tend to be more hidden. The mild climate is illustrated by the occurrence (albeit scarce) of Swallow, House Martin and Sand Martin even in the middle of winter, when the rice fields are a stronghold for the Black-tailed Godwit.

Continue and park near Barroca d'Alva (GPS: 38.732889, -8.893784).

2 Here there are more fields and channels to check for the aforementioned birds. On the other side of the farm buildings lies a rough terrain with Cork Oaks and tracks for horse riding. Here you may find

Freshwater marshes are few and far between in southern Portugal, but always a delight for birdwatchers. Barroca d'Alva is one of those sites, where birds like this Purple Heron can be seen.

Black-winged Kite, Azure-winged Magpie and Red-rumped Swallow. Return to the N118 and turn right. Just after passing over the IC3 you arrive at a roundabout where you turn right onto a dead-end street (not signposted) and directly turn left again. Park at the T-junction of this cul-de-sac (GPS: 38.746518, -8.929492).

3 Walk along the street to the right towards the ruins of a bridge some 600 metres ahead. This little used road gives panoramic views over the nearby rice-fields and fish pools called *Ribeira das Enguias*. Scan for Osprey, Peregrine Falcon, Black Kite, herons, egrets and Flamingos. It may be difficult to identify waders that hide in the fields.

There is a large area of montados around Pancas (bottom), where, in winter, the Black-winged Kite is a frequent sight (top).

At the bridge look at the river that fills up during flood. At low tide look for feeding waders here. Also look for Crested Coot, which is rare but more often seen in recent years. The surrounding fields hold Crested Lark, Zitting Cisticola, Spotless Starling and Corn Bunting.

Go back to the roundabout and take the exit for the N118 to Porto Alto. After 5 km you pass the turn to Coruche. Ignore it and continue to Porto Alto. After 5 km beyond the turn to Coruche, turn left on a small sign that reads *Pancas* (GPS: 38.828617, -8.881196). From this turn, the recommended strategy here is to make frequent stops. Note that on the following stretch, both the state of the road and access regulations may change. Don't proceed if the situation is not good to do so.

4 The track bends to the right, and you reach a beautiful but fenced Cork Oak forest where cattle graze and where Woodchat Shrike, Bee-eater, Melodious Warbler, Iberian Green Woodpecker and Iberian Chiffchaff breed.

5 You reach a gate (private property but you are allowed to continue on foot) and a hamlet with farm buildings called Bate-Orelhas. This is about a 2 kms walk. If you pass through the hamlet you will find salt-pans behind it. Turning left at the saltpans will bring you in 4 km to the point where river Sorraia flows into the Tagus estuary, opposite the Ponta da Erva plains (see site C on page 136).

Go back to your car and proceed on the sandy track, exploring the surroundings.

6 Cork Oak groves and open fields alternate. In winter and spring, you find puddles of water and flooded lands with Little Egrets. All this is good for raptors such as Black-winged Kite, Booted and Short-toed Eagle and for Iberian Grey Shrike and other Mediterranean species mentioned above. Both European and Red-necked Nightjar breed and on a late evening trip you can hear them both singing.

The Sharp-lipped Tongue Orchid* *(Serapias strictiflora)* grows abundantly at point 7.

7 Around the farm buildings of Pancas, the landscape is more open. Walk the smaller path to the west. The ground towards the Tagus is lower. In the abundant vegetation, Quail and Corn Bunting breed. Lots of Iberian Hare and Rabbit live around here as well.

Proceed on the track. There is a line of Eucalyptus trees on your right. Behind it are fields and the Tagus in the distance. Further ahead, a fence appears, also on the right.

8 Behind the fence, in the fields below the Cork Oaks, there are many wildflowers, including some stout Sharp-lipped Tongue-orchids* (*Serapias strictiflora*).

The last part of the track goes a bit up and down along the Tagus estuary. It ends where the track, now a small tarmac road, reaches the N-118.

Route 3: The northern Sado estuary and Palmela

46 KM: SADO SITES
21 KM: PALMELA LOOP

A diverse route that combines birdwatching with orchids and butterflies.

Best season
September-October
and February-May

Habitats: salt marsh, freshwater marsh, cork oak montado, limestone grass-lands, scrub, cliffs, limestone grasslands
Selected species: many orchids, including Black Spider, Giant, Mirror, Yellow Bee and Pyramidal Orchid, Spoonbill, Greater Flamingo, Marsh Harrier, waders, Waxbill, Iberian Green Woodpecker, Azure-winged Magpie, Spanish Festoon, False Baton Blue, Green-striped White, Spanish Marbled White

This is the first of three routes that start from Setúbal and which can be linked together if you want. It brings you east to the marshes of the north-ern Sado estuary and later visits the pretty valley of Palmela. The first part of the route is a bird heaven, the second a splendid site for orchid and but-terfly lovers. This route is set up as a string of short rambles. You'll need a car to go from one site to the next.

Starting point Setúbal. Drive the N-10 from Setúbal eastwards, direc-tion Alcácer / Algarve. Pass the Ibis hotel and turn right on the next road (GPS: 38.540338, -8.835476), the M536 signposted *Praias do Sado*. On the next roundabout go left, to Moinho da Maré (GPS: 38.528713, -8.805938).

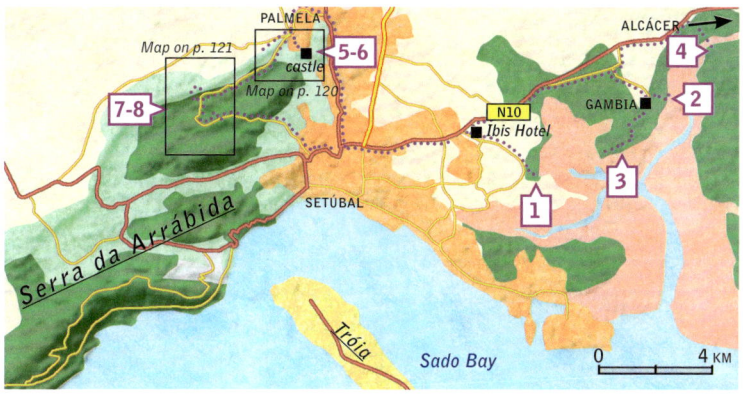

1 Moinho da Maré is an old tidal mill. Under the building you can see the six holes through which the tidal waters flowed four times a day providing the mill with what we'd now call sustainable energy. Today it is a visitor centre. There is an observation hide, a path and good views over the estuary. Feeding waders can be observed from close distance and thanks to high tide roosts, this place is interesting for birding all day. During upcoming and lowering tide you can see how the water moves in and out and how the highest parts, where glasswort grows, become islands during high tide.

Return to the N10, turn right and after 4.2 kms, turn again right at the sign to Gambia. When you come to a roundabout, go right and after another 1.7 kms, just before reaching the first houses of Gambia, turn left.

2 A little further lies a small harbour with small fishing boats (GPS: 38.548686, -8.758988). Enjoy the laid-back atmosphere and explore the track to the left that leads through meadows, salt marsh and reedbeds with views on the river. Reptiles that are listed for this general area are European Pond Terrapin, Ocellated Lizard and Viperine and Grass Snakes, so keep your eyes open and check the banks of the ditches. Breeding birds include Purple Heron, Marsh Harrier, Waxbill, Reed and Great Reed Warblers, Black-winged Stilt and Black-winged Kite. The saltmarsh is 'high ground' in comparison to most of the Sado estuary, so when the tide is high, masses of waders flock in to roost. In the montado around Gambia village, look for Booted Eagle, Hoopoe, Azure-winged Magpie and Cirl Bunting.

Return to the crossing turn left to proceed through the village. The road brings you to the edge of the estuary and continues as a track, which you can follow to the end (GPS: 38.533316, -8.779514).

3 Scan for waders, Spoonbills, Flamingos and herons. On the right side of the road is a Holm Oak montado where Great Spotted Cuckoo, Iberian Green Woodpecker and Azure-winged Magpie occur. There are several picnic spots along the track and about half way there is a deserted building on the edge of the marsh, the first floor of which serves as an excellent viewpoint. With a telescope, thousands of waders may be found. In winter and on passage, Dunlin, Redshank, Curlew, Grey Plover, Avocet, Greater Flamingo and Spoonbill can be seen plus, with luck, an Osprey.

The track ends at a picnic spot that is popular with clam fishers (see box on page 112). This is another viewpoint with roughly the same birds.

Return to the roundabout, go right and left at the next roundabout to connect with the N10 again. Go right. After 2.8 km on the N10, just before km post 54, turn right (signposted *Reserva Natural*) onto a small and rather bumpy tarmac road that takes you to the Zambujal bridge (GPS: 38.548686, -8.758988). Careful, this turn is easy to miss.

4 From the bridge you overlook excellent habitat once again, with meadows, saltmarsh and the Zambujal river which is still tidal at this point. Kingfisher, Purple Heron, Little and, in winter, Great White Egret live along the river and in the pools. Hundreds of estuarine birds can be seen including Avocet and Black-tailed Godwit as well as Spoonbill and Greater Flamingo. Groups of waders spend high tide on the old saltpans north of the bridge. The fields may hold groups of Waxbill and breeding Yellow-crowned Bishop. In the past Black-headed and Scaly-breasted Munia have been seen here too.

Return to the N10 and turn left to drive back towards Setúbal. After passing the Ibis hotel again, go right at the roundabout (direction Lisbon-Algarve motorway). Keep driving straight on until you hit a T-junction and are lead to the right, out of town, direction Palmela. Before heading out to the orchid sites in Serra da Arrábida, visit the castle of Palmela (GPS: 38.565378, -8.898709)..

The beautiful, warm grassy hillsides in the Serra da Arrábida at point 7. In the background the traditional windmills on the ridge and Palmela castle on the right.
This place is a delight for those interested in orchids, butterflies and other insects.

5 Palmela itself is a pretty town, built on a hill with a 12th century castle that dominates the top. It was founded by the Romans, but later occupied by the Visigoths and later still by the Moors, who greatly extended it. The park just beneath the castle is beautiful in spring, when the Judas Trees are in flower. The founders of the castle chose a strategic spot – the views are excellent in every direction. To the south you overlook Setúbal and the Sado bay, with the Tróia Peninsula beyond (the goal of route 6). Towards the north, you see the lowlands of Seixal and further on, across the Tejo, Lisbon. To the west lies the valley you will explore on the remainder of the route, overlooked by a crest on which stands a row of windmills, all dating back to the mid 19th century. At this time, the wine blight (*phylloxera*) destroyed the vines forcing the entire region to switch to growing wheat, which the mills ground.

Leave Palmela in direction Azeitão/ Sesimbra and at the roundabout just west of town, take the track up the ridge (signposted *Serra do Louro*). Park where a track goes left (with the no entry for motorised traffic sign; GPS: 38.568542, -8.910564) and walk up the track to the windmills.

6 You have splendid views over Palmela, the plain towards the north and the Serra da Arrábida to the south. Between March and May there are many orchids along the path, mainly

Two-tailed Pasha (top) and False Baton Blue (bottom) – two frequent butterflies in the Serra da Arrábida.

From the castle of Palmela you have a good view over the windmills of Serra do Louro (point 6).

Mirror, Yellow Bee and Sombre Bee, plus a few Giant Orchids. The third windmill you encounter is still functioning and sells bread from wheat flour that is ground at this mill. If you wish, you could follow this track over the ridge on foot all the way to the next point.

Return and take the first right. After 4 km, the tarmacked road makes a sharp left turn, while a broad track continues. Park at this junction and walk the trail up the hill from here (see map; GPS: 38.551183, -8.942306).

7 This little triangle (which brings you to four more traditional windmills on the top) offers a wealth of orchids and a great number of butterflies and other insects. Out of the many attractions, Black Spider and Giant Orchid deserve a special mention, as do the masses of Pyramidal Orchids that grow in the field west of the orchard. The upper part is best for butterflies, with Green-striped and Spanish Marbled Whites, False Baton Blue and Spanish Festoon among the more common ones.

Follow the road further.

8 Basically the entire stretch up to the highest point is superb for orchids. Either walk this stretch (there is very little traffic) or make regular stops. In spring, there should be plenty of Yellow Bee, Bumblebee, Sombre Bee, Common Bee, Woodcock and Black Spider Orchid, plus a few Naked-man, Small-flowered and Sharp-lipped (*strictiflora*) Tongue Orchids. There are many other attractive plants as well. The birdlife, meanwhile, consists of Turtle Dove, Iberian Green Woodpecker, Iberian Grey Shrike and various warblers.

Continue on the road to return to Setúbal.

The orchid *Ophrys bilunulata* has a yellow margin around the lip which distinguishes it from the more common Sombre Bee Orchid (*Ophrys fusca*).

PRACTICAL PART

Route 4: Serra da Arrábida and Cabo Espichel

Best season
September-October
and February-May

FULL DAY, 55 KM

Superb landscape of oceanside cliffs.
Many great sites for wildflowers, above all orchids.

Habitats: Mediterranean scrubland, limestone grassland, coastal cliffs
Selected species: Naked-man Orchid, Man Orchid, Two-leaved Gennaria, Sombre Bee Orchid, Hoop-petticoat Daffodil, Wild Tulip, Gannet, Shag, Subalpine Warbler, Crag Martin, Pallid Swift, Alpine Swift, Two-tailed Pasha

The second route out of Setúbal leads west, through the beautiful Serra da Arrábida over to the promontory of Cape Espichel. To the west and south the promontory is bordered by cliffs (mainly limestone), which rise up steeply from the sea. Spectacular views over the ocean are a dominant theme of this route, but those with an eye for them, will find large numbers of wildflowers (particularly orchids) and a good range of birds.

Starting Point Setúbal

Leave town following the main boulevard westwards (N10-4) from the town centre. Beyond a large picnic site in a secluded bay, turn right towards Lisboa / Arrábida (GPS: 38.504286, -8.927867). At the next junction, turn left onto the N379-1 to Arrábida / Convento. This small winding road takes you to the heart of the park. It climbs for about 4.5 kilometres with the view becoming increasingly superb as you go up the mountain.

1 Stop after approx. 2.5 km near a derelict building in a hairpin bend (GPS: 38.491023, -8.937354). Beyond it is a ruined building from which views over the Arrábida hills, the ocean and the Tróia Peninsula are beautiful. Walk back along the main road and in the first 500 metres on the left, there are good numbers of orchids and other wildflowers, including large numbers of the otherwise rare Two-leaved Gennaria, Mirror, Giant, Sombre Bee and Yellow Bee Orchids, masses of Wild Tulips and the squill *Scilla ramburei*.

Continue along the road. A series of small car parks dictate where you can park.

2 One is on the right, a little past the radio tower on the top (GPS: 38.494008, -8.966968), with views over the Rasca valley, the north slopes of Arrábida and even Lisbon. Look for Dartford and Sardinian Warbler as well as raptors (Bonelli´s Eagle is sometimes seen), Pallid and Alpine Swifts. Two-tailed Pasha sometimes flies by.

3 Another parking spot is a few kilometres further and has fabulous views over the Sado estuary, the south facing slopes of Arrábida Natural Park and the ocean (GPS: 38.481387, -8.989288). Man and Naked-man Orchids can be found in the roadside.

Again lots of orchids on this route, with the rare, winter-flowering Two-leaved Gennaria (top) and the Naked-man Orchid (bottom) being two of the attractions.

4 The last part of this road drops down and on both sides you see small, cultivated fields. This section is especially good for Azure-winged Magpie and Red-necked Nightjar. The latter often rests on the road at night. In Casais do Serra, you can connect with route 5.

At the T-junction turn left on the main road N379 towards Sesimbra.

5 Downhill from the main road lies the laid-back seaside town of Sesimbra. To visit the small harbour, follow the signs *Porto*. In winter, Great Cormorant and many hundreds of Lesser Black-backed and Yellow-legged Gulls are around, sometimes joined by Red-throated

PRACTICAL PART

124

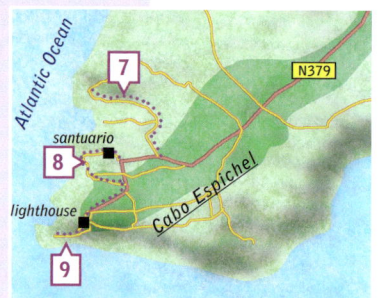

Diver or Red-breasted Merganser. A few Crag Martins winter here as well, while in spring and summer, Pallid and Alpine Swift may be seen.

From Sesimbra, follow the signs on the N379 towards Cabo Espichel. Just after the turn to Pinheirinhos, you pass a large hotel (*Dos Zimbros*) on your right. Beyond it, park at the side of the road (or onto a rough track) and explore the rough grassland on either side of the road, just west of the hotel (GPS: 38.446392, -9.155364).

6 This is probably the easiest place to see lots of orchids close to a road. Pyramidal, Naked-man, Bug, Yellow Bee, Bumblebee and Mirror Orchids are all present in good numbers, plus a few more. You'll also notice the first spiny cushions of Dense-flowered Gorse* (*Ulex densus*), an endemic spiny shrub of the capes of central Portugal.

Dinosaur footprints on the cliffs of Cabo Espichel.

Continue towards Espichel. Six kilometres beyond the hotel (and about 350m before the Santuario de Nossa Senhora do Cabo Espichel), park at the start of a walking trail on your right (GPS: 38.420205, -9.208296).

7 This is a circular trail and we advise to walk at least the first 1.5 km, to the cape just north of Espichel, from which you can see petrified dinosaur footprints on the cliffs. There are two sites within metres from one another (both with signs). The first overlooks the footprints

from a distance, underneath the Santuario. The second is much nearer, just beyond the noticeboard. The noticeboards explain where to look. The trail over has the 'regular' orchids plus Small-flowered Tongue Orchids. The area around the dinosaur cape has a different bedrock, with Umbel-flowered Heath, Myrtle and various cistuses common. The birdlife is not particularly rich, but look for Cirl and Rock Buntings, Crested Lark, Sardinian Warbler, Black Redstart and during autumn migration, Subalpine and Bonelli´s Warbler, Pied Flycatcher and Woodchat Shrike. Keep in mind the potential for rarer birds (Richard's Pipit and Alpine Accentor have, for example, been seen).

Continue to the lighthouse and monastery.

The sanctuario of Cabo Espichel, with hundreds of thousands of wild Hoop-petticoat Daffodils flowering in March.

8 The Santuario buildings and their surroundings should be examined for Little Owl, Blue Rock Thrush and Peregrine Falcon. Crested Myna, a cagebird which has a feral population in Sesimbra and Setúbal, has been seen here. Seawatching is possible from this point and views over the cliffs are magnificent. In March-April there are hundreds of thousands of Hoop-petticoat Daffodils in flower in the grassy parts of the cape, near the sanctuary and behind the lighthouse.

9 Behind the lighthouse, walk down to the tip of the cape (with the ruins of some buildings). This is an excellent place for seawatching particularly during onshore winds. Gannet and Cory´s Shearwater are regular and sometimes abundant, Balearic Shearwater, Great Shearwater and Great Skua are often seen on migration. Common Scoter, Razorbill and Puffin are mostly winter birds, while Shag may be seen year-round. Cape Espichel is not so often visited by birders as Cape St. Vincent, but remember that nutrient-rich sea canyons are close by, which attract many pelagic birds, so there is a great potential for rare seabirds.

Return via the way you came or visit the nearby freshwater lagoon of Albufeira (site E on page 137).

PRACTICAL PART

Route 5: A Walk in the Serra da Arrábida

Best season
April and May

3-4 HOURS, 4.5 KM
EASY

A ramble on foot with large numbers of orchids.

Habitats: scrubland, flowery grassland, stony areas, umbrella pinewood
Selected species: Pink Butterfly Orchid, Yellow Bee Orchid, Bug Orchid, Champagne Orchid (and many more), Palmate Anemone, Western Peony, Bonelli's Eagle, Iberian Chiffchaff, Red-necked Nightjar, Large Psammodromus, Horseshoe Whip Snake, Ladder Snake, Bedriaga's Skink, Spanish Festoon, Lorquin's Blue

Oddly enough for an area that begs to be explored on foot, there are only few walking trails in the Serra Arrábida. This is one of them – an easy route to an area of meadows with tall Umbrella Pines. This route is superb for its flora (especially orchids) and a fine range of butterflies, birds and reptiles. The route follows a way-marked horse-riding track. There are many side-tracks in the area, which can also be explored. Be careful not to lose yourself in the myriad of trails, although with the hills in the south, a large quarry in the west and the road in the north and east, you won't get lost for long.

Starting point the hamlet of Casais do Serra (38.461437, -9.056497).

Getting there Drive south for 4.2 km along the N379-1 after it comes off the N379 and take the first right, about 250 m past the restaurant *Bom Petisco*. Continue on this dirt road for 2.6 km until you see an information board on the left (facing away from you, Casa de Calhariz). On the hill on the right lies a large, conspicuous finca. Continue on foot.

1 Within the first 100 metres, you should be able to spot the first populations of Yellow Bee and Sombre Bee Orchid. Check the skies for birds – Bonelli's and Booted Eagle breed in the area and Pallid and Alpine Swift often fly by.

Where the track splits into three leave the horse-riding route (which goes right) and take instead the left-hand branch.

2 The next km is a veritable wildflower heaven. In the verges beside the track and in open patches, there are good numbers of Pink Butterfly Orchid. This magnificent species, rare in Portugal, occurs here as the variant *grandiflora* and the plants more than live up to the name. Bumblebee, Yellow Bee, Sombre Bee, Sawfly and Mirror Orchids form drifts in the open patches, where they are joined by the stout yellow Palmate Anemones. Further on, the vegetation changes and the above mentioned orchids give way to Champagne and Small-flowered Tongue Orchid. Locally, the pretty blue squill *Scilla ramburei* can be found here too. The scrub and Umbrella Pines are home to a large population of Iberian Chiffchaff (recognisable by their distinctive song), Red-necked Nightjar (which is not hard to find at dusk from late April onwards into the autumn), Crested Tit, Firecrest and Short-toed Treecreeper. Any of the lizards and snakes of Arrábida can be found on the route.

3 Following the signs for the equestrian route (which has joined your path again), you'll arrive at a large area of meadows. Continue to the area by the ruin of *Casal do Meio* (which has an information panel) and explore this area for butterflies. Spanish Festoon, Baton Blue, False Baton Blue and Lorquin's Blue can be found here. In spring check the south-facing walls of the ruined farmhouse ruin as, if you approach carefully, you may catch basking Moorish Geckos and Geniez's Wall Lizards – the form of wall lizard found across most of the area.

On the trail, you can see Pink Butterfly Orchid (top), Champagne Orchid (centre) and the hybrid between both species (bottom).

Return and once you come to the crossing (see map), turn left.

4 This last part of the loop brings you to an abandoned quarry. The flowery, stony area with its many sheltered excavations is a great terrain for butterflies and reptiles. In the last part before returning to the road, look for Western Peony.

Route 6: Sado Estuary and Tróia Peninsula

Best season
March-April
(wildflowers)
Of interest
Autumn-spring

On weekends and
during summer
months there may
be a long queue
for the ferry.

40 KM

*A great introduction to the different habitats of the Lisbon area.
Masses of birds and plenty of dune wildflowers.*

Habitats: salt marsh, rice paddies, dunes
Selected species: Bottlenose Dolphin, Purple Heron, Dartford Warbler, Purple Gallinule, Glossy Ibis, Greater Flamingo, Bar-tailed Godwit, Spiny-footed Lizard, Yellow Cistanche

This car-and-walk route offers splendid overall views of the Sado Estuary and takes you to some of the region's finest deserted beaches and dunes, mudflats and salt marshes. The route starts at the harbour of Setúbal where the ferry to the Tróia peninsula departs on the half hour (return from Tróia on the hour, with extra ferries between June – September; see **www.atlanticferries.pt**). If you have to wait for the ferry – have a coffee at the small booth and check between the spaces the cobble stones of the terrace for the diminutive Mossy Stonecrop, whose claim to fame lies in being one of the smallest flowering plant(s) of Europe.

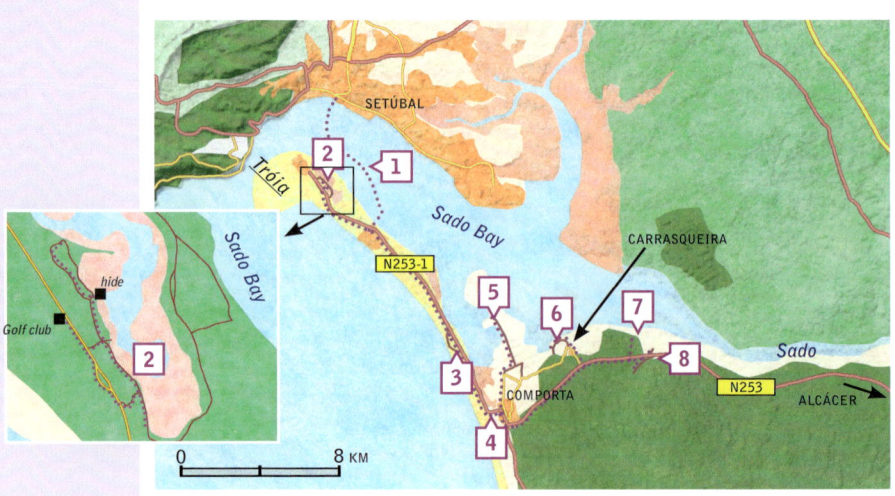

1 Look for a place on the upper deck and keep your eyes open during the 20 minutes crossing for Bottlenose Dolphin and Mediterranean Gull and in winter Black-necked Grebe, Common Scoter, Red-breasted Merganser and Great Black-backed Gull, only a handful of which winter this far south in Portugal.

The ship docks 5 km south of the tip of the peninsula. On reaching the N253-1 (500m) turn right towards the head of the peninsula and after 3 km, park at the Golf Course Restaurant. Walk back some 250 metres, take the track on the opposite side of the road and follow the circuit on the in-set map (GPS: 38.477093, -8.887701: access point to the dunes).

2 This short walk (which can be extended if you like) explores a unique area of dunes and a secluded lagoon – all superb for wild-flowers, birds and reptiles. Large Psammodromuses are common and Spiny-footed Lizard also occurs. Among the birds there are Hoopoes, Woodchat Shrikes, Sardinian and Dartford Warblers, Zitting Cisticola, while the lagoon can be full of waders (depending on the water level) and Little Egrets. The flora is absolutely superb, with many Yellow Rockrose* (*Halimium calycinum*) and some Yellow Scrub Rockrose* (*H. halimifolium*), French Lavender, the toad-flaxes *Linaria platycalyx* and *Linaria bipuntata glutinosa*) the latter endemic to the Portuguese coast, Pink (*Silene col-orata*) and Seaside Catchfly* (*S. littorea*), Yellow Restharrow, Scrambling Gromwell* (*Lithodora diffusa*) and many more. Close to the edge of the lagoon, there are hundreds of the stout yellow parasitic Yellow Cistanche.

Head back south passing the junction for the ferry as you go.

Yellow Rockrose is a conspicuous dune flower on the Tróia Peninsula.

3 After 6.3 kms from the turning to the ferry, you have excellent views over the Sado bay on your left and you can safely park off the road to the right (GPS: 38.425974, -8.824037). From here, you overlook the vast mud banks and beautiful salt marshes. In winter and during pas-sage periods check for groups of Sanderling, Dunlin, Little Stint, Ringed Plover, Black-tailed Godwit and other waders. See how the birds retreat to still exposed sandbars on a rising tide and how the longer-legged birds – Whimbrels, Little Egrets, Flamingos and Spoonbills – remain on these temporary refuges longer than the smaller waders.

View over the Sado Bay from Tróia (point 3).

On the opposite side of the road, follow the path through the dunes to the sea. Portuguese Crowberry, Shrubby Figwort, Sea Daffodil, Sea Holly, Seaside Catchfly and Cottonweed are some of the frequent wildflowers here. Look out too for Large Psammodromus and Spiny-footed Lizard.

Continue along the N253-1 road to Comporta and park next to the rice museum, which lies on your right, just before you enter the village.

4 From here you may have, at high tide, closer views of waders as Dunlin, Greenshank, Redshank, Spotted Redshank, Avocet and Black-winged Stilt. On the other side of the road, there are rice paddies. When wet (see page 37), they often have Black-winged Stilts, Glossy Ibis, White Stork and other birds.

Enter the village, turn left past a bend to the right (sign for *Aldeia do Possanco*). Then take the second left at the sign *Cambado*. After 2 km, you enter the rice paddies. The track bends to the right. After 500m, take the first left to enter the peninsula.

5 You cross excellent habitat for Marsh Harrier, White Stork and Black-winged Stilt, the Iberian race of Yellow Wagtail and Short-toed Lark. During migration, Northern Wheatear is frequent and in winter look for Bluethroat and Water Pipit. We've seen Egyptian Mongoose here as well.

Go back to the N253-1 road at Comporta and turn left. Just after the village turn left to Alcácer do Sal and after 4.8 km through open pinewoods (excellent for Red-necked Nightjar) turn left on the sign to Carrasqueira. Cross the village to park near the moorings (GPS: 38.412738, -8.756506).

6 This photogenic place forms an excellent viewpoint for the estuary and a starting point to explore the fields and reeds from the dike. The salt marshes called the *Sapal de Carrasquerio* are among the best in the estuary. Behind the village there is a mosaic of rice-fields, small agricultural lands, pastures, pools, reedbeds and channels.

Stilts and plovers feed in the harbour and can be very close to the observer, Flamingos, gulls and ducks are generally more distant. The reeds are home to Purple Gallinule, Water Rail, Great Reed Warbler and Black-headed Weaver. On passage and in winter, groups of Glossy Ibis can be seen in the fields. In winter a few Short-eared Owls, Reed Buntings and Penduline Tits appear and hundreds of herons and egrets occupy the area.

Go back to the N253 and turn left. Drive for 3.3 kms and just after passing kilometre post 8, turn left to a farm at the edge of the rice paddies (GPS: 38.407790, -8.707057).

7 Check the rice paddies and the reedbeds here for Marsh Harrier, Glossy Ibis, egrets, Spoonbills, Reed and Great Reed Warblers and Waxbills. If the water conditions are right, this area is alive with birds. You can follow a trail along the canal to cover some ground and view other rice paddies. Look for Viperine Snakes and Stripeless Tree Frogs too.

8 Walk back to the N253 and follow it some 350m back to the bottom of the shallow valley. From here, a sandy track leads to the left along a stream (Stripeless Tree Frog, Royal Fern, lots of Nightingales and a potential for interesting dragon-flies) to a reedy reservoir where Little Bittern, Purple Heron and both Cattle and Little Egrets breed. Be careful not to disturb the birds.

This is the end of the route. Either return or proceed to Alcácer do Sal to connect with the motorway back to Setúbal.

Traditional fishing boat in the harbour of Carrasqueira.

Route 7: Lagoa de Santo André

Best season
Autumn to spring

FULL DAY, 12 KM BY CAR
4.9 KM ON FOOT - EASY

Several small walks along Portugal's largest coastal lagoon.
Attractive birdlife, reptiles and wildflowers of the dunes.

Habitats: reed beds, sand plates, dunes, woodland
Selected species: Three-leaved Snowflake, Shrubby Pimpernel, *Linaria ficalhoana*, Rouyan's Thrift, *Silene littorea*, One-leaved Squill, Purple Heron, Hobby, Purple Gallinule, Little Tern, Red-necked Nightjar, Spiny-footed Lizard, Large and Smaller Psammodromus, Carbonell's Wall Lizard

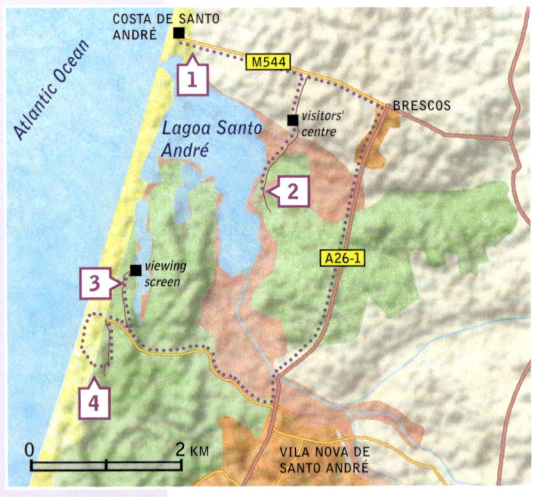

Lagoa de Santo André is somewhat forgotten by naturalists, presumably because it is a little off the usual itineraries. The area is certainly worth a visit, though, especially for birdwatchers. In contrast to the wetland sites further north, Saint André has a good stretch of reedbeds, which harbours species like Purple Heron and Purple Gallinule, which are rare or absent further north. The highest number of species can be seen at migration times (March-April and August-September) when pretty much anything can turn up. With birds arriving and departing at any time, every day has new surprises. Passerines on passage are most abundant in autumn and numbers of ducks, herons, egrets and Glossy Ibis are peak in winter.

The impressive dune strip is great for wildflowers and reptiles, while, in season, the sea invites for a dip – this part of Portugal sees rather few beach tourists and is a wonderful and laid-back area.

Starting point Car park at Costa de Santo André (GPS: 38.11407, -8.79614).

Getting there From Vila Nova de Santo André, follow the main A26-1 in northern direction to the T-junction with the M544. Turn left here to Lagoa de Santo André.

1 From Costa de Santo André you have an overall view of the lagoon to the south. This is the most open and sandy part of the site and often has gulls and terns. In summer, it is one of the few points with beach access that may become quite crowded. The light conditions for birdwatching are best early and late in the day.

View over the northern edge of the Lagoa de Santo André.

Take the car and head east to the visitors' centre, which is signposted from the road (GPS: 38.104269, -8.779814). It is one of the few places selling natural history books (bring cash!). Behind it runs a short trail.

2 From this trail, you can see good numbers of Three-leaved Snowflake and Shrubby Pimpernel which put on a great show in early spring. On the way you have good views over the lagoon (best light in the morning – early afternoon). Towards the end of the trail there is a freshwater marsh with some reeds.

The visitors' centre and the walk give good views of the lake. You will be

surprised by the number of Coots, which have surpassed 25,000 birds. Use a telescope to search for Garganey (March), Red-crested Pochard (especially winter) and waders (any month). In spring, Great Reed and Savi´s Warbler can be heard from the reeds where Little Bittern and Night Heron are uncommon but regular visitors. Little Tern breed and other terns are found on passage.

Large numbers of Cattle Egret stroll through the grasslands in search of insects.

Return to the main road (M544) and head inland, turning right at the *Café Arsénio* onto the A26-1 (direction Sines). Continue all the way to the large, elongated roundabout (4.4 km) and turn right. About 2.5 km from

the roundabout on a hilltop, 400 m before the end of the road, there is a car park on your right, from which a linear walk to a viewing screen starts (GPS: 38.079116, -8.805356).

Some of the more conspicuous wildflowers of the dunes: Shrubby Pimpernel (top), Capeweed* (*Arctotheca calendula;* centre) and Three-leaved Snowflake (bottom).

3 The walk leads through pine clad dunes, with the laguna to your right and the sea to your left. In early spring, there are plenty of One-leaved Squills flowering here. After 850m you reach the viewing screen on your right that overlooks the laguna. This is the best place for Purple Herons, Gallinules and reedbed songbirds.

4 Return to the car and continue to the car park at the end of the road (400 m), follow the circular route towards the south (4 km) that leads past two small reedy freshwater lakes and a third that is usually dry. Note how the dunes nearly swallow the small lakes

as the dominant westerly winds are pushing them inland. On the other hand, the dunes feed the lakes with fresh rainwater which seeps out of the porous sand and into the lake.

Along the stretch back to the car park on the seaward side of the lagunas, you cross a wonderful area of dunes with a rich flora. At the edges of the car park, the curious and diminutive Pygmy Cudweed grows.

Additional sites Setúbal

A – Fossil cliffs of Costa de Caparica

Erosion has sculpted unusual shapes in the fossil dune cliffs of Costa de Caparica, which rise abruptly from the sea along a 13km stretch of coastline. The cliffs look particularly striking when bathed in the golden tones of the setting sun. The jagged ochreous cliffs, which drop down from woodland and scrub towards the sea, wear a petticoat of scrub at their base. The usual bird species of such woodlands are present (Tawny Owl, Red-necked Nightjar), but above all, it is the landscape that is most remarkable. It is best enjoyed by walking along the beach from Fonte de Telha southwards, towards the Laguna de Albufeira. There is a fine dune flora at the base of the cliffs.

To get to the site, follow Fonte de Telha (separate exit off the A33) or the coastal road from Costa de Caparica. Continue to the beach of Fonte de Telha and continue down the track until it ends at a car park. Start the walk there (GPS: 38.558769, -9.189715).

B – Baía do Seixal and Rio Coina

The Baía do Seixal, south of Lisbon and at the mouth of the Tagus, is mainly fed by the Rio Coina. It is full of mud banks that attract waders at low tide and is therefore very interesting

The fossil dune cliffs of Costa de Caparica.

for birders. It is surrounded by urban areas and it is not always easy to get to good viewpoints. There are high tide roosts for waders and gulls near the villages of Coina, Seixal and Corroios. Grey and Kentish Plover, Dunlin, Little Stint, Curlew Sandpiper and other waders can be found. The Ring-billed Gull, native to North America, is seen here regularly during winter (but hard to locate amongst the numerous gulls). Exotics as Crested Myna occur around the estuary. Access and parking safely is not always simple. Good views can be obtained just west from Palhais (GPS: 38.622214, -9.053991), 600 m south of Palhais (GPS: 38.605813, -9.048447), and from a track along the sandy spit (Ponta do Corvos) at the mouth of the bay where there are information boards and a new viewing screen (*Observatório de Aves no Sapal de Corroios*; GPS: 38.652997, -9.125073).

C – Ponta da Erva plains

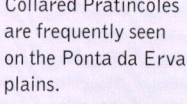

GPS: 38.950084, -8.971698. Most of what is known as the Ponta da Erva plains (a part of the Tagus Estuary Natural Reserve) is dominated by intensive farming with large agricultural tracts intersected by unpaved tracks. Its interest lies in its marshes and dikes at the edge of the rivers and its views over the Estuary. This triangular area is bordered by the Tagus, the small Rio Sorraia and the N-10 between Vila Franca de Xira and Porto Alto. Access is not straightforward. Because of the heavy traffic, make sure you approach from Vila Franca de Xira to avoid having to cross a busy carriageway. We advise you to take the track (signposted *Cabo*) just east of the bridge over the Tagus.

Collared Pratincoles are frequently seen on the Ponta da Erva plains.

At the gate, a panel welcomes the visitor and informs that after 12.5 km you will reach a futuristic style visitors centre. On the way there and back there are several sites of interest.

Take the track heading south, and go right at the first junction. Continue for about 9 kms to a farm house where the road turns left. You can visit some marshes following the first track on your right (point 1). Continue and after 3.2 kms, a track branches off to the visitors centre (2), from where there is access to a path around three ponds and hides (open November – February from 10 – 17 h. and March – October from 9 – 19 h.; entrance € 3.00). Return to the junction and turn right and again right and explore the dike and the marshes (3). Look here for Purple Heron, Great Reed Warbler, Iberian Yellow Wagtail (summer), Marsh Harrier, Cetti´s and Sardinian Warbler (all year) and Penduline Tit and Bluethroat (winter). Continue to an amazing point called *Ponta da Erva* (4), with more reedbeds where Bluethroat are often abundant in winter. Scan the mudflats for terns and, at low tide, for waders. Passerines frequent the low vegetation during migration. Turn around and go straight on to return to the main road about 5 km east of where you entered. The fields and rice paddies may yield Purple Heron, Collared Pratincole and Whiskered tern in spring and summer and Glossy Ibises and Black-tailed Godwits outside the breeding season (5).

D – Montijo harbour

If you are based at Lisbon, the regular ferry from Cais do Sodré (in the heart of Lisbon) to Montijo (€ 2.75 one way for foot passengers, **www.ttsl.pt**) offers a fine excursion, especially in winter and migration periods. During the 20 minutes crossing, Shag, Mediterranean Gull and Red-breasted Merganser may be encountered. From the Montijo harbour you have good views over the estuary and you can explore its shores on foot. A great variety of waders can be expected, especially at low tide. Bluethroats overwinter in the vegetation, while during migration, groups of Yellow Wagtails stay here and other migrants can show up.

E – Lagoa de Albufeira

GPS: 38.521722, -9.143442. The large Albufeira lagoon is situated on the seashore between Cabo Espichel and Costa Capparica. Albufeira is in fact a complex of three lagoons. The big lagoon (*Lagoa Grande*) is an open lake separated from the sea by a sand bar. *Lagoa Pequena*, actually an eastern extension of the main lagoon, has more vegetation and pastures on its southern shore. The innermost lagoon (*Lagoa da Estacada*) is separated by a bund from Lagao Pequena and covered in reeds and fringed by poplars and willows. The lagoons are surrounded by mixed and pine woodlands.

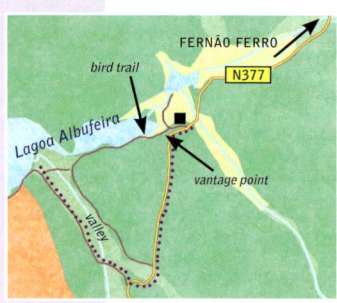

Thanks to its strategic location near the sea, many migrating birds use the area to feed or rest. Migration starts early (Feb-March), when thousands of Barn and Red-rumped Swallows, House, Sand and Crag Martins sweep across the lagunas. In April, groups of Common and Pallid Swift cross the sky and waders as Greenshank, Bar-tailed Godwit and Dunlin visit the shore. Sandwich, Common and Little Tern regularly fly in from the sea. Albufeira is a good area for raptors with regular presence of Buzzard, Goshawk, Booted and Short-toed Eagle. Marsh Harrier breeds, as do Little Bittern, Purple Heron, Water Rail and Purple Gallinule. Other birds include Turtle Dove, Nightingale, Reed and Cetti's Warbler, Zitting Cisticola, Cuckoo, Iberian Chiffchaff and Cirl Bunting. Among the amphibians are Iberian Water Frog, Western Spadefoot, Natterjack Toad, Tree Frog and Iberian ribbed Newt.

The lagoon can be viewed from a hide and a bird trail, plus a vantage point from the road. If you come from the north on the N377, park by a bend (4.5 km from the roundabout as you leave Fernão Ferro) under the pines from where you can overlook the lake and scan for birds. Continue by car for another 500m to reach the sign *Observacao de Aves – Lagoa Pequena*.

A walk along the Logao de Albufeira always turns up something special. Sometimes it's waterfowl, which includes the rather scarce Red-crested Pochard (right), the next time it is much closer to your feet as you stumble upon an Iberian Midwife Toad (left).

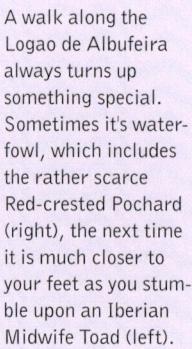

Unfortunately, the site only opens for paying groups but sometimes it is possible to enter. Another spot to explore the lagoon lies another km further where a track turns off to the right into a valley. Leave your car there and walk along the western edge up to the big lagoon. There turn left to reach the beach by its southern shore.

F – The eastern bank of the Sado estuary

  The area east of the Sado estuary is worth exploring for its dense woodlands of Cork Oaks and Umbrella Pines, its rice paddies, its agricultural fields and the shore of the estuary. This place is certainly off the beaten track and most of it is private land so should not be entered without permission.

A good road to explore this habitat branches off the N5 just south of Palma, signposted *Monte Novo* (GPS: 38.475874, -8.594669). You will see several tracks enter old Umbrella Pine and Cork Oak woods that are full of birds. Make lots of stops here and walk along the sandy track. Azure-winged Mapie, Lesser Spotted Woodpecker, Hawfinch and Crested Tit can be seen all year round. Booted Eagle, Bonelli´s Warbler, Woodchat Shrike and Wryneck are interesting summer birds. Red Fox, Iberian Hare and Egyptian Mongoose can be encountered in these parts. Among the birds, Booted Eagle, Great Spotted Cuckoo and Azure-winged Magpie are noteworthy.

Monte Novo village has 50 small houses and is situated close to the estuary. We advise to search the surroundings of the village and to take a path that takes you to the saltpans. The old saltpans and rice fields are visited by hundreds of White Storks, Glossy Ibises, Little Egrets and Cattle Egrets. Passerines on migration rest on the shores and you will find waders on the estuary.

G – The saltpans at Setúbal

  Most of the old salt pans of the Sado estuary are on the southeastern outskirts of Setúbal near *Praias do Sado*. The area contains a mixture of saltmarshes, shallow creeks, fish farms and abandoned saltpans. These salt pans produced up to 400 tons of salt each year before they were abandoned around 1900. Lots of waders and herons look for food in the old pans and in the mud of the creeks during low tide. Most important is the area's function as a high tide roost. Thousands of waders rest on the dikes between the pans and fields. Some of the saltpans have been converted into fish farms. You can easily recognise such a fish farm at low tide as they retain their water.

It is not easy to provide directions in this maze of little streets through the villages and the salt marshes. Perhaps the easiest way is to navigate to either GPS 38.520801, -8.791535 or GPS 38.516748, -8.823063, both of which are the starting points of tracks that enter the saltpans.

H – Visiting Lisbon

One of the great attractions of the Lisbon area is that it is easy to combine wildlife watching with time on the beach or being a 'culture vulture' in a beautiful city. If you are not based in Lisbon, do as the local commuters do and park at a convenient train or bus station and visit the town by public transport. Information about buses in Lisbon is found on **www.carris.pt/en**. For info about the metro (underground), check **www.lisbon.net/tram** and don't forget to try the famous Tram 28 through the old city. It is beyond the scope of this nature travel guide to discuss the many attractions of the capital. However, we make an exception for the botanical garden (just outside the town centre), which is a leafy haven of tranquillity amidst the hurly-burly of a busy city. It has a splendid collection of palms and other tropical trees. Unseen by the gardeners, whose task to maintain the garden is beyond daunting, in a lost corner of the 'Monocot garden', we found some native plants creeping up in the garden: a small population of Small-flowered Tongue Orchids had invaded the flower beds!

In the old city centre of Lisbon you may also encounter some interesting birds. Pallid Swift and Black Redstart breed in old buildings (Common Swift is more confined to modern buildings). In green oases you may find Serin, Sardinian Warbler, Firecrest and Spottless Starling. Crested Myna are becoming easier to find as is Ring-necked Parakeet (but other species of parrots may also occur).

The diminutive Geranium Bronze is a recent colonist of Portugal. Originally from South Africa, it lays its eggs on Garden Geraniums, which, among other places, are plentiful in Lisbon. From late spring into autumn, you may see this little butterfly flying around the terraces of Portugal's capital.

Routes in the Alentejo

The Alentejo is southern Portugal's vast and wild back garden – sizzling hot in summer but green and painted with flowers in winter and spring. The landscape is hilly, pretty and thinly populated. The unique land use of montados and steppes (described in detail on pages 38 to 45), gives this region a special atmosphere redolent of an ancient rural culture. The aromatic cistus scrub fills the air with its herbal scent. Small rivers, fringed with dense beds of white flowering Water Crow's-foot, lace the region. Despite a gently rolling, flower-rich spring landscape, the sudden rocky canyons, thin slate soils, the baking summer sun and vast horizons give this part of Portugal its unique and paradoxical mix

Overview of the Alentejo. The letters refer to the sites on page 158-162.

of harshness and loveliness that never ceases to astonish. In this way, and also in its geology and land use, the Alentejo resembles the adjacent Spanish region of Extremadura.

The natural inhabitants of this world are similar too – the birdlife is rich with very large populations of steppe birds, large numbers of storks, Azure-winged Magpies, Hoopoes, Bee-eaters, shrikes, and birds of prey for which this is Portugal's best region. The richest areas for naturalists are in the southern Alentejo, which is why we focus on that area.

For a birdwatcher a visit to the Alentejo is a particularly enriching experience as birdwatching is simply splendid almost anywhere. The best area for steppe birds is near Castro Verde (route 10), while raptors are best seen on routes 8, 9 and 11. Sometimes the roads that connect you to these sites and routes in this book can be as exciting as the destinations themselves. Any track or side road may be worth to explore.

The Alentejo is not only about birds but also has beautiful landscapes. Reptiles and amphibians are plentiful and in spring, wildflowers bloom in profusion, but with a generally poor and acidic bedrock, the flora and butterfly fauna is not very diverse, except for a few pockets where limestone comes to the surface (route 9).

142

Route 8: The Moura area

Best season
March-May
Of interest
October-June

FULL DAY, 67 KM

A dip into interior Portugal.
Splendid birdlife of the montados and steppes.

Habitats: cereal steppes, river valley, holm oak montados
Selected species: Otter, Little Bustard, Black Stork, Crane (winter), Red Kite (winter), Black-winged Kite, Woodchat Shrike, Bee-eater, Hoopoe, Black-eared Wheatear, Calandra Lark, Thekla's Lark

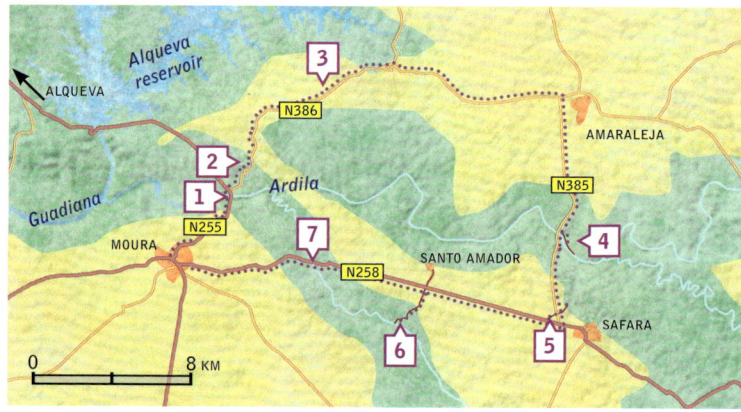

Moura is a small town in the heart of the Alentejo. It lies in a rugged landscape with woods and montados of Holm Oak, pastures, cultivated fields and olive groves. Due to the poor soils, agriculture is traditional and many areas are used for grazing cattle. The area is best explored by car, making stops at appropriate points to look for birds or just to enjoy the landscape. This route is good for steppe birds, raptors and other birds of the montados.

Starting point Moura.
Drive north on the N255 direction Alqueva and Amareleja.

1 After 5 km, park just before the bridge over the beautiful Ardila River, which holds water even in summer. Scan the area and explore the path down to the water (remembering to close the gate behind you). On both sides, Holm Oak and Olive dominate the landscape. Great Spotted Cuckoo, Bee-eater, Red-rumped Swallow, Crag Martin, Black-eared Wheatear, Woodchat Shrike, Rock Sparrow, Subalpine and Melodious Warbler breed along the river, where Black Stork and Otter hunt for fish in the crystal-clear water.

Continue and a little further, turn right towards Amareleja. If you want to visit the immense Alqueva dam first ignore the turning and proceed along the N255. The dam is 9 km further ahead.

2 Along the road to Amareleja there are many places to park safely and we advise you to do so several times to scan the area. The road passes through an area with Holm Oaks, olive groves and fields with cattle. Spanish Sparrow, Thekla's Lark, Calandra Lark (plentiful!), Stone Curlew, Red-legged Partridge, Iberian Grey Shrike and Corn Bunting can all be seen here. Booted and Short-toed Eagle, Black Kite, Black-winged Kite and Buzzard frequently cross the sky. This is also one of the best places for wintering Cranes in Portugal, with several hundreds present in the area. Flocks and families can be seen feeding in the fields and flying over. Red Kites and Hen Harrier also winter.

The lovely Ardila River flows gently through the vast Holm Oak montados near Moura.

3 At km 24.2 (GPS: 38.214539, -7.363209) there is another good spot to stop, with cereal fields, Olives and big Holm Oaks. Explore the tracks that branch off at this point on foot to find more birds. You have a chance of seeing Little Bustard and Montagu´s Harrier here.

Cross the village of Povoa and continue to Almareleja. Just before this village turn right on the N385 towards Safara.

4 After another 7.5 km you reach the Ardila River for the second time. Park before the bridge and walk the path along the river to search for birds – the same species are possible as mentioned at point 2.

After crossing the bridge on foot, a path goes left down to the river, which we also recommend. Eagle Owl occurs in this area.

Continue for 4 km from the bridge and at km post 35, park on the right side of the road.

5 A broad track crosses some extensive, rolling cereal fields. This is a good area for Little Bustard, Montagu´s Harrier, Quail and Black-bellied Sandgrouse. Take your time to search for them, along the track. We also found Badger footprints here.

Proceed to the next junction (500m) and turn right to Moura. After 7 km turn left opposite the junction to Sto. Amador (GPS: 38.125432, -7.312687).

6 Explore this quiet road for several kilometres. Old olive groves and montados alternate with small agricultural fields. Similar birds as at point 2 and 5 can be found here.

7 A few kilometres further, at km post 66.1, there are two more side tracks, both to the left and to the right, which offers another shot at the aforementioned birds (GPS: 38.133287, -7.339698).

Return to the junction and turn left to Moura.

Male (top) and female (bottom) Little Bustard.
The great attraction of this route is the combination of birds (and other wildlife) of both montados and steppes.

Route 9: From Sobral da Adiça to Barrancos

FULL DAY, 80 KM

Exploring splendid holm oak montados.
Rich sites for wildflower and butterflies.
The best route for vultures and eagles.

Best season
February-May
Of interest
Year-round

Habitats: cereal steppes, river valley, holm oak montados
Selected species: Fan-lipped Orchid, Mirror Orchid, Spotted Green-winged
Orchid* (*Anacamptis picta*), Wild Boar, Red Deer, Griffon Vulture, Black
Vulture, Little Owl, Crane, Stone Curlew, Azure-winged Magpie, White-
rumped Swift, Aetherie Fritillary, Portuguese Dappled White

This route explores a hidden and
relatively unknown part of the
lower Alentejo near the Guadiana
river and the border with Spain.
It combines superb montados
and pasturelands – like on the
previous route – with pockets of
limestone which are attractive
for wildflowers and butterflies.
In comparison with the previous
route, this one covers less ground
by car and offers more options to
explore on foot.

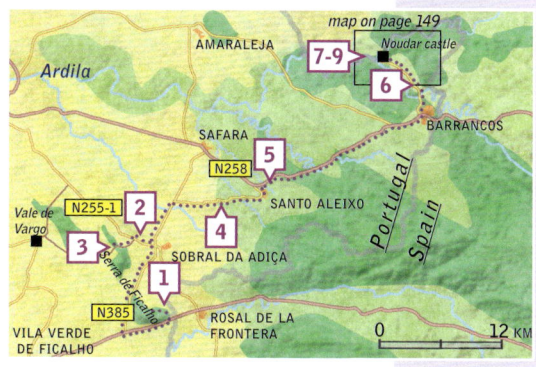

The Barrancos area is a lost corner of Portugal that juts into Spain between the regions of Extremadura and Andalucía and that feels equally
far from civilization. Few people live in this area and there is little traffic.

Starting point Vila Verde de Ficalho (GPS: 37.946603, -7.298548)

Drive in the direction of Spain. On your left is the conspicuous hill
of the Serra de Ficalho, one of three limestone ranges in a vast area
of schist. Within sight of the border, park at the car park on the left
side, close to a derelict white building and a bus stop sign. Just behind
the building, a track runs off into the olive groves (GPS: 37.960102,
-7.253276). Follow it for a kilometre or two.

Yellow Lupin is frequently planted in the montados of the Alentejo and puts up a spectacular show in March and April. The Red-legged Partridge occurs here in high numbers (top).

1 Nothwithstanding the somewhat tacky starting point, the olive groves here are superb. The ground is home to a rich flora with a good number of orchids. Follow the track along the dry stream on the right (which is actually the border with Spain), past a white building and at the fork, wander into the groves on the left. There are good numbers of the very rare Fan-lipped Orchid here in late winter (Feb-March), followed by equal numbers of Naked-man Orchid and, more thinly, Woodcock Orchid. Following the other fork, continue to a saddle dividing the hills for wonderful views over the area. You may spot the first vultures or other raptors here, enjoy views of Azure-winged Magpies and Hoopoes, or look out for Ocellated Lizard. Lataste's Viper has been found in the hills and Genet occurs here too.

Return to the car and drive back to Vila Verde de Ficalho and turn right onto the N385 towards Mourão. After 9 km, turn left at a crossroads towards Moura on the N255-1.

2 This is a superb montado, one of many you'll be crossing this day. Corn Bunting, Iberian Grey and Woodchat Shrikes, Hoopoe, Bee-eater and

Azure-winged Magpie are all regular here. After 1.5 km check the low ruins on a hill to your right for breeding Little Owl, while in winter, Cranes regularly feed in the open pastures (GPS: 38.026922, -7.287263). Keep an eye on the sky as well. Here and on the remainder of the route, you have a good chance of spotting Griffon and Black Vulture, Short-toed and Golden Eagle. Check the latter carefully as Spanish Imperial Eagles (mostly immatures) are turning up more often in this part of Portugal.

At the crossing, turn left towards Vale de Vargo and follow the somewhat bumpy tarmac road uphill. Park at a track on the right, just over the hill (GPS: 38.021566, -7.314851).

3 Follow this track for about 100 metres, examining the olive grove for orchids. Late winter sees more Fan-lipped Orchid, there are masses of Mirror Orchids and lower numbers of Yellow Bee and Sawfly Orchids. Portuguese Dappled White flies here in April and May. Return to explore on foot for some 300 metres along the road you arrived by, for wonderful views over the olive groves and montado. There is a good chance on raptors here while in the roadside on the right, there are good numbers of Spotted Green-winged Orchid* (*Anacamptis picta*).

Return to the N385 and head north. After 4.8 kms, turn right onto an again somewhat bumpy minor road to Santo Aleixo.

4 This stretch passes through pastureland and montado. Scan for raptors (including Black-winged Kite) and birds of the montado. Butterfly aficionados would do well to check the areas with Cardoon, the host plant of the rare Aetherie Fritillary, which is seen along this road. Further ahead (6.4 km from the turning), you cross a beautiful stream to which, sadly, there is no access but it's worth checking it from the bridge.

Once in Santo Aleixo, turn left and shortly thereafter right, to Barrancos on the N258.

5 The next stretch has more montado, but also some dull Eucalyptus stands. There are two rivers which are worth a stop. The first is close to

147

A spectacular rarity that grows only in a handful of sites in Portugal is the Fan-lipped Orchid (top). It flowers from late January to late March.
More common is the Spanish Marbled White (bottom), a spring butterfly, here on the flower of a Galactitis Thistle.

Santo Aleixo (GPS: 38.076641, -7.154007). The gentle slopes, verdant pasture and the river lined with Oleanders you can explore freely in either direction. The common montado birds are present, plus Spanish Sparrow which breeds in the Eucalyptus.

The second bridge (GPS: 38.089286, -7.102431) is at about a third of the way to Barrancos. It spans a stunning river that is easily seen from the road, but is unfortunately inaccessible.

At Barrancos, turn left off the N258 just before a petrol station and follow the signs to *Castelo de Noudar*. After 3 km, this winding road brings you to a very narrow bridge over the Ribeiro de Murtega. Park by the bridge.

The border area with Spain, which this route explores, is one of the best areas in Portugal for raptors. You have a good chance on seeing vultures like Griffon and this Black Vulture.

6 On the roadside in spring, there are clumps of the pretty Champagne Orchid. On foot, follow the road to the riverbank, some 200 metres. The rocks here are rich in ferns and in the riverside cliffs and vegetation look for Cirl and Rock Bunting, Golden Oriole, Bee-eater, Nightingale, Orphean Warbler and Red-rumped Swallow.

Cross the bridge by car and continue the 10 km long stony track to Noudar Castle. The views over the hills and Holm Oak forests (which are excellent here) become increasingly magnificent.

7 Make a stop at the observation tower (*Torre* – signposted) on the left. Although concealed from view from the road, it offers excellent 360° view over the area, making it a good viewpoint for raptors. Black Vulture is regular and Griffon Vulture is more common here than in other parts of southern Portugal. Other soaring raptors, which can be spotted from any viewpoint along this road, include Spanish Imperial, Booted, Short-toed, Bonelli´s and Golden Eagle.

8 Just before the castle there's a ruin on the left, from where two walking trails start – one to the left and the other to the right. Although both are worth walking, we advise taking the one on the left.

This 4 km, moderately difficult walk leads through beautiful holm oak woodland down to the river. Bee-eaters breed, you have a chance of seeing Black Stork and any of the other montado birds. Above all, though, this is an excellent way to breathe in the sweet scent of the Gum Cistus, to marvel at the surprisingly dense, lichen-clad woods on north slopes and to see some of the butterflies (plenty of Spanish Festoons) and reptiles (numerous Large Psammodromuses) – in other words, to take in the montado from up close. Look out for mammals as well. Red Deer are common and, although elusive, all the other montado-species (e.g. Badger, Fox, Genet, Otter, Egyptian Mongoose) occur here.

9 The walled fortress Castelo de Noudar is located between the two rivers Ardila and Murtega. Originally a Moorish castle, for centuries it served as border fortress (it was occupied by Spain several times until it definitively returned to Portugal in 1715). It was the municipal seat until replaced by Barrancos in the 1700s, the village was

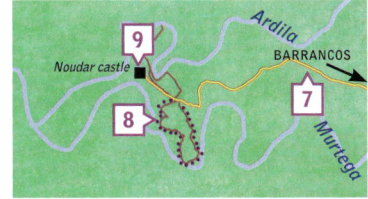

abandoned in the early 19th century. Herpetologists note that a legend tells that the castle is inhabited by an enchanted Moorish princess in the form of a serpent! From the hilltop you look out over Spain and this is again a good place to scan for large raptors. Walk the path around the walls and enter into the castle (entrance free, but closed on monday). In and around the castle Blue Rock Thrush, Thekla's Lark, Black Redstart, Crag Martin and sometimes Black-eared Wheatear breed. From the car park you can walk a short path that leads down to the river, where Black Stork often feeds.

Noudar castle, set in a paradisiacal landscape.

Route 10: Castro Verde plains

Best season
February-May
Of interest
Year-round

5 HOURS, 78 KM

Superb area for steppe birds – among the best in Europe.

Habitats: steppes, holm oak montados
Selected species: Crane (w), Golden Plover (w), Black-winged Kite (w), Red Kite (w), Hen Harrier (w), Spanish Imperial Eagle, Lesser Kestrel, Montagu's Harrier, Great Bustard, Little Bustard, Great Spotted Cuckoo, Black-bellied Sandgrouse, Stone Curlew, Roller, Calandra Lark, Spanish Sparrow, Spanish Terrapin

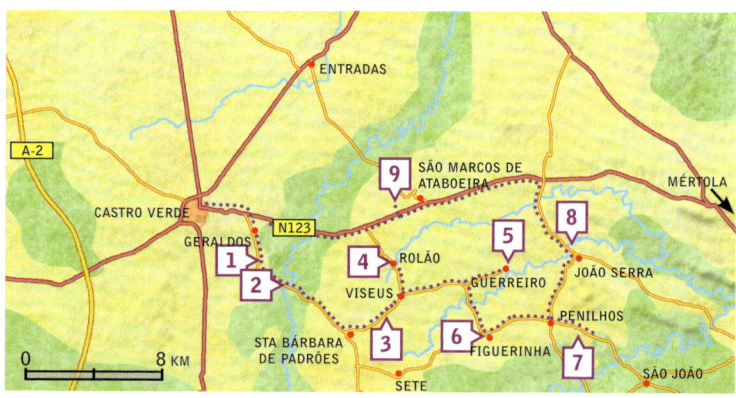

Between Castro Verde and Mértola there are roughly 50 x 25 km of pastures, cereal fields and fallow lands on poor and dry soils: the Castro Verde plains. This region is undoubtedly the best area for steppe birds in Portugal and measures up to those of the neighbouring Extremadura in Spain. Small, white-washed villages dot the plains, connected by narrow, little-travelled roads. There are a few streams, some holm oak montados, areas of cistus scrub and Eucalyptus trees along the roads, but otherwise it is all steppe pastures. Following the winter rains, the rolling landscape is splashed with colour with the meadows turning purple with Purple Viper's-bugloss and white and yellow from the marigolds, chamomiles and hawk's-beards.

Birds of the Castro Verde plains

The Castro Verde plains are home to high densities of steppe birds and raptors. It is the most important place in Portugal for Great and Little Bustard, Black-bellied Sandgrouse, Montagu´s Harrier and (with Mértola) Lesser Kestrel. Many hundreds of pairs of Quail, Stone Curlew, Black-eared Wheatear, Tawny Pipit, Spanish Sparrow and plenty of Iberian Grey Shrike breed. There are numerous Little Owls and (in season) Great Spotted Cuckoos whilst pairs of Thekla's, Calandra and Short-toed Lark number in the thousands and Corn Bunting is even more abundant. It is the main Portuguese site for Roller. The only steppe bird that is missing is Pin-tailed Sandgrouse which is now virtually extinct in the coun-

try. The whole area is an important hunting ground for young and sub-adult Golden and Bonelli´s Eagle, Griffon and Black Vulture and, increasingly, for the Spanish Imperial Eagle. In winter, raptors such as Black-winged Kite, Hen Harrier, Marsh Harrier, Red Kite, Peregrine Falcon and Merlin scout the plains, where Lapwing and Golden Plover abound. The resident larks congregate in large groups and are joined by Meadow Pipits.

The landscape is impressive, but this is above all a birdwatching route. It pays (enormously) to be out and about early, preferably at sunrise. Note that finding steppe birds is challenging and that birdwatchers are advised to do this route twice, perhaps varying the itinerary somewhat, to get the most out of what this splendid area has to offer. This route is described from Castro Verde, but if you are based in Mértola, it can easily be done in reversed order.

The colourful Roller breeds near São Marcos de Ataboeira.

Starting point Castro Verde (note the Lesser Kestrels here).
Take the N123 to Mértola and roughly 2 km from the edge of Castro Verde, turn right to Geraldos.

1 On this first stretch, montados dominate the landscape. It should be not too hard to pick up the first Azure-winged Magpies, Red-legged Partridges, Hoopoes, Red-rumped Swallows, Bee-eaters and Woodchat and Iberian Grey Shrikes.

2 After crossing the bridge south of Geraldos, park your car and explore. Nightingale, Melodious Warbler and Golden Oriole breed in the riverine vegetation. Further afield, there are Iberian Grey and Woodchat Shrikes.

Proceed to Sta. Bárbara de Padrões and continue to Viseus.

3 From Sta. Bárbara onwards, you are in prime steppe habitat. From here it is important to make regular stops to search for Little and Great Bustards, Black-bellied Sandgrouse, Stone Curlew, Little Owl, Calandra Lark and Great Spotted Cuckoo and the other steppe birds named above (see also page 230 for tips on watching steppe birds). Along the road there is cereal cultivation and fallow land. Montagu's Harrier is particularly abundant here.

4 When you reach Viseus, there is a road to the left (80m beyond a bus shelter), which leads to Rolão (not signposted; GPS: 37.675118, -7.960163), a tiny village only 2 km from the junction. Head along this road stopping to scan the fields as the habitat here is also very good for the above mentioned steppe birds.

5 Return to Viseus and proceed to Guerreiro for more steppe habitat. At Guerreiro, the tarmac ends and you are in one of the most lonely places in a vast area. Park your car at the edge of the village, walk around and explore both village (Spanish Sparrow breeds) and tracks leading into the fields – again it is the steppe birds that form the main attraction.

A flock of Black-bellied Sandgrouse.

6 Retrace your route and take the left-hand turning to Figueirinha. There is a great vantage point just before you reach the crossroads next to the village where we had both Great and Little Bustard. At this crossroads you turn left towards Penilhos.

7 Another good stretch of road is the one east from Penilhos towards São João dos Caldeireiros (on the N267 Mértola road). We advise you to explore the first 4.6 km and turn around before the bridge over the river.

Returning to Penilhos take the road north towards to João Serra where you bear left towards Castro Verde.

8 Just outside the village, park before the bridge and make a walk along the small stream to explore. You can find Spanish Terrapin, lots of Bee-eaters, Woodchat Shrike. Spanish Sparrows breed in the White Stork nests.

On reaching the N123 turn left towards Castro Verde. Continue westwards for 10 km until, 3km beyond the village of São Marcos da Ataboeiera, the road passes through a shallow cutting where you turn right onto a track signposted to Monte de Apariça. Park 100m further up, before the sign *pista privada* (GPS: 37.696937, -7.970252).

Great Spotted Cuckoos are quite common on this route. Check the fences, poles and electricity wires carefully and you make a good chance to find it.

9 There are several nest boxes on the telephone poles where Roller, Little Owl and Lesser Kestrel breed. As the nest boxes are close to the road and the birds are shy, it is vital not to approach too closely as it will severely disturb the breeding birds!

Continue along the N123 to return to Castro Verde. Alternatively, you can go back to turn left towards São Marcos da Ataboeiera but before you reach the village, go left on a minor road to Entradas (site G on page 162) for more steppe habitat. Note that in wet winters, this road may be flooded.

In spring, the plains are awash with wildflowers.

154

Route 11: Pulo do Lobo

**32 KM, ONE WAY
EASY-MODERATE**

*Drive to and walk along a beautiful river valley.
Excellent birdwatching and dragonflies in late spring.*

Habitats: river valley, cliffs, extensive agricultural patches, Holm Oak montados
Selected species: Red Deer, Spanish Imperial Eagle, Golden Eagle, Bonelli´s
Eagle, Little Owl, Azure-winged Magpie, Rock Bunting, Blue Rock Thrush,
Iberian Grey Shrike, Woodchat Shrike, Spanish Terrapin, Northern Banded
Groundling

Pulo do Lobo is in the heart of the Vale do
Guadiana natural park, and, together with
Mértola village and the Mina São Domingo, is
one of the few sites in this part of the Alentejo
that attracts even a modest number of visitors.
It is indeed an enchanting site – a rocky tour-
niquet squeezing the Río Guadiana through a
narrow canyon as it drops some 15 metres over
a short stretch. It is proudly described as the
largest waterfall on the river, but it would be
more accurate to describe it as an impressive
series of narrow, steeply tumbling rapids.

This short car route and walk along the river
is highly recommended to birdwatchers and
general naturalists alike. The drive to Pulo do
Lobo is as much a part of the experience as
the destination itself.

Starting point Mértola
Head towards Castro Verde (N122) and after
4 km, turn right onto a road signposted to
Corte Gafo de Cima and Pulo do Lobo (note,
en route, the warning signs for Lynx, which
were recently reintroduced in the area). For
the rest of the route, keep following the Pulo
do Lobo signs.

1 The first stretch is dominated by fallow land, some pastures and abandoned slopes, covered in Gum Cistus scrub. Soon you'll enter open montados. Black-winged Kite may be seen, there are large flocks of Azure-winged Magpie and high numbers of Red-legged Partridge. Iberian Grey and Woodchat Shrikes are common. Cattle Egret, Turtle Dove, Great Spotted Cuckoo (uncommon), Little Owl, Hoopoe, Iberian Green Woodpecker, Thekla's and Woodlarks, Corn and Cirl Buntings are all here, while Black Kite and any of the eagles, may soar by. Keep an eye out here and further along this route for raptors anyway – this general area has a high concentration of eagles, particularly Bonelli's and Golden Eagles. Red Kite, Hen Harrier and Meadow Pipit are among the winter birds. The montados are a paint box of wildflowers. Some have crops of Yellow Lupin, which are planted both as

Montados along the way to Pulo do Lobo (top). There are two interesting wild-flowers here: the Green-flowered Lavender (centre) is often considered a separate species from the French Lavender with which it often grows together. The Spiny Greenweed (bottom) is a common plant in this region, but one that is confined to southwestern Iberia.

In late summer, the boldly patterned Northern Banded Groundling is frequent along the Guadiana. It is often found resting on the ground in areas with lots of cattle.

livestock feed and to improve the fertility of the soil by nitrogen fixation.

2 Before entering the village Corte Gafo de Cima turn right onto the small road towards Corte Gafo Baixo which is the starting point of a walk to the Río Guadiana. Look out for grazing Red or Fallow Deer (this is a hunting area between the 15th of August and the 28th of February). Hunting has made Wild Boar and Iberian Hare very shy. The Red-legged Partridges and Quails are hunted after the breeding season.

Park on the other side of Corte Gafo Baixo and follow the 4.5 km signposted walk to the old watermill on the river.

3 This trail leads you through a landscape of Mediterranean scrub, wild olive trees, juniper and broom. The scrub is a good place for the Spectacled Warbler and the sites with more trees are good for Subalpine Warbler.

Head back towards Corte Gafo Cima but before you reach the village, turn right at the crossroads for Amendoeira do Serra and Pulo do Lobo.

Drive through Amendoeira do Serra continuing for another 6km to the end of the tarmac road where there is a small car park. The route continues on a well-maintained but steep track down to Pulo do Lobo. It is drivable with a normal car (but take care). If you are here in low season, it is advisable to walk down, as you will be able to see far more.

4 At Pulo do Lobo, walk the concrete track to the waterfalls. This is a stunning place – rocky with swirling, roaring water which contrasts the still water-carved half-filled hollows in the rocks. Pulo do Lobo means Wolf's Leap, as the ravine is so narrow that it seems it could be crossed in one giant leap. This is a good spot to look for Black Stork, Raven, Grey Wagtail, Blue Rock Thrush, Rock Bunting, Subalpine Warbler, and Bonelli's Eagle plus any of the raptors noted elsewhere in this account.

On the cliffs near the river Red-rumped Swallow and Crag Martin build their nest. Viperine Snake lives among the rocks on the waterside.

5 You can follow a trail (red-and-yellow markings) upstream, to increase your chances of finding the species mentioned previously. Look in the river for Spanish Terrapin. Spanish Marbled White, Black-eyed Blue, Cleopatra, Spanish Festoon, Green-striped White and Small Heath are frequent butterflies. Dartford, Subalpine and Sardinian Warbler breed in the scrub and woodland on the slopes.

After a few hundred metres, the trail becomes increasingly hard to follow until eventually it simply disappears. Go as far as you feel like.

Between May and July, the Guadiana river at Pulo do Lobo is attractive for dragonflies as well. Northern Banded Groundling and Broad Scarlet are frequent, while Green Hooktail and Pronged Clubtail are also listed for this area.

The wild Pulo do Lobo gorge (top) is a rough note amidst the colourful montado landscape (bottom).

PRACTICAL PART

Additional sites in Baixo Alentejo

A – Lagoa dos Patos and Albufeira de Odivelas

  'Albufeira' originates from the Arabic word for 'marsh' (*al buhayrah*) and is now applied to marshland along reservoirs and rivers. Shallow, marshy reservoirs can be very rich in birds when there's just sufficient water to expose muddy shores and shallow puddles yet maintain a healthy lakeside vegetation of reedbeds and tamarisk. About 25 km northeast of the city of Beja, three waterbodies often contain just the right amount of water to be attractive to birds and birdwatchers alike.

The small *Lagoa dos Patos* (Duck Lake) and the adjacent *Lagoa do Peneireiro* (Kestrel Lake) are reservoirs that, together with some rice paddies downstream, hold the highest concentrations of ducks in the Alentejo in winter. Several thousands can be present, mostly Gadwall,

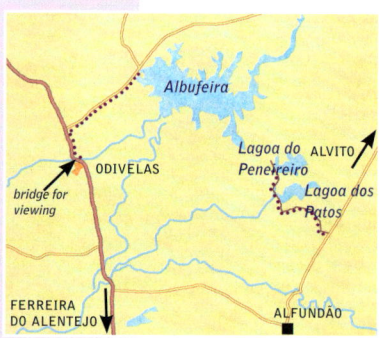

Mallard, Teal and Shoveler. Great White Egret, Great Crested Grebe, Cormorant and Coot are abundant in winter too, when Snipe, Common Sandpiper, Kingfisher and Water Pipit can also be found. Other birds that are regularly seen include Little Egret and Purple Heron, Spoonbill (mostly winter) and Flamingo and there is a Cattle Egret colony. Collared Pratincole and Little Ringed Plover breed on the shore. During the breeding season the surroundings are attractive for Montagu´s Harrier, Short-toed Lark and Black-eared Wheatear. Gull-billed Tern visits the lakes on passage and of course during migration more species show up. In spring, the large numbers of Stripeless Tree Frog make themselves heard.

Access is from the road between Ferreira do Alentejo and Odivelas. Coming from Ferreira, turn right after about 9 km to Alfundão. At the entrance of the latter, turn left to Alvito. Where the road crosses a track, about 3.5 km from the village, turn left (GPS: 38.148888, -8.048668) and after 1 km you will see Lagoa dos Patos. Lagoa do Peneireiro is behind it, hidden by a line of trees.

To reach the far end of the Albufeira de Odivelas, you need to return to Alfundão and take the road to Odivelas. Stop first in the village and park behind the bridge over the river (GPS: 38.171403, -8.149910). The riverine vegetation is rich and attracts passerines. Look for Hawfinch in the trees. We found Otter droppings and a nest of Red-rumped Swallow under the bridge. Two km further north along the N2, a side road sign-posted *Barragem* (dam) leads to the reservoir. Park at the end of the dam and explore the area on foot (GPS: 38.184086, -8.113733).

B – Canais do Guadiana

    GPS: 37.693291, -7.654004 A beautiful track leads to a rocky stretch on the Guadiana river. The site is somewhat similar to the Pulo do Lobo, but it is much less visited. At the river, you can find Rock Bunting, Blue Rock Thrush, Subalpine Warbler, Black Stork, Bonelli's Eagle – in other words all the attractions of Pulo do Lobo.
To get to Canais, take the exit to Corvos / Canais, 5 km east of Mértola on the N265. At the roundabout of Corvos, go left (Corte Pequena) and after 3.2 km left again, following Canais. This well-maintained track ends at the hamlet of Corte Pequena, from which you can walk (or carefully drive) the steep track down to the river.
Between the main N265 road and Corvos village, you'll see the reservoir (*Barragem*) of Corvos on your right – it is difficult to access but sometimes hold Marsh Harrier and some other birds of freshwater marshes, rare in the interior of the Alentejo.

C – Sapos – Santana de Cambas

   GPS: 37.649897, -7.533584. Like Guerreiro on the Castro Verde plains, Sapos feels like one of the most remote and lonely parts of Portugal. The open country, pastures, scattered trees and a beautiful small river are full of birds during spring. At this time, the green grassland is also a wildflower paradise. Quail, Red-rumped Swallow, Bee-eater, Woodchat Shrike, Woodlark, Thekla's Lark and Corn Bunting, common birds on the Portuguese steppes, are especially abundant here. The fields are also very good for Iberian Hare. In the river you may see lots of Spanish Terrapin. To get to the tiny village of Sapos (not to be confused with a village of the same name just west of Mértola) take a sideroad south from the N265, 13 km east of Mértola. The tarmac turns into a stony track and ends in Santana de Cambas.

The Blue Rock Thrush is found in rocky terrain but sometimes chooses (hilltop) villages as a substitute habitat. You can find it both in Mértola town (site E) as well as in the Guadiana river valley (site B).

160

D – Mina de São Domingos

GPS: Between 1855 and 1966, many workers lived in a crowded village near the São Domingo mines where they excavated the open cast diggings. Most of it was sent to the UK. Many old buildings and the open mine now remain in a deserted landscape of deep red rocks dotted with Eucalyptus. There is a small museum on the mining history. The area is popular among birdwatchers because it is a well-known site for the rare White-rumped Swift. There are regular sightings between May and August and it seems that at least several pairs breed in the surroundings. Black Vulture, Short-toed Eagle and Golden Eagle are also regular and Red-rumped Swallow (whose nests the White-rumped Swift uses), Blue Rock Thrush, Black-eared Wheatear, Spanish Sparrow and Red-necked Nightjar breed. The mines are 17 km east of Mértola on the N265. In São Domingo, opposite the church follow the sign Montes Altos.

Mértola town (bottom) is, together with the village of Castro Verde, the best place to observe the graceful Lesser Kestrel (top), which breeds in a loose colony in and around the walled town.

E – Mértola town and walk along the Guadiana river

The attractive white buildings of the historic town of Mértola are built on the west bank of the Guadiana. Each morning the sun rises from behind the hills and sets the town afire in a warm glow, best seen (and photographed) from the opposite bank of the river. In ancient times, despite being 70 km from the ocean, this was the highest navigable point in the river so trade with the Phoenicians and Carthaginians thrived. Later it became a Roman settlement and later still the Moors arrived. The Moors built the walls that still remain as does the mosque they built which is now a remarkable church (*Igreja Matriz*). The castle dates from after the reconquista of 1238.

Mértola is not only picturesque and historically interesting, it is a great place
for birdwatchers too. With
several dozens of pairs,
Mértola has one of the largest Lesser Kestrel colonies
in Portugal. They nest in
the old buildings (in particular the castle walls),
hover and cavort over the
streets, rest on the rooftops
and the whole town echoes
with their excited calls. You can sit and watch them whilst enjoying a
beer or coffee in a convenient bar. An important conservation project for
this species has boosted the number of pairs breeding on the Convento
São Francisco (just outside the town walls) from a handful to 65 pairs.
Blue Rock Thrush, White Stork, Hoopoe and Spotless Starling are other
rooftop birds of Mértola. All can be seen on the church, while Black-eared
Wheatear may hold territory near the castle. Barn and Scops Owl can be
heard at night. Night is also the time to search for the Moorish Gecko on
walls near streetlights hunting for insects, or maybe even in your own
hotel room.

Viperine Snakes are
the most frequently
seen snake in the
Alentejo. In contrast
to the other species
(except Grass Snake),
it is found in or near
water.

What makes Mértola even more attractive is its position by the river,
where Crag Martin, Red-rumped Swallow, Grey Wagtail and Kingfisher
can all be seen, while Subalpine Warbler frequents the bushes on the
bank opposite the village. Cormorant and Cattle Egret have a roost by
the river further downstream and can be seen commuting in the morn-
ings and evenings. The nearby gardens, trees, bushes and fields are good
for Golden Oriole, Iberian Green Woodpecker, Nightingale, Sardinian
Warbler, Woodchat Shrike, Bee-eater, Thekla's Lark, Spanish Sparrow,
Long-tailed Tit, Serin, Azure-winged Magpie and Rock Bunting. In winter Hawfinch, Bullfinch and Lesser Spotted Woodpecker may show up.

There is a walking trail off the N122 just south of town (about 800 m.
beyond a bridge over a tributary of the main river) which starts at the
Poço dos dois Irmãos (The well of the Two Brothers; GPS: 37.633688,
-7.673231) and leads down to and along the Guadiana. It is a scenic walk
on which many of the aforementioned birds can also be seen as well as
the typical flora of the region. The route is linear and the first 1-2 km is
the best section.

162

F – The Azinhal steppes

  GPS: 37.759710, -7.824406. From the hamlet of Azinhal, a track cuts through the steppes and connects with the local road between Corte Pequena and Viegas. It is a great area for steppe birds. Drive slowly and scan the area for Little and Great Bustards, Black-bellied Sandgrouse, Little Owl, Montagu's (summer) and Hen Harrier (winter), Calandra Lark and Stone Curlew.
Azinhal lies 20 km northwest of Mértola on the N122. The track is signposted with wooden signs *birdwatching walk*, the first of which is at the main road in the middle of the hamlet of Azinhal.

G – Entradas

  The fields surrounding the village of Entradas are among the best places to find Great Bustard. Up to date information can be had in the *Centro de Educação Ambiental de Vale Gonçalinho* (Environmental Education Centre of Vale Gonçalinho), run by the LPN (*Liga para a Protecção da Natureza*). The centre, situated off the E802/IP2 road 6 km north of Castro Verde (but note that you have to turn onto the track running parallel to the main road 2 km earlier). The centre, which houses a small exhibition, is open Tuesday to Saturday, 09:00-13:00 and 14:00-18:00.
There are good areas to explore around Entradas. At the Entradas junction on the IP 2 (the southern one of two), you have two options. The first is to turn left (as you come from Castro Verde) towards Carregueiro. After 1 km a track signed *Monte das Mouras* appears on your left. Here you can park safely to scan the area. Follow the track (by car) and look at the terracotta pots at the walls of the buildings that are used as nest boxes by Lesser Kestrel (GPS: 37.779533, -8.026359).
Back on the tarmac road, only 250m further on, a track heads off to the right. It ends at a gate, but the first part is excellent for steppe birds and raptors. Return to the tarmac road and continue. The whole of this 10

km road (which ends at the N2) is worth exploring. The second option is to head into Entradas and turn right just past a small chapel onto the main street and then immediately left onto a minor road which passes a water tower and, after about 10 km, reaches São Marcos da Ataboeiera. The first stretch is steppe bird country again. The scarce and declining Rufous Bush Chat has bred along the river here (GPS: 37.766010, -8.009700).

Routes in the Algarve

Splendid, sandstone cliffs, beautiful beaches, a sun that never seems to cease shining, mild winters and more golf courses than you can dream of (even in your worst nightmare): coastal Algarve has all the trimmings of a traditional A-star tourist destination. Add to this the relatively cheap flights and hotels or apartments, then it is no wonder that it is the most popular destination in southern Portugal. Less well known is what a great area this is for naturalists. Granted, you'll have to be able to stomach some ugly overdevelopment but if you look past that, you'll find bird-packed marshlands, both freshwater and saline, and some very fine areas with dunes, plus, of course, the beautiful and famous Algarve cliffs. An attractive aspect of the southern coast of the Algarve, is that it takes just a short drive inland to escape the hustle-and-bustle of coast and discover peaceful, orchid-rich hillsides, woodlands, carob groves and cliffs.

The following routes explore all the major estuaries and salt marshes of the southern Algarve: Castro Marim (route 13), Ria Formosa (route 14 and 15), the Arade (route 19) and Alvor estuaries (route 20). The few, but excellent, freshwater sites feature on route 15 and sites A and B on pages 195-196. For the famous coastal cliffs, look at sites D and F on pages 197-198 and for dunes, routes 14 and 15.

Heading into the interior, routes 16 and 17 offer short but fine walks in the botanically rich limestone hills. Routes 12 and 18 explore some of the most attractive rivers of the southern Algarve, with route 18 also bringing you to the highest peaks of the region, near Monchique.

The famous cliffs of the 'Golden Coast' of the Algarve. In the evening sun, the sandstone is of an unforgettable colour.

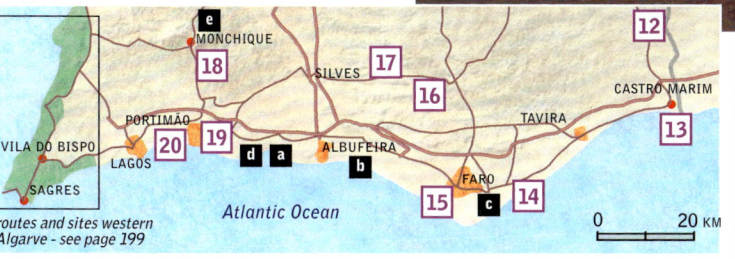

routes and sites western Algarve - see page 199

Overview of the southern Algarve. The letters refer to the sites on page 195-198.

Route 12: The Guadiana river near Alcoutim

Best season
March-July

36 KM, ONE WAY
EASY

Fascinating landscape on the border with Spain.

Habitats: broad river valley, riverine woodland, flowery fields
Selected species: Barbary Nut, Champagne Orchid, Andalusian Birthwort, Rufous Bush Chat, Kingfisher, Melodious Warbler, White-rumped Swift, Rock Bunting, Mediterranean House Gecko, Spanish Terrapin, Violet Dropwing, Keeled Skimmer, Northern Banded Groundling

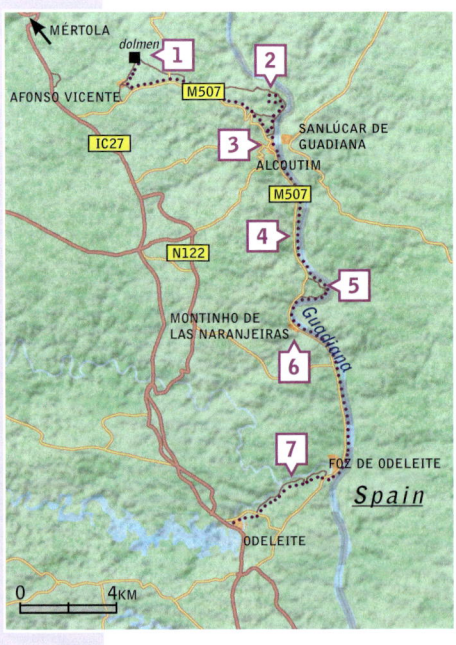

From the village of Alcoutim southwards, the Guadiana is much deeper and wider than further north, near Mértola. Sailing boats travel between the riverside villages, which are an attraction of their own. As the river has been the border between Spain and Portugal for centuries, castles and fortifications are frequent along its banks. The river is also fringed by a lush forest of Poplar, Ash and Willow, providing a sharp contrast with the surrounding dry hills clothed in holm oaks, scrub and olive groves.

This route explores this section of the Guadiana, including its tributaries. The main attraction is the landscape (which is quite different from the rest of southern Portugal) and the birdlife that goes with it (including several species that are rather rare in Portugal). There is also a good sideshow of reptiles and amphibians, butterflies and dragonflies.

Starting point Afonso Vicente (GPS: 37.492694, -7.540567)

Getting there The village of Afonso Vicente, between the main IC27 road and the village of Alcoutim on the bank of the Guadiana. The *Menires de Lavajo* here are signposted from afar (GPS: 37.50143, -7.53373).

1 The first short walk starts in the village of Afonso and is a 1.3 km linear walk to the menhirs of Lavajo. The standing stones are between 3500 and 2800 years old. Although of great historical interest, from a naturalist's point of view it is the walk to the stones that is of most interest. The vegetation here (and on the rest of the route) is typical for the schist soils of the Alentejo – Gum and Narrow-leaved Cistus, French Lavender, Mediterranean Mezereon and here or there the odd Brown Bluebell, Barbary Nut or Gladiole. The flat schist stones are excellent to turn in search for amphibians (in the dry streambed) and reptiles on the hillsides. We found Mediterranean House Gecko here, but anything may turn up. The region is known for the presence of Iberian Painted Frog and Iberian Midwife Toad, and perhaps they occur here too.

Follow the M507 east to Alcoutim, which is the least densely populated municipality in Portugal. As you enter the village, turn left following the sign *Posauda Juventude* (Youth Hostel) to explore the riverside to the north on a clearly signposted loop to the ruins of an old castle. (GPS: 37.480989, -7.472431)

The ruins of the old Alcoutim castle.

2 There is a castle in the centre of Alcoutim as well as the older Castle just north of the village. This last one was built during the Reconquista on an older fortress and was used to guard the border until the 17th Century. The place lost its importance, and today little remains of this medieval castle. It is worth visiting the old ruins that have great views over the surroundings. In late spring, look around the castle and the lands along the river for Rufous Bush-chat, Melodious Warbler, Crag Martin and Kingfisher. Golden Oriole, Eagle Owl and Rock Sparrow also occur. Spring visitors will enjoy the fort's wildflowers – again the typical scrubland species occur, with addition of Purple Jerusalem-sage and Andalusian Birthwort, the latter being the host plant of Spanish Festoon which is plentiful in spring.

Brown Bluebell (top) and Champagne Orchid (bottom) are two spring wildflowers you can find in the Guadiana river basin.

3 Alcoutim is a lovely village that warrants a stop for its own sake. It was once an important port and border town, as is demonstrated by the centuries old castle in the middle of the village.

From the *Praia Fluvial* (river beach) you can walk along the San Marcos river, a wonderful small tributary to the great Guadiana. Keeled Skimmers and Violet Dropwings are noteworthy among the dragonflies, but Western Clubtail and Northern Banded Groundling are listed for the area too. Look for Spanish Terrapins and Viperine Snakes, while the birds are represented with Iberian Green Woodpecker, Kingfisher, Golden Oriole and Grey Wagtail.

Continue south along the M507.

4 Park at the second bridge (GPS: 37.440032, -7.462006), about 4 km south of the roundabout on the south side of Alcoutim) and follow the track down to the river to explore. The scenery here is verdant with olive groves and Mediterranean woodland. All the typical scrubland birds of south Portugal are possible here, but most attractive are the Bee-eaters and the Red-rumped Swallows that nest under the bridge. Occasionally, White-rumped Swift breeds here as well.

5 After 6.4 km after leaving Alcoutim, in the curve to the right, park at the viewpoint on the left that overlooks the Guadiana (GPS: 37.422554, -7.454662). From here you can walk a 4 km loop that leads down to the Guadiana. There are Champagne Orchids here in spring (in the trackside close to the floodplain) and all the aforementioned birds. The fields and (lovely) olive groves may host Rufous Bush-chat and Melodious Warblers.

6 Just a little further you arrive at Montinho das Laranjeiras, where there are ruins of an old Roman villa on the left side of the road. Just beyond the ruins, on the other side of a bridge (again with Red-rumped Swallow), you can follow the dry streambed uphill. The first part runs through small orchards and alllotments and has an attractive birdlife, with similar birds as in the previous sites.

Continue on the M507.

7 Just past Foz de Odeleite village, park beyond the large bridge (about 7 km south of Montinho das Laranjeiras) and follow the track on your right (GPS: 37.352417, -7.453600). It follows a broad floodplain along the large Odeleite river. In spring, there are masses of the small, pale-blue iris Barbary Nut. Rock Bunting, Thekla's Lark, Nightingale and Golden Oriole breed here and you have another chance on seeing the aforementioned birds.

You can walk (or drive) the track as far as Odeleite village (6 km), from which you can complete the loop.

The spectacularly coloured Violet Dropwing flies along the banks of the Guadiana.

The picturesque Guadiana near Alcoutim. Opposite the river lies Spain, with the village of Sanlúcar de Guadiana.

PRACTICAL PART

Route 13: Castro Marim salt marshes

Best season
Autumn to spring
Of interest
Year-round

HALF A DAY, 18 KM
EASY

Salt marshes, creeks and high tide roosts.

Habitats: pastures, salt marsh, salt pans, creeks
Selected species: Greater Flamingo, Avocet, Dunlin, Greenshank, Grey Plover, Kentish Plover, Audouin's Gull, Slender-billed Gull, Little Tern, Caspian Tern, Lesser Short-toed Lark, Spectacled Warbler, Chameleon

The *Reserva Natural do Sapal do Castro Marim e de Vila Real de Santo António*, situated on the Spanish border is, thankfully, usually just called Castro Marim. It is a flat area at the mouth of the Guadiana river and consists of saltmarshes, mudflats, creeks, canals, pastures and saltpans, many of which are still in use. Castro Marim is hugely important for birds, above all waders, that use this site as a stop-over. The numbers of waders peak in April and again between July to November. The site is at its best at high tide, as birds use the reserve as a high tide roost. The core area of 149 ha is protected both as Natura2000 sites and as the Castro Marim Important Bird Area (IBA), but the attractive area is much larger. The reserve is surrounded by pastures and Umrella Pines.

Castro Marim is best visited in autumn (best period for gulls and terns and great for waders), in winter (waders, Stone Curlews and Little Bustards) and spring.

This route describes the few roads and trails that offer access to this site. Note that the surrounding coast is pretty built-up with large, busy and chaotic tourist resorts. Hence, we advise you to stick to the described route.

The saltpans of Castro Marim are full of waders.

Starting point The village of Monte Francisco

Getting there Monte Francsico is 200 m north of the A22 motorway. Take the track off the N122 opposite the entrance to the village signposted *reserva natural* (right when coming from the motorway). After 550 m you pass underneath the motorway and this is where you start birding (GPS: 37.234333, -7.441313).

1 The first of the salt pans are very close to the track and here, by using your car as a hide, you can get the closest views and, if you have a camera, the best photographs of Dunlin, Little Stint, Curlew Sandpiper, Black-winged Stilt, Kentish and Ringed Plover and more.

Continue to the visitors' centre of the Natural Park.

2 The centre offers, in addition to information and coffee, good views from the windows at the back over the Guadiana, the bridge to Spain, creeks and saltpans. Depending on the tide and the time of the year you see waders such as Greenshank and Spotted Redshank, Common and Green Sandpiper, plus Grey Herons and Little Egrets.

3 Look around the visitors' centre and walk up the low hill behind the car park. In spring, look for Lesser Short-toed Lark in the low saline vegetation and singing Spectacled Warbler in the tamarisk bushes, plus migrating passerines. Other birds are Iberian Grey Shrike, Woodchat

PRACTICAL PART

Castro Marim is the best place in Portugal to find the rare Audouin's Gull.

Shrike, Black-eared Wheatear, Iberian Yellow Wagtail, Sardinian Warbler, Thekla's Lark and Red-necked Nightjar. Spanish Sparrow is a winter bird here.

4 The track traverses a low hill, from which you overlook the pools and saltpans to the east. A telescope is needed here to get decent views of Audouin's (late summer/autumn) and Slender-billed Gulls, Caspian and Little Terns, Spoonbill, Greater Flamingo, Avocet, Whimbrel, Black-tailed Godwit, Ruff and other waders. On the fields behind the pools, Stone Curlew and Little Bustard are usually present but difficult to find. Thanks to your strategic position near the coast you can see flying raptors as Short-tailed and Booted Eagle, in summer Montagu´s or in winter Hen Harriers.

Go back as you came, turn left on the N122 in the direction of Castro Marim, pass under the A22 viaduct and turn right on the roundabout. Continue, going straight on the roundabouts until you come to an elongated one. Turn right there and after 600 m, go left on the roundabout at the sign *Altura* (GPS: 37.216901, -7.465392).

5 On your left are the salt marshes *Sapal do Castro Marim* and the saltpans of *Cerro do Bufo*. Stop beside the road where it is safe (and legal) to do so and scan the area. Piles of salt and resting birds are still quite far away, but you have a good overview. 80% of Castro Marim's roosting waders stay in this area during high tide.

Take the track to the left after crossing the bridge *Ponte da Esteveira* (check beneath it for Red-rumped Swallow nests).

6 On the track make several stops to scan the marshes and check the creeks.

Park near the gate of the salt production company. Note that entering the salt storage area is not permitted.

7 Walk the 4 km trail that has been set out for birdwatchers. It goes around the north of the saltpans and connects with the Castro Marim – Vila Real de Sant Antonio road. Enjoy this rare opportunity to enter deep into an area of salt marshes and saltpans. The path brings you closer to the Spoonbills, Greater Flamingos and the waders. It is possible to see Collared Pratincole, Slender-billed Gull and Audouin's Gull (a small colony of which now breeds in the area). Spectacled Warbler can be present in spring and Black-necked Grebe might been seen in winter.

8 Back at the car, note that the track that brought you here, turns into a footpath that can be walked for 1 km. Similar birds as at the previous points can be seen here.

Additional remarks
You can explore more saltmarshes and saltpans east of Castro Marim and North of Vila real. If you try it please be very careful as the road is very busy and dangerous and there are no lay-bys. The pinewoods of nearby Monte Gordo host the largest population of Chameleons in Portugal. These are best found in late summer.

The Mediterranean Chameleon has been introduced to the Iberian Peninsula by the Moors. There are only a few populations in Portugal, here in Monte Gordo and another one in the pinewoods of Quinta de Marim (route 14).

Route 14: Ria Formosa East

Best season
Autumn to spring

5 HOURS, 28 KM
EASY

Excellent birdwatching with a reptile and wildflower sideshow.
Versatile route that includes walks, birdwatching and a boat trip to one of the islands of the Ria Formosa.

Habitats: salt marsh, saltpans, dunes, pinewood
Selected species: Limoniastrum, Yellow Cistanche, Mirror Orchid, Sea Holly, Sea Daffodil, Azure-winged Magpie, Audouin's Gull, waders, Spoonbill, Spectacled Warbler, Greater Flamingo, Spanish Terrapin, Chameleon, Spiny-footed Lizard, Large Psammodromus, African Grass Blue

This route explores the part of the Ria Formosa east of Faro and consists of three equal parts – a walk through the Parque Natural da Ria Formosa (a 3km, easy stroll), which should be the start of any visit to the area. The second part is a visit to some salt marshes and, last but not least, a boat trip and walk to one of the sandy islands that shelters the Ria Formosa bay from the ocean. This route is first and foremost a birdwatching route, but there are several botanical delights, reptiles and a great landscape in general to see.

Lagoon at the Quinta do Marim reserve, with the hide in the background.

Starting point Quinta de Marim visitors' centre (GPS: 37.0328, -7.8218).

Getting there From Olhão, follow the main N125 east. Just out of town turn right following the signs Ria Formosa natural park and *Campisimo* (camper site). After 650m you cross the railway and 350m further, the Quinta de Marim visitors' centre and headquarters of the Parque Natural da Ria Formosa are on your left. The site is open between 8:00 and 19:00 and the entrance fee is € 2.60 (2017).

The Quinta de Marim reserve is the Ria Formosa in miniature – all habitats handed to you on a plate on a relatively small, fenced reserve. Potter around at your leisure along the paths and explore all the sites (see inset map).

1 The pine woodlands are nice and shady. Look for Azure-winged Magpies, Serins, Sardinian Warblers and migrating songbirds in spring and autumn. In early spring, especially after wet winters, there are many orchids in the grassy sides of the tracks – Mirror, Bee, Bumblebee and Sombre Bee are among the species that can be found here. Lizards are common too, in particular Large Psammodromus, but Spiny-footed Lizard, Moorish and Mediterranean House Gecko are present and even a small number of Chameleons hide in the bushes. Apart from the common Spanish Festoon, look out for rare southern butterflies like African Grass Blue and Monarch.

2 A small quarry next to the Roman salt pans is home to a very large number of Spanish terrapins which are basking on the edge of the quarry. Little Grebe, Shoveler, Gadwall and other ducks are present, especially in winter and spring. Kingfisher and Purple Gallinule are sometimes seen. This is one of the few freshwater sites in the Algarve.

3 Depending on the state of the tide and the season, saltmarshes are home to a fluctuating range and number of waders. Ringed Plover, Sanderling, Dunlin, Little Stint, Whimbrel, Grey Plover, Common Sandpiper, Redshank and Greenshank are amongst 'the usual suspects'. Close by, on the low scrub, there are many Sardinian Warblers and sometimes Spectacled Warblers as well. Limoniastrum (a bush with small pink flowers, related to the sea-lavenders; p. 28) and the Stout Yellow Cistanche are common plants. Look out too for Fiddler Crabs. Don't forget to climb the bank to look into the Ria, where gulls, terns and a different set of waders may be found (e.g. Curlew and Bar-tailed Godwit). Have a look at the tidal mills too, both for the elegant system of the mills themselves and for the wonderful viewing platform on top of the building.

Spanish Terrapins are easily seen from the hide that overlooks the old quarry in the Quinta do Marim reserve (point 2).

4 The small area of sand dunes is worth a quick look, but better examples are to be found outside the reserve, at the final stop on this route.

Back in the car, return to the N125 and continue eastwards (Tavira). Ignore the first turn to Fuseta, but take the second (6.5km). Just after crossing the railroad, turn left and on your right, there are several tracks into a complex of salt pans (GPS: 37.063100, -7.752784).

5 The saltpans hold good numbers of waders. In contrast to the previous site, these saltpans frequently hold Avocet, Black-winged Stilt and Kentish Plover in addition to the typical mix of stints and sandpipers.

Continue along the N125 and turn right to Santa Luzia.

6 Just across the railroad tracks, have a brief stop to admire the remnant groves of olives and Carob Trees. There are some old specimens here.

7 Further on towards Santa Luzia you follow the edge of the Ria Formosa salt flats for several kilometres. Black-winged Stilts, Flamingos and Little Egrets are usually present, but of course, other species may turn up.

8 In Santa Luzia, follow the boulevard along the Ria Formosa until you find the signs to Tavira. Follow these through the village. A few hundred metres outside town (you are following the M515 now), take the first track that turns right and cuts deep into another complex of salt pans, which is again attractive to waders (GPS: 37.106834, -7.654428).

Along the way you pass a beautiful old Carob grove – one of the few that are still in use.

Return to the M515 and turn right to Tavira. In town, turn right on a signpost to *Ilha de Tavira*. Follow the road to the quay (*Cais das Quatro Aguas*; GPS: 37.116648, -7.629362), where a pedestrian ferry takes you to the island.

9 Take the ferry (€ 2.50 return price in 2023) to visit the island. There, take a stroll through the dunes and over the beach. Keep an eye out for Audouin's Gull, once an extreme rarity in Portugal. A small colony has es-tablished itself in the area and there are post-breeding flocks of several hundred strong now with a handful staying to winter. Scan the ocean for Gannet and other sea-birds. The dunes have a number of interesting wildflowers, like Sea Holly and Sea Daffodil, Three-lobed Stock* (*Malcolmia triloba*) Nice Catchfly (*Silene nicaeensis*), The Stitchwort-leaved Allseeds* (*Polycarpon alsinifolium*) and Milkwort-leaved Toadflax* (*Linaria polygalifolia*).

Two of many attractive dune flowers of Ilha de Tavira: Milkwort-leaved Toadflax* (*Linaria polygalifolia*; top) and Three-lobed Stock* (*Malcolmia triloba*; bottom)

176

Best season
Autumn to spring

Route 15: Ria Formosa West

**5 HOURS, 18 KM
EASY**

*Two walks with a superb birdlife of both salt and fresh water habitat.
An attractive accompanying flora.*

Habitats: saltmarsh, saltpans, freshwater marsh, umbrella pine woods, dunes
Selected species: Cistanche, Bumblebee Orchid, Three-leaved Snowflake, Sea
Daffodil, Sea Holly, Sea Bindweed, Azure-winged Magpie, Booted Eagle, Osprey,
Purple Heron, Purple Gallinule, Red-crested Pochard, Black-headed Weaver,
Waxbill, Caspian Tern, Bar-tailed Godwit, Greater Flamingo

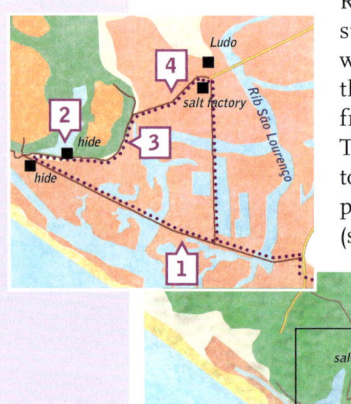

Right next to Faro airport lies one of the finest
stretches of wetland of southern Portugal. This
western part of the Ria Formosa has, compared to
the eastern part of the previous route, a larger area of
freshwater marshes.

This route connects several sites, most of which are
to be explored on foot. Take your time for. If bird
photography is what you're here for, plan several
(short) visits to this part of the Ria Formosa as a lagoon

Don't forget to check the margins of the embankments. In places, such as point 5, there are drifts of Bumblebee Orchids (top). A bit further down in the salt marsh, the parasitic Yellow Cistanche is a con-spicuous sight (bottom).

here is great for photography (Purple Gallinule, for example, often poses at close range).

This route has been well known and used by the public for at least 25 years. All facilities along the route are freely accessible, despite what some handwritten no entry signs of unknown provenance state.

Starting point Faro airport.

At the large roundabout at the airport take the exit signposted *Praia de Faro* and turn left at the second roundabout (signposted *estaciomento da praia de Faro*) and park (GPS: 37.014611, -7.986028)

Walk back some 400 metres and turn left at the large sign Ludo.

1 From the causeway you overlook the Ria Formosa on both sides. Depending on the time of year, there should be lots of waders, sometimes flamingos and possibly Caspian Tern and Mediterranean Gull. The embankment itself is also worth exploring. On the Ria-side (the left), there is Limoniastrum (p. 28) and, at the bottom, the iridescently yellow, parasitic Yellow Cistanche (p. 22). On the northern side, there are orchids growing on the patches that haven't been overgrown by Cape Sorrel. There

The freshwater lagoon on this route is probably the best place to see Purple Gallinules in Portugal (top).

are some large patches of Bumblebee Orchids in early spring, plus a few Spotted Green-winged* (*Anacamptis picta*), Yellow Bee and Mirror Orchids.

Ignore the first turn right (this will be your way back) but take a sharp right after 2.5 kms near the first bird hide.

2 The small freshwater lake on your left is a highlight of the route. Little and Great Crested Grebes, Shoveler, Pochard, Red-crested Pochard, Teal and sometimes Ferruginous Duck are seen here, but the great attraction is the large number of Purple Gallinules, which show themselves very well. Kingfisher and (in spring) Purple Heron and Little Bittern are usually about and a small population of Black-headed Weavers add an exotic tone. Many sun bathing Spanish Terrapins can be seen and the exotic Red-eared Slider is also present. From May onwards, look for the rare, essentially African dragonfly Black Percher (p. 102). There is an excellent two-storied hide – the top for the best overview and the bottom best for photography.

3 On the far side, you pass through a strip of pinewood. Azure-winged Magpies and Waxbills are frequently seen. Note the Gum Cistus and, in spring, the rich flora with Three-leaved Snowflake, Brown Bluebell and Andalusian Birthwort* (*Aristolochia baetica*; p. 70). This is one of the areas where we've encountered Monarchs, although this wonderful butterfly may turn up in many places in the coastal Algarve.

Go right (GPS: 37.027972, -8.004861) and follow the track through the salt pans. At the next junction (near some large salt pans) turn right to return to the causeway, where you go left to retun to the starting point.

4 In the saltpans, look for more waders (e.g. Kentish Plover and Black-winged Stilt), plus Spoonbills and Little Egrets.

Either take the car or walk on towards Praia de Faro the beach, turn left and continue all the way to the end of the road. Continue on foot on a boardwalk (GPS: 36.998445, -7.980183).

5 The boardwalk that leads to the seaside that is great for the dune flora. There is Sea Spurge, Sea Daffodil, Sea Holly, Cottonweed and Sea Bindweed, but also scarcer plants like Portuguese Crowberry and the Milkwort-leaved Toadflax* (*Linaria polygalifolia*).

Another boardwalk (much longer) follows the Ría-side and is best for birds. Depending on the water level, waders can come close to the shore (e.g. Whimbrel, Sanderling, Dunlin, Curlew Sandpiper, Kentish Plover, Bar-tailed Godwit, Grey Plover). Further into the Ría, there are Greater Flamingos, while terns and gulls patrol the length of the waterway. The light here is best in the evening and a telescope is handy. The landscape is something special too – a superb and wild maze of saltmarsh with the high-rise buildings of Faro in the background and planes landing in front of you at regular interval.

Bar-tailed Godwits and Grey Plover on the Praia de Faro (top).
Praia de Faro, with the Atlantic on the right and the lagoons of the Ria on the left (bottom).

PRACTICAL PART

Route 16: Fonte de Benémola

Best season
Late February-
early June

**4 HOURS, 5 KM
EASY**

Pretty river valley with a splendid flora, including lots of orchids.

Habitats: woodland, scrubland, river
Selected species: Naked-man, Man, Mirror, Sombre Bee, Lusitanian Mirror
Orchids, Portuguese Squill, Marsh Marigold, Golden Oriole, Crag Martin,
Melodious Warbler, Two-tailed Pasha, Black-eyed Blue, Western Spectre

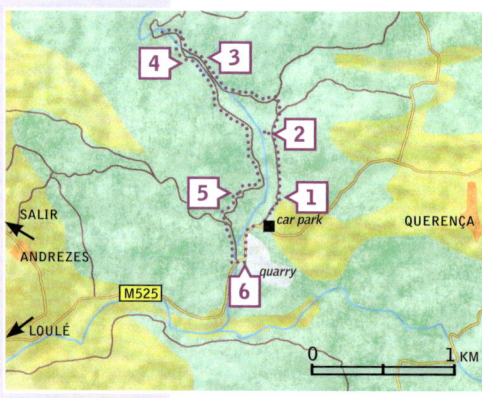

The springs (*fontes*) collectively called *Fonte de Benémola*, are the main source of the Ribeira de Algibre. At the height of summer, as the river dries out further downstream, this section still flows with water, making it a veritable oasis in the dry Algarve hinterland.

This is above all a very scenic site, with its terraced fields and orchards, and can be explored in an easy, 4.5 km loop. The spring flora is superb, in particular for orchid lovers, while in late spring and early summer, this is a great site for dragonflies.

Starting point Benémola car park on the M524 (GPS: 37.19856, -8.00440).

Getting there From Loulé, follow the M525, direction *Salir*. After 5.8 km, just beyond the bridge over the Algibre river, turn right to Fonte de Benémola. The car park is another 2.6 kms further on your left.

1 The route starts splendidly. On your right, you'll find the first Mirror and Man Orchids. Further on, there are plenty of Sombre Bee, Man and Naked-man orchids, growing in open patches on either side of the track. In total, 14 species have been noted here, including the rare Lusitanian Mirror Orchid which is almost restricted to southern Portugal. Also note the large Carob trees – relics of old cultivation – and Strawberry Trees.

From spring into autumn, this is a good route to see Two-tailed Pasha (p. 99).

2 Just before another parking area, there is a small trail that goes down to the river. There are some terraced fields here full of Mirror and Naked-man Orchids.

3 The section close to the river has a splendid scenery. This is where the majority of the springs are. The tall Narrow-leaved Ash trees and Mediterranean Willow bushes are alive with the songs of Cetti's and Melodious Warbler, Golden Oriole and Nightingale. Marsh Marigold is a 'northern' plant that finds refuge here in the permanently wet terrain. At the picnic spot, you reach the final spring and in late spring you can enter the riverbed and follow it upstream.

4 On the other side of the stream, the slopes are more shaded. This is another good stretch for orchid hunting. A couple of the robust Portuguese Squills are also present.

Although the springs of Benémola (bottom) are the goal of this walk, the orchids that grow all along the route are the true highlight. This is one of the spots where the rare Lusitanian Mirror Orchid grows (top) – a species endemic to southern Portugal and adjacent Andalucía.

5 A sudden change in flora heralds the change to another, much more acidic, schist-like soil. Gum Cistus and Tree Heath are the dominant plants, but there are Spotted Green-winged Orchids* (*Anacamptis picta*) too, as well as Poplar-leaved Cistus.

6 The bridge at the road and the basins at the abandoned mill offer a great finale. The emergent vegetation in the river (which flows slowly here) offers a different dragonfly habitat with Western Clubtail, Small Pincertail, Orange-spotted Emerald and Western Spectre.

Turn left and follow the road to the starting point.

Route 17: Rocha da Pena

Best season
Mid February-May

**3-4 HOURS, 6 KM
MODERATE**

A fine walk along cliffs and hills with a rich flora and butterfly fauna.

Habitats: oak woods, scrubland, cliffs, riverine forest
Selected species: Southern Early Purple Orchid, Mirror Orchid, Bee Orchid, Narcissus calcicola, Bellevalia, Portuguese Squill, Western Peony, Wild Boar, Blue Rock Thrush, Rock Bunting, Woodlark, Cirl Bunting, Jay, Ocellated Lizard, Iberian Scarce Swallowtail, Marsh Fritillary, Panoptes Blue

The Rocha da Pena is a small (roughly 2 x 1 km) limestone plateau, which rises above the surrounding hills like a table mountain. It is the goal of a splendid, 6 km circular walk. You cross a lovely landscape with scrubland, old carob tree groves, cliffs and beautiful views from the plateaux.

Rocha da Pena is famous for its flora, but it also has an interesting birdlife, plenty of reptiles and butterflies.

Starting point The da Grutas café in the village of Pena (GPS: 37.250315, -8.098176).
Getting there From Benafim, follow the N124 east and turn left on the sign *Rocha da Pena*. Follow these signs to the hamlet of Rocha da Pena where the car park and bar are situated. There is only one signposted, circular walk – follow it.

1 Check the flowery grasslands, in particular the sunny and wind-free corners, for butterflies, which include Panoptes Blue, Iberian Scarce Swallowtail, Marsh Fritillary, Black-eyed Blue and Spanish Festoon.
About half way up you have a splendid view on the cliffs. Look and listen for Blue Rock Thrush and Rock Bunting, while Cirl Bunting, Woodlark

On the way to Rocha da Pena (top), where Portuguese Squill (centre) grows and Spanish Scarce Swallowtail flies (bottom).

and Jay are calling from the Carob Trees. Keep an eye out here and for the remainder of the trip for raptors. Though rare in the Algarve, Short-toed and Bonelli's Eagle are sometimes seen at Rocha da Pena. The first attractive wildflowers should be present here as well. Look for Bellevalia (a grape-hyacinth that is endemic to southern Portugal; p. 68), Green-winged Orchid and Western Peony.

2 At the plateaux, follow the side-trail to the viewpoint *Norte*. There are masses of Southern Early Purple Orchids* (*Orchis olbiensis*) here. The rutted soil betrays the presence of a significant population of Wild Boar.

3 Return to the loop and continue. Early spring visitors (February) will be able to see the rare daffodil *Narcissus calcicola* near the clifftops. Mirror, Bee, Yellow Bee and Bumblebee orchids are growing here and there along the trail.

The trail descends to the village of Penina where you follow the road back to Rocha da Pena (signposted). Portuguese Squill grows in the roadside here.

Route 18: Odelouca valley and Serra de Monchique

Best season
Year-round

Prepare rain-coat
and jersey for lower
temperatures and
possible rain.

**FULL DAY, 78 KM
ONE WAY**

*The highest top of the Algarve.
Splendid views, beautiful river valley and old cork oak forests.
Unique flora and rich birdlife.*

Habitats: Cork Oak, mixed forest, Mediterranean scrub, agricultural fields
Selected species: Rock Bunting, Bee-eater, Iberian Chiffchaff, Spanish Terrapin, Schreiber's Green Lizard, Monarch, Two-tailed Pasha, Orange Featherleg

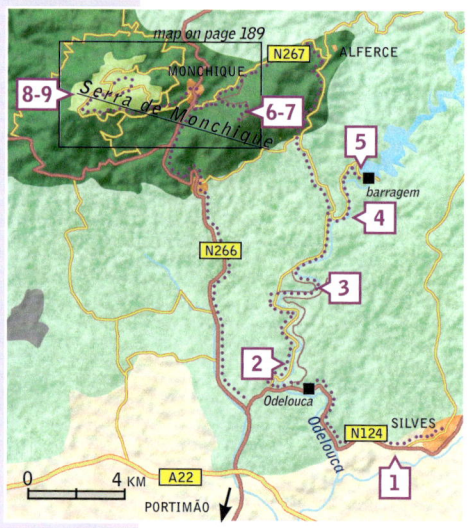

The Serra de Monchique, an isolated mountain range, includes the highest point of the Algarve – the *Fóia* (902 m). Just east of Fóia lies the second-highest peak, the *Picota* (773 m), and the village of Monchique is located in the pass between the two.

Due to its geology and its relatively wet climate (twice the annual rainfall of the coast) it is a very special place, where an ecosystem of dense cork oak woods thrives with many special plant species. Sadly, the Serra de Monchique has been largely destroyed by the pulp and paper industry – many of its slopes are subject to what can only be described as brutal rape: the natural vegetation completely razed and replanted with Eucalyptus, which is in turn harvested by clearcut.

A visit to the Serra de Monchique is therefore a bittersweet experience: on the one hand, there are lovely sections where much of the remaining attractions of the range can be seen, on the other hand, one cannot escape the depressing result of the commercial despoliation of the area. This route takes you to some of the best places, avoiding the Eucalyptus stands as far as possible. It is a car route that follows the lovely Odelouca valley, enabling you to see the changes in landscape from coast to mountain top.

Starting point Silves which has, besides the distinction of being the old Moorish capital of the Algarve and a pretty town, a large population of White Storks and a reedy riverside which should be checked for terrapins and dragonflies.

Leave town on the N124, direction Monchique.

1 This first stretch of road is interesting as it is in the area where Monarch butterflies are seen most often. The numbers gradually build up during spring, increasing your chances on this butterfly as

the season progresses. The Monarch is a recent colonist from America via the Atlantic islands. Unlike the American populations, the European Monarch do not migrate. A little further on, there are several spots where you can pull over to the left to overlook the Odelouca river and its banks. Even though you are well inland, the tidal influence is still very visible here, with saltmarsh vegetation on the river's edge.

The Odelouca river

Just after crossing the Odelouca river, turn right to Laranjeiro and Alferce.

2 This is a wonderful and quiet road that follows the Odelouca river up to its source in the Serra de Monchique. The strategy for a visit in Odelouca valley is making roadside stops and getting down to the river. Especially in spring, the valley is an ornithological delight where you can spend several pleasurable hours in search of Hoopoe, Bee-eater, Black-eared Wheatear, Azure-winged Magpie, Turtle Dove, Woodchat Shrike, Iberian Green Woodpecker, Iberian Chiffchaff, Cetti's and Melodious Warbler, Zitting Cisticola, Serin, Cirl and Rock Buntings and Common Waxbill. Little, Scops and Tawny Owl and Red-necked Nightjar also breed but you have to go out for them at nightfall.

PRACTICAL PART

Old Cork Oak on the track up to the Picota. Note the original creviced bark in the top, the dark bark in the area that was debarked several years ago and the fresh, light bark where the cork was recently peeled.

Five km from the junction with the N124, you arrive at a junction where you turn right to Alferce and Barragem de Odelouca. Proceed 650 metres and turn right onto an unsignposted track that follows the river (GPS: 37.245081, -8.513651).

3 This quiet track offers great views over the river. Look and listen here for the aforementioned birds. A few hundred metres along this track, near an orange grove, you can walk to the river and explore. Look here for Little and Cattle Egret, Common Sandpiper, Grey Wagtail and Bee-eater. Spanish Terrapin can be found in the river and it is a good spot to search for amphibians or just for taking in the landscape.

The track reaches the road again. Turn right. After 3.5 km, a road branches off to the right, signposted *Barragem de Odelouca*. Follow it.

4 After 1.8km, at the bridge, you have more opportunities to explore the riverside (GPS: 37.283618, -8.486155).

Continue along the road.

5 The dam and reservoir (*barragem*) is only a couple of kilometres from the previous spot. There is a car park and small picnic site on the edge of the lake. The deep reservoir with surrounding, Eucalyptus-clad hills is a forlorn place. Both the lake and the Eucalyptus forest are alien habitats where very little of the native flora and fauna is able to survive. The clearly newly constructed but otherwise deserted site in an ecologically dead surrounding gives an otherworldly feeling. The omega to the alpha of the riverside delights described earlier.

Return to the junction before point 4 and turn right. The landscape gives way to Eucalyptus plantations.
Continue to Alferce but as you enter the village, turn sharply left down to the N267 towards San Marcos da Serra and Monchique. This road leads through

a beautiful cork oak forest. Continue until you're almost in Monchique. Just beyond the right turn to Brejo (which is part of Monchique), there is a restaurant on your left. Turn left here onto a road signposted to Picota, the second highest peak of the Serra de Monchique. Take this pretty road through shady cork oak woods. Take a right at the next junction and continue to the top of the mountain (note that the road first drops down again before bending to the left and up to the peak. When in doubt, check your maps app; GPS: 37.308226, -8.530739).

6 Picota is with 774 m the second highest point of both the Serra de Monchique and the Algarve. The north slope you are following is still covered in the cork oak woods that once cloaked the whole of the Monchique range. Due to the altitude and the proximity to the ocean, this modest range catches far more rain and fog than the nearby lowlands, allowing for a special micro-climate that is not as harsh as that of the lowlands. Various plants and animals of more northern origin occur here and nowhere else in the Algarve – ranging from mundane species like Nuthatch to rare specialties like the carnivorous Portuguese Sundew (p. 67) and Schreiber's Green Lizard.

Rock Buntings are common on Foía mountain.

7 On the summit you will find a small path upward to the fire tower, built only a 100 m from the car park in a stony area above the timberline. This point gives excellent overall views of the surroundings including Monchique village. It is also a good watch point for raptors (Short-toed Eagle, Buzzard and Kestrel). In the scrub and woodland, Crested Tit, Subalpine and Bonelli´s Warbler, Great Spotted and Iberian Green Woodpecker all breed. There are some attractive wildflowers as well, such as (in spring) Sand-crocus (p. 202), Yellow Rockrose (p. 129), Spotted Green-winged Orchid* (*Anacamptis picta*), One-leaved Squill, Heather, the Iberian endemic buttercup *Ranunculus bupleuroides*, Mediterranean Quillwort* (*Isoetes histrix*) and the dwarf bushes of the Algerian Oak, to name but a few.

Foía, the balcony of the Algarve. From the mountain you can see the whole western part of the Algarve, all the way to the ocean.

It is also a good spot to watch butterflies. You can see an interesting phenomenon here: hill-topping butterflies. Many butterflies in search for a mate, fly uphill to congregate at the top. In late spring and summer, the hill-topping behaviour can be obvious. Two-tailed Pasha and both Scarce and Common Swallowtails are among the butterflies that can be seen.

Return to the main road and turn left to Monchique, the village that has given its name to these hills. Head into the village and loop through it following the signs to Fóia.

8 About 6 km along the winding road from Monchique you reach a fine viewpoint on the left. The point has a natural spring where people fill their water bottles. It has good views to the south. With favourable weather you can even see Algarve coast.

Proceed to Fóia, park your car and walk around (GPS: 37.316264, -8.593238).

9 The summit area of Fóia is something special – a large granite outcrop with boggy grasslands (unique this far south!) and a superb view over the Algarve and the ocean. At 902 metres Fóia is high enough to give you that 'mountain feeling'. The birdlife helps with that as well – Woodlark, Rock and Cirl Bunting, Dartford Warbler, Whitethroat, Linnet and Blue Rock Thrush can be seen. Although the Algarve isn't rich in raptors, Fóia is one of the best places in the region. Short-toed Eagle and Griffon Vulture are regularly seen. Alpine Accentor and Ring Ouzel have been recorded in winter. Birding during migration periods can be very entertaining as many passerines of different species rest here during daytime.
Follow the trail indicated on the map, looking for birds, Schreiber's Green Lizard, Bellevalia, One-leaved Squill, Meadow Saxifrage and lots of Green-winged Orchids.

Return to Monchique and follow the road south towards Portimão and turn left onto the N124 to return to Silves.

Route 19: The Arade estuary

HALF A DAY, 25 KM
MODERATE

Best season
Autumn-spring

A good route for shorebirds.

Habitats: mudflats, creeks, salt marshes, salt pans
Selected species: Greater Flamingo, Greenshank, Grey Plover, Caspian Tern, Gannet, Epaulet Skimmer

The rivers Arade, Monchique and Odelouca come together in the Arade estuary near the old fishing port of Portimão. With the large tidal differences in this part of the Atlantic, the sea water flows surprisingly high up the creeks and channels of the estuary, covering the extensive mud banks at high tide and exposing them to thousands of waders as it drops. The tidal movements are felt up to Silves (see previous route). The most extensive salt marshes and mud flats are just north of Portimão and at the confluence of the Odelouca and Arade rivers. Waders are one of the main attractions of the estuary.

Arade and Alvor (route 20) are often compared. Generally speaking, the latter is better for birds, but the Arade estuary is limited as less visited and is therefore more likely to offer some surprises.

Starting point Portimão

Head north on the N124, the main road through town. Just short of the junction with the N125 (by a large hospital) go right at the roundabout to Companheira. After 200 m go left under the N125, continue beyond the small urbanisation of Companheira and park at the end of the road (GPS: 37.156527, -8.523095).

1 From the end of this road you have superb views over the Arade estuary. The light conditions are best in the afternoon and best birding is at low tide. Walk up the track to the left and scan the creeks, salt marshes

Tidal marshes in the Arade river.

and mudflats. At low tide, many waders (e.g. Greenshank and Redshank, Green and Common Sandpiper, Dunlin, Ringed Plover) and Little Egret are to be seen. Further out are groups of Flamingos and gulls. During migration, hundreds of House Martins and Swallows fly over the estuary.

Return to the roundabout, turn right, pass under the N125, continue straight on over two roundabouts and go right round a third one just before the A22 to reverse direction (360°). You cross a creek and at the end of the bridge turn sharp right and park near the old bridge (out of use).

2 A track (GPS: 37.171751, -8.533277) leads a few hundred metres along this creek and into the fields. It is a small area, but at low tide water flows out of the creek and you can observe waders, Kingfisher and Little Egret at close range.

Greater Flamingos occur in large numbers in the Arade estuary.

Drive back in the direction of Portimão and follow the N125 towards Faro. When you have crossed the impressive suspension bridge, turn right (Ferragudo) and after 1 km right again to arrive in the village of Mexilhoeira da Carregação. Take the second street right towards *Club Náutico* and *salinas*.

3 A short distance along the road you reach a complex of saltpans with views on the estuary (GPS: 37.148856, -8.502256). Park along the road and look for waders, Spoonbill and Grey Heron. Whimbrel, Black-winged Stilt and Caspian Tern are often seen here.

Continue and go left at the junction.

4 You now cross over the N125 whereupon the road becomes a track, one with still more saltpans and even better views. Crested Lark breeds, Bluethroat is a winter visitor and you can expect migrating passerines such as Yellow Wagtail in autumn.

Go back to the roundabout of Mexilhoeira and turn right. Go straight at the next two roundabouts and then take the first right, towards the riverside and *Restaurante Vista Rio*. Follow these signs across the railway to the river (GPS: 37.142337, -8.517028).

5 The short pier is about the best place to see the wide mudflats and the saltpans on the other side of the river. Depending on the time of the year, hundreds of flamingos, storks, gulls, terns and waders can be present, but for the most part, the birds are quite distant and you will need a telescope to see them well.

Return to the main road and turn right. From the second roundabout, signs will bring you to Ferragudo by the M530 and further signs *campismo* and *praias* will bring you eventually to *Praia do Molhe* and the breakwater at the mouth of the Arade (GPS: 37.110135, -8.519145).

Resting Sandwich Terns with Portimão in the back.

6 Walk the breakwater that juts into the ocean and protects the Portimão harbour. On one side there is the mouth of the river, on the other side the ocean. Shag is present all year. Outside the breeding season, you may see Turnstone searching for food on the stony pier, Mediterranean Gull resting on the estuary and Sandwich Tern, Gannet and Cory´s Shearwater flying over the ocean.

Route 20: The Alvor estuary

**HALF A DAY, 20 KM
EASY**

*Another good route for watching shorebirds.
Relatively quiet area of dunes and beaches.*

Habitats: fields, estuary, salt marsh, dunes, beaches
Selected species: Flamingo, Dunlin, Greenshank, Grey Plover, Kentish Plover,
Audouin's Gull, Caspian Tern, Little Owl, Red-necked Nightjar

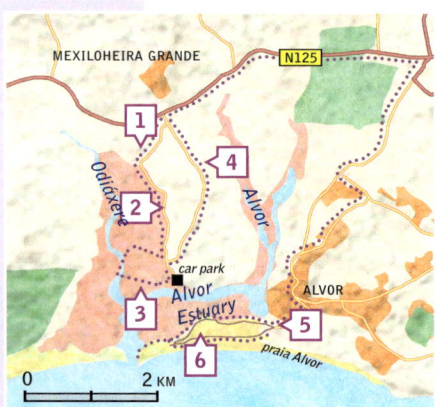

The Alvor estuary is an oasis of tranquillity on the urbanised Algarve coast. Its lagoons, dunes and salt marshes offer a great variety of wildlife, especially birds. The central lagoon of Alvor is actually the joint estuary of two rivers: Odiáxere and Alvor. The lagoon is separated from the ocean by a broad row of dunes. Two breakwaters protect the mouth of the estuary into which the salt water flows twice a day. Further into the estuary there are salt marshes and grasslands backed by low hills with orchards and fields. Both aspects offer wildlife attractions of their own.

This route consists of two parts: first a visit to the peninsula between the Odiáxere and Alvor estuaries and second a walk through the coastal dunes. It is a great route for the bird orientated, with several excellent viewpoints to look for shorebirds and, in atumn, Audouin's and Slender-billed Gulls.

Starting point Mexiloheira Grande (roundabout on the N125 south of the village; GPS: 37.153970, -8.613753).
Head south (estacioua), cross the railway and turn right onto a dirt track running parallel to the railway (*Caminho da Espargueira*).

1 You are now on the peninsula between the rivers Odiáxere and Alvor. The landscape is dominated by olive groves and fields, where Azure-winged Magpie, Hoopoe, Little Owl, Red-necked Nightjar, Black-winged

Kite and Sardinian Warbler can be found. Osprey is increasingly seen in winter.

2 This is an excellent viewpoint to scan the estuary and to search the pools in the salt marshes. Feeding Flamingo and Black-winged Stilt can be seen in the saltmarshes, together with other waders like Curlew, Whimbrel, Greenshank, Redshank, Wood Sandpiper, Dunlin, Kentish Plover, Grey Plover. During migration, the numbers and variety of waders increases and you have a chance to spot Caspian Tern and Audouin's Gull during migration.

Walk the circuit through the saltmarsh, which at leisure is a roughly one hour walk.

3 You'll find more waders on this trail (best at high tide), plus Zitting Cisticola and Bluethroat in winter. We also found several singing Lesser Short-toed Larks in early spring. In spring and early summer, this is a good dragonfly spot as well.

Return to your car, drive back and after 200 m, turn right.

4 This section crosses fields again. Look for a place to park your car and search for birds. Similar birds can be seen as at point 1.

Return to the N125, turn right and follow the signs to Alvor. Subsequently,

The Alvor estuary on a September evening, with Greater Flamingos.

Sandwich terns at the coast.

follow signs *Praias* and then *Praia Alvor* (Alvor beach). Just before reaching the beach, you come to a T-junction. Instead of parking at the beach (left), turn right to park, only a bit further ahead at the *zona ribeirinha* (GPS: 37.126698, -8.595818).

5 You in the small harbour of Alvor. This place still retains some of the atmosphere of the Algarve of decades ago, when there was little tourism and only small fishing communities dotted the coastline. During low tide you can see the clam collectors out on the bay (see text box on page 112); their spoils can be enjoyed in several small restaurants in the harbour. From the harbour you have good views over the inner estuary and its sand bars (including its birds). There are boat trips from here to the Arade estuary and Silves and the nearby ocean.

6 A boardwalk through the 200-300 m wide dunes starts next to the car park and leads you to the mouth of the estuary, the breakwater and a quiet beach. The absence of beach restaurants near the breakwaters makes this 4 km walk on these broad and calm beaches a delight.
Crested Lark breeds in the dunes and from September to March you may expect Mediteranean Gull and Sandwich Tern here. Where the route runs along beside the estuary, you again have the opportunity to enjoy the waders and watch their feeding behavior. There is lots of Sea Holly, Dune Galingale and other dune plants here in spring.

Additional remark the nearby cliffs of Portimão are part of The Golden Coast (see page 197) and deserve a visit at low tide.

Additional sites in the Algarve

A – Lagoa dos Salgados

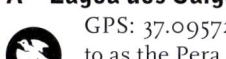 GPS: 37.095722, -8.336328. Lagoa dos Salgados (often referred to as the Pera Marshes) is a small coastal lagoon that is fantastic for birdwatching. It is situated at the confluence of two seasonal streams: *Espiche* and *Vale Rabelho*. Since 1980, the waste water treatment plant has supplemented the natural water flow and the lagoon does not dry up in summer anymore. Although the water is brackish near the beach, a thick freshwater vegetation of rushes and reeds has developed, which harbours herons and ducks that are uncommon in southern Portugal. The surroundings of the lake consist mainly of agricultural fields and orchards in the west and north, and a golf resort to the east. The site has a boardwalk and the observation points from where you can get good views on the lake and its rush and reedbeds.

Birding starts already on the car park at the north-western shore from where hundreds of ducks, herons and waders can be seen. Marsh Harrier, Purple Heron, Little Bittern, Ferruginous Duck and Purple Gallinule breed. Squacco Heron, Little Egret, Glossy Ibis and Spoonbill are regular. Numbers of Greater Flamingo peak in winter, as do those of Kingfisher, Teal, Pintail, Shoveler and Wigeon. Black-winged Stilt is resident and Avocet, Black-tailed Godwit, Ruff, Dunlin, Little Stint and Collared Pratincole are some of the waders seen frequently during migration. Zitting Cisticola, Cetti´s Warbler, Great Reed Warbler and Black-headed Weaver breed in the reeds and tamarisks. Red-necked Nightjars and Little Owls can be heard at night. Thanks to the geographical location of the lagoon, many rarities have been found here.

Lagoa dos Salgados

196

In winter, Kingfishers are often found at the coast, where they fish in brackish or even saline water.

To get to the site, take the exit 7 to Armação de Pêra from the A22. When you reach Camping *Canelas*, turn left at the next roundabout and right at the second roundabout and follow the signs *Praia Grande* that lead you to the lagoon.

B – Vilamoura wetlands

 GPS: 37.092958, -8.135756. Just southwest of Vilamoura lies a small freshwater wetland named *Parque Ambiental de Vilamoura*. This reserve is a small, natural oasis in a huge area of tourist resorts and golf courses and attracts birds thanks to its reedbeds, small-scale agricultural fields and the Carob, Fig and Almond trees. For birdwatchers, there is an observation tower near the entrance and there are two hides in the reeds. Marsh Harrier, Little Bittern, Purple Heron, Purple Gallinule, Great Reed Warbler and Black-headed Weaver and Waxbill breed in the reeds. In the fields, there are Little Owl, Hoopoe and Turtle Dove, plus, during migration, Booted Eagle, Night Heron, Black-winged Stilt, Red-rumped Swallow and various passerines may be seen.

From the A22, take exit 11 to Boliqueime, turn left on the N125 (direction Faro) and after 3.5 km, on the 2nd roundabout, turn right to Vilamoura. After passing three roundabouts, you take the first turn right, signed *Golfes*. After the bend to the right, a track goes left where you can park your car. We advise to walk the 3.5 km loop.

C – Faro city shoreline

  GPS: 37.012378, -7.935577. Though not nearly as good as the two described routes in the Ria Formosa, the shoreline in Faro city is actually not a bad place for birdwatching. Take the promenade along the city´s edge, right next to the old city centre and look for waders, Little Egrets, the occasional Flamingos, plus Osprey on migration and Peregrine in winter. It is also possible to rent a bicycle. If you do, don't forget to visit the harbour.

An evening stroll along the stacks near Portimão.

D – Walk along the Algarve cliff coast – Praia Marinha

   GPS: 37.090138, -8.412698. The ramble over the limestone cliffs at *Praia Marinha,* which are among the very few on the south Algarvian coast that are not heavily developed, makes for a wonderful coastal walk. The views are sublime, with beautiful stacks, secluded beaches, arches, caves and sinkholes all visible on the trail. There are quite a few breeding birds in inaccessible places, in particular on an off-shore islet, where Jackdaw, Rock Dove and – somewhat unexpectedly – a large colony of Cattle Egrets are found. At sea, Gannets frequently fly by. The flora is attractive too, especially for visitors in (late) winter – the orchids on this trail start to flower as early as February.

To get to Praia Marinha, follow the signs to Benagil from Lagoa and pick up the signs to Praia Marinha. From the car park you can make a 'long' (approx. 3 km) walk in eastern direction, and a short (approx. 1.5 km) walk to Benagil in the west.

E – Searching for the jewel among the butterflies

The Spanish Fritillary is a very rare butterfly that occurs in just a few mountain ranges in Spain, one small spot in the French Mediterranean and a handful locations around Monchique in Portugal. Its larval food plant is a local species of teasel, which grows along some small brooks.

198

One such site is just east of the village of Nave Redonda, north of Monchique. Follow the road to São Marcos and after 900 metres from the junction in Nave Redonda, turn left onto a track signposted *Pereiras*. Park after 100 metres and explore the soggy meadows along the stream (GPS: 37.399615, -8.473635). In April, Spanish Fritillary flies here together with Spanish Marbled White, Spanish Festoon and Swallowtail. Small-flowered Tongue Orchid, Shrubby Pimpernel and the Mediterranean form of Marsh Marigold are noteworthy flowers.

Spanish Fritillary

F – The golden Coast

If you google 'Algarve' you are inundated with images of the beautiful beaches, with sandstone cliffs and stacks bathed in the golden evening sun. This is the great trademark of the Algarve tourism (next to golf) and draws thousands of sun-seeking visitors from all over Europe. Not the kind of place for the naturalist, you may think. And still we advise you to go. The scenery is just too beautiful to miss. In the high season the trick is to visit these sites in the evening, when most tourists have gone and the light is at its best. In winter and spring (say October to early May) these places are not so busy. The *praias* can best be visited at low tide as at that time, you are able to walk around the cliffs. Some companies offer boat trips to the less accesible cliffs.

Apart from the beauty of the landscape, the praias are actually a textbook example of coastal erosion in all its forms. As the tide is rising, you can see for yourself how the ocean is carving out tunnels and caves, gradually undermining the cliffs until they collapse. Birdwatchers will find interest in the Gannets, Cormorants and Shags that pass by, while the cliffs themselves usually hold a few plants of interest too.

Ponta da Piedade, Praia Tres Irmãos, Praia Tres Castelos and Praia Marinha are the most attractive ones.

Costa Vicentina – the southwest coast

How different is the southwest coast from the 'classic' Algarve! A wild ocean, rugged cliffs, small villages and a green hinterland is what constitutes the *Costa Vicentina*. The atmosphere and the tourists are different too. Whereas the 'Golfer's Algarve' (roughly from Lagos to the Spanish border) is the realm of pensionados and sun-seekers, the Costa Vicentina is the 'hippy Algarve', where mobile homers, surf dudes and peace-seekers huddle together on beach-front car parks.

Naturalists have only recently discovered the Costa Vicentina, a natural park that stretches from Vila Nova de Milfontes in the north to Lagos in the south.

The most famous part of the area is Cabo São Vicente (route 21), whose superb cliffs and position as southwesternmost point of mainland Europe draws many tourists, but which is for natural-

Overview of the western Algarve. The letters refer to the sites on page 212-214.

ists above all famous for its outstanding cliff flora. In autumn, it draws birdwatchers too, to watch migration.

North of Cabo São Vicente, the attractive areas are nearly all to be found at the coastal dunes and cliffs, which have a spectacular landscape and outstanding flora (routes 21, 22 and sites A, D, E, F, G and H on pages 212-215). The river valleys are hotspots too, with their lovely areas of meadows and riverine woodland (routes 22 and 23). The hillsides and plateaux are less attractive, with lots of Eucalyptus and scrubby pastures, mixed with smaller areas of native pinewoods and stands of Cork Oak.

Although the Costa Vicentina is great for hikers and for those interested in wildflowers, it admittedly has less to offer to birdwatchers.

Route 21: Cabo São Vicente and the Sagres Peninsula

**4 HOURS - FULL DAY
30 KM, EASY**

*Europe's southwesternmost tip with a spectacular flora.
Exciting autumn migration.*

Habitats: coastal cliffs, dunes and beach
Selected species: Saint Vincent Cistus, Saint Vincent Bucklar-mustard,
Bellevalia, Algarve Toadflax, Portuguese Crowberry, Shrubby Violet, Red-billed
Chough, Shag, Gannet, Black Redstart, Short-toed Lark, Lorquin's Blue, raptors
and passerines on migration

Best season
Mid-February to
mid-May (flora)
September-October
(migration)
Of interest
Year-round

Cape St. Vincent (*Cabo de São Vicente*) is the southwesternmost point of
Europe. The place has a mythical ring to it due to its geographical location and its history. Called by the Romans *Promontorium Sacrum* (or
Holy Promontory) and named af-
ter a fourth century saint, Cabo São
Vicente was regarded as a holy place
thanks to the idea that it marked the
edge of the known world.

Cape St. Vincent lies on the Sagres
Peninsula, named after the village
just east from the cape. High cliffs
mark the edge of the otherwise flat
and barren peninsula. Due to the
porous limestone, low rainfall, extreme winds, the peninsula is dry and
rocky, with low bushes (*matos*) at the
coast and cereal cultivation, pastures
and fallow land. There are only a few
woodlands (all pine plantations) on
this flat land, and they are a magnet
for migrant birds. Bird migration,
both on and off-shore, forms one of
the great attractions of the Sagres
Peninsula, but to appreciate it in
full, you need to be here in autumn

Cabo São Vicente is a wildflower paradise, with, in March to early May, the dome-shaped, spiny *Staurocanthus spectabilis* (top), the Spiny Thrift (centre) and the white-flowered shrub *Prasium majus* (bottom).

(see page 91), when an estimated 4000 raptors belonging to 20 or more species pass over the Sagres peninsula.

The other magical time to visit this area is in spring (early March – mid May) when the matos along the coast are alive with wildflowers. Of all the Algarve's wildflower haunts, Cabo São Vicente is the top site and early spring is the time to experience it.

Starting point Vila do Bispo

Take the N268 to Sagres, turning left to Martinhal after 7 km.

1 Praia do Martinhal is a small beach next to a new, upmarket resort, with dunes and a small lagoon behind it. The beach retains a laid-back atmosphere. In spring, look for Kentish Plover, which sometimes breeds near the lagoon. On the islands off-shore there is a colony of Yellow-legged Gulls and Shags. During autumn migration, the sheltered bay attracts all sorts of migrating birds: not only waders, herons and egrets, but also passerines.

PRACTICAL PART

Return to the N268 and turn left to Sagres. Follow the signs *Baleeira* (later *Porto do Baleeira*) to the harbour.

2 The harbour can be good in autumn. Look for gulls and terns that take shelter in the harbour. Whale and dolphin trips start from here (see page 213).

Return to the village and proceed south to the old fortress, which is the most outstanding building.

3 Sagres fort it situated on the southernmost headland of mainland Portugal. The fort and adjacent village were long of strategic importance following the voyages of discovery initially sponsored by Henry the Navigator who used Sagres as his base. The fortifications helped to protect the coast from pirates whilst the cape offered a safe haven for ships waiting for favourable winds around Cape St. Vincent. The fort was largely destroyed in the Great Earthquake of 1755 (the one that also destroyed much of Lisbon). The current fort was rebuilt in the mid 20th century. There is an entry fee (€ 3.00).

Follow the signs *Cabo do S. Vicente* and *Forte do Beliche*. At the first option, just beyond a fence, park on the left side of the road and follow the cliff coast on foot (GPS: 37.013584, -8.952280).

Sandcrocus on the sandstone near Sagres (top).
The continuous beating of the surf has created large holes in the bedrock, where the water breaks through with force, almost like a geyser (bottom).

4 This fine walk gives you your first view of the cliffs. Spectacular sink-holes, cliffs and caves (careful!) give a good insight in how the erosion of such coasts takes place (see page 17). Off-shore, there are Shags (which breed on the cliffs), there is a chance on Gannets and other seabirds, although this is not the best location for them. Peregrine Falcon inhabit the cliffs and hunt above both the sea and land.

In spring this is a first opportunity to see some of the impressive wildflowers. The limestone cliffs have a scant growth of windswept bushes, in which the endemic Saint Vincent Cistus* (*Cistus palhinae*; p. 60), Sage-leaved cistus, Kermes Oak, the white-flowered, sage-like shrub *Prasium majus* (p. 201) and Phoenician Juniper are key players. Note the clear difference in flora between of the cliffs and that of the small dunes, where more sandy spots, there is Yellow Rockrose (*Halimium calycynum*; p. 129), Portuguese Crowberry (p. 66), Spiny Thrift (*Armeria pungens*; p. 201), Sand-crocus, Snapdragon (p. 63), the pretty purple Algarve Toadflax (*Linaria algaviense*), the bright blue Saint Vincent's Squill, the dark, white-edged flowers of Bellevalia (p. 68) and the spiny, white-flowered cushions of *Astragalus tragacantha*, the latter four endemic to south Portugal, the latter even to the cape itself.

Explore as far as you wish. The trail leads as far as *Beliche Praia*.

Return to the car and drive to Beliche Praia. Just before the bend in the road, turn right onto a sandy track.

5 This is an autumn site. The track leads through uncultivated fields and bushes to a pine forest which is attractive for bird migration (esp. during easterlies). The area is a little elevated and the best point to scan for raptors. Take your time here. Search for migrating passerines that hide in the vegetation, numbers vary each day. Both Long-eared and Short-eared Owls on migration roost in the trees and bushes, but they are more difficult to find. In spring the fields often have Short-toed Lark and in winter, look for Little Bustard.

Algarve Toadflax*
(*Linaria algarviense*)

Turn back to the tarmac, turn right and park after 1.5 km near the fortress.

6 The 16th century Forte do Beliche (or Belixe) was built as a defence against pirates. Now it is a home to Blue Rock Thrush, Black Redstart and Stonechat. Again, you have superb views on the coastline.

Between the fort and the lighthouse of Cape St. Vincent there are a number of trails you can follow through the flower-rich matos. You can make them a loop (see map on following page), or choose for short rambles on the following points.

Cabo São Vicente
(top).
The white leek *Allium subvillosum* is restricted to the Iberian south coast, northwest Africa and the Canary Islands (bottom).

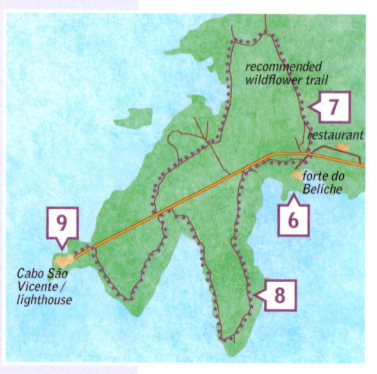

7 Follow the track inland that starts from the road west of the restaurant. This is a splendid area for dune flora (which is just as attractive as the cliff flora). On the first 500 m. you should find lots of Snapdragon, French Lavender, Wrinkle-leaved Cistus, Yellow Rockrose, Creeping Gromwell* (*Lithodora prostrata*), the white leek *Allium subvillosum* plus Saint Vincent / South Portuguese endemics like Saint Vincent Bucklar-mustard* (*Biscutella vicentina*), Saint Vincent Germander* (*Teucrium vicentinum*), Algarve Toadflax, Saint Vincent Squill and Spade-leaved Weld* (*Sesamoides spathulifolia*). Furthermore, keep an eye out for the diminutive Lorquin's Blue, a rare butterfly of the extreme south of Portugal and Spain.

8 From Forte do Beliche along the road and then southwards, you follow the cliffs through low matos. The views are superb, the unique cliff flora surrounds you and you have again a chance on Lorquin's Blues. In autumn and winter, Stonechat and Black Redstart are common and Water Pipit, Alpine Accentor and Thekla's Lark are regular.

9 The lighthouse is a major tourist attraction and at sunset the place can even be crowded. At night its light is visible at 60 km distance.

Although you are a little high above the sea, this is the best place for sea-watching. Autumn is the best period for this. The best strategy is to sit and wait, binoculars or telescope directed to a fixed point. Take care with strong winds and keep an eye open for seabirds that pass very close (especially during or after strong westerly winds). Hundreds, even thousands of Gannets have been counted in a single autumn or winter morning. Hundreds of Cory´s Shearwater can be seen daily in summer and autumn. The Balearic Shearwater is most abundant after the breeding season, when the birds move from their Mediterranean breeding colonies up to the Atlantic coast to complete their moult. Other shearwaters and storm-petrels are more difficult to see from this point. Great Skua is regular throughout the year, while Arctic Skua can be seen during autumn migration.

Sandwich Tern, Yellow-legged and Lesser Black-backed gull are common at sea. In winter, look for Alpine Accentor around the lighthouse.

In westerly winds in autumn, the Gannets are flying right over your head at Cabo São Vicente.

Go back along the same road and after 2 km turn left on the narrow tarmac road that heads north (GPS: 37.028098, -8.971555).

10 The fields can hold interesting birds throughout the year. Stop regularly to look Red-legged Partridge, Thekla's Lark, Corn Bunting and Red-billed Chough. Low numbers of Little Bustard winter in these fields and during autumn migration, anything can turn up.

11 If you're game for more exploration, follow the bumpy track to the left at the ruins of the Vale Santo farm and proceed to the coast where the track ends (GPS: 37.046566, -8.976642).
This is a beautiful spot that is little visited. A trail (signposted) runs all along this coastline. Note the different geology of the cape to the right. In spring the flora is again rich, with similar species as in the previous spots, plus a local specialty: the Shrubby Violet (p. 65). This plant is endemic to Cabo São Vicente and Cabo Trafalgar in Spain and grows a little beneath the end point of the track.

Return to the Vale Santo farm and turn left to return to Vila do Bispo.

Route 22: Aljezur – river and dunes

Best season
March-July
Of interest
Year-round

3-4 HOURS, 15 KM
MODERATE

Unspoilt river valley and estuary.
Splendid dunes on top of the sea cliffs, with a spectacular
flora.

Habitats: riverine woodland, meadows, salt marsh, primary and secondary dunes, pinewoods, pastures
Selected species: *Linaria ficalhoana*, Sticky Dwarf Campion, Stinking Broomrape, Two-leaved Gennaria, Heart-flowered Tongue Orchid, Sharp-lipped Tongue Orchid, Otter, Wild Boar, Golden Oriole, Melodious Warbler, Little Egret, Bee-eater, Tawny Pipit, Knapweed Fritillary, Black Pennant, Pronged Clubtail

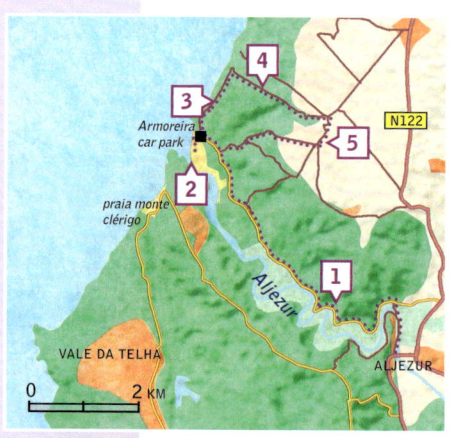

The Aljezur river is one of the gems of the Vicentina natural park – a small stream that snakes its way through a fertile valley down to the coast. The transformation of the river from a forest-fringed, freshwater stream to an increasingly saline area is very special. It is a textbook example of a natural river illustrating the ecological change from woodland and meadows to brackish tamarisk scrub and saltmarsh to a lagoon and beach (see illustration on page 18). All this is easily visible from the minor 7 km road that leads to the quiet beach. It is most attractive to do this short route on bicycle (for rent in Aljezur) but it is just as easy to drive it. From the car park at the beach there is a lovely, 6.5 km easy circular walk through the dunes and over the cliffs.

Starting point bridge of Aljezur (GPS: 37.316656, -8.803219)

The old part of Aljezur (with the castle on the highest point) lies on a low hill around which the river snakes.
The most attractive route to Praia da Amoreira is to follow the road north from the west end of the bridge, along the river and through the old part of the village. However, the first kilometre is very narrow and

more suited for a bicycle. Alternatively, cross the bridge to the newer part of the village, follow the main road north towards Odeceixe and turn left outside the village at the sign *Amoreira*.

1 Make regular stops along the road to see the changes in the river as described above. The valley is not terribly rich in birds, but Iberian Green Woodpecker, Blackcap, Nightingale, Cetti's Warbler and, further down in the saltmarsh, Little Egret, Bee-eater and waders on migration are possible finds. Small-flowered Tongue Orchids grow in the roadside. Spanish Marbled White, Knapweed Fritillary and, later in the season, Marsh Fritillary may be found.

The estuary of the Aljezur river.

2 At the car park near the beach, explore the dunes. There is a great flora of primary dunes here, including Spiny Thrift* (*Armeria pungens*; p. 201), Coastal Crucianella, Shrubby Figwort* (*Scrophularia fruticans*) Sea Holly, Sea Bindweed, Sea Daffodil and Sea Spurge,

Superb flowery *matos* on the cliff dunes of Aljezur (bottom). Close to the coast, the small Seaside Catchfly* (*Silene littorea*) grows. It is sticky all over except for the pink petals (top).

with, as you proceed a bit further inland, Seaside Catchfly* (*Silene littorea*), Chalk Alkanet* (*Anchusa calcarea*), and the diminutive The Stitchwort-leaved Allseeds* *(Polycarpon alsinifolium).*

3 The coastal path (with green-blue signs) starts at the beginning of the car park (GPS: 37.351836, -8.842668) and leads up the cliff. This is one of the areas in the Costa Vicentina where dunes have established on top of the cliff. It is a veritable wildflower paradise. In spring (March-May) the matos are extremely colourful, with the spiny, dome-shaped 'greenweed' *Stauracanthus genistoides*, the tall Round-headed Knapweed (*Centaurea sphaerocephala*), Snapdragon, Yellow Rockrose (p. 129), Brown Bluebell (p. 129), Portuguese Crowberry (p. 66), Three-leaved Snowflake (p. 134), Spotted Rockrose, the stout Stinking Broomrape (p. 66) and the small, yellow toadflax *Linaria ficalhoana* (p. 65), endemic to the Portuguese southwest coast, just a few of the highlights.

4 As the trail bends inland, you cross a pinewood where you can find a small population of the rare green-flowered Two-leaved Gennaria Orchid (p. 123).

Continue through a rather dull clearcut before entering the grassy plateaux. At the T-junction, turn right (signposted Aljezur) and further on, turn right onto the track with the sign *Campo de Treino de Caça*, which leads back to the road.

5 This entire stretch runs through open grassland where lots of tongue orchids grow. The most common is Sharp-lipped (*strictiflora*), but there are some Heart-flowered and Small-flowered here too. Don't forget the birds on this stretch either. Short-toed Lark and Tawny Pipit breed, the latter often walking on the track itself. Iberian Grey Shrike, Bee-eater, Stonechat and Sardinian Warbler are frequent as well.

Thekla's Lark

Route 23: Along the Ceixe river

4 HOURS, 22 KM

Best season
March-July
Of interest
Year-round

Unspoilt river valley with lush riverine vegetation.

Habitats: riverine woodland, meadows, cork oak montado, scrub
Selected species: Green-winged Orchid, Heart-flowered Tongue Orchid, Sharp-lipped Tongue Orchid, Green Lavender, Royal Fern, Monchique Spurge, Yellow Iris, Otter, Iberian Chiffchaff, Kingfisher, Iberian Grey Shrike, Spanish Terrapin, Large Tortoiseshell, Large Pincertail, Small Pincertail, Western Demoiselle, Copper Demoiselle, Splendid Cruiser, Western Clubtail

The Ceixe is perhaps the prettiest of the rivers that flow out into the ocean in the Vicentina nature park. It is larger and more powerful than the Aljezur stream (see previous route) and lined with dense ash and alder woods. This route follows the last stretch of its course to the ocean, passing, midway, the village of Odeceixe.

This route is perfect for cyclists, but equally feasible by car. Although there is an attractive mix of birds, wildflowers and insects, this route is above all a scenic trip.

Starting point Maria Vinagre (GPS: 37.397117, -8.782280; 3.5 km south of Odeceixe). Leave the village in eastern direction, to Zambujeiro de Baixo. At the next junction, go left to Zambujeiro de Baixo.

1 The first part of the route is not exceptional. You cross a plain with fields and pinewoods, the most remarkable feature of which is the non-Mediterranean look and feel of the area. Nevertheless, there are a number of interesting birds, such as Azure-winged Magpies, Zitting Cisticolas, Iberian Grey Shrikes and, with some luck, a Tawny Pipit or Short-toed Lark.

The valley of the Ceixe River is beautiful and unspoilt. In the Ash trees along the river, the Golden Oriole is common (top), while the Heart-flowered Tongue Orchid grows (centre and bottom) in the grassy slopes over the river, together with several other orchid species.

As the road winds downwards you have your first views of an exceptionally green river valley.
In the hamlet of Zambujeiro you cross a small ridge. Park at the high point on the left, near a white, abandoned house (GPS: 37.396565, -8.727634) and walk the track towards the river.

2 This short and easy walk follows the ridge to a bend in the river. Note the many Green-winged (March-April) and tongue orchids (April – May); the latter mostly Sharp-lipped (*strictiflora*), but also Heart-flowered and Small-flowered. Towards the end of the track, you descend to the river. Moisture-loving trees like Portuguese Oak, Alder, Narrow-leaved Ash and Mediterranean Willow cloak this site and the rest of

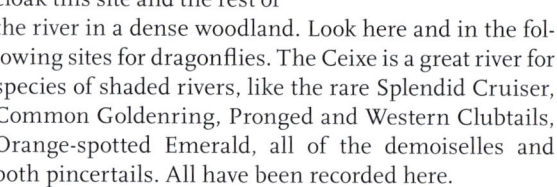

the river in a dense woodland. Look here and in the following sites for dragonflies. The Ceixe is a great river for species of shaded rivers, like the rare Splendid Cruiser, Common Goldenring, Pronged and Western Clubtails, Orange-spotted Emerald, all of the demoiselles and both pincertails. All have been recorded here.
If you're very lucky, you may even see an Otter – the Ceixe has a healthy population of the species.

Return to your car or bicycle and head back the way you came. At the hairpin bend, follow the track to the right (GPS: 37.404233, -8.738609).

3 You cross a cork oak montado with a small pond, where several dragonflies, Viperine Snake and Spanish Terrapin can be seen. In spring and summer Iberian Chiffchaffs are common in the woods.

Shortly hereafter, the track splits. Take the right branch, signposted *Crato*.

4 You continue along the river. Make stops here and there to explore, for example near the side track to *Vida Pura*, where Monchique Spurge* (*Euphorbia monchiquensis*), endemic to the wider Monchique area, grows along the river, together with Royal Fern.

Continue to Odeceixe, cross the N120 and follow the road to the Praia de Odeceixe.

5 Note how the river changes as the maritime influences increase. The streambed widens and the riparian vegetation gives way to the more salt-tolerant tamarisks which are replaced further downstream by saltmarsh. A large sand bar marks the high tide line. In the river valley, look for Waxbills and at sea, Gannets and (in winter) Sandwich Terns.

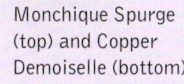

The kiosk and viewpoint over the Ceixe estuary marks the end of this route.

Monchique Spurge (top) and Copper Demoiselle (bottom)

Pristine beach at the mouth of the Ceixe river.

212

Additional sites in the Costa Vicentina

A – Migration and orchids at Boca do Rio

GPS: 37.066598, -8.809726. Boca do Rio is a splendid and unspoilt valley, the merger of two small rivers which join together to form a wide valley. There are fields, salt marsh, reedbeds and some riparian

woodland, with hills with matos on either side. The limestone hills are very rich in orchids. There are masses of Bumblebee and Naked-man Orchids and lower numbers of Yellow Bee, Sombre Bee and Mirror Orchid. The rare Cadiz Daffodil* (*Narcissus gaditanus*) also grows here. You can see it all on the short, two km educational trail that starts at the rivermouth. Explore the valley itself as well – the reedbeds and saltmarsh are attractive for passerines on migration, while Viperine Snakes can be found in the river.

Trail through the Vila do Bispo woodland (site E), where the Two-leaved Gennaria grows in large numbers (bottom).

To get there, take the road down from Budens signposted *Boca do Rio*. It branches off the N125 just west of the roundabout with the large supermarket.

B – Wildflower-hunting in the Barrocal

GPS: 37.123806, -8.768389. The barrocal is the narrow limestone belt just inland of the Algarve, which extends roughly north of Faro to Budens near Cabo São Vicente. Much of it is a wildflower heaven, especially rich in orchids, although many sites are lost to either agriculture, infrastructure or real estate developments.

A wonderful, original stretch is found on either side of the road between Bensafrim, Barão de São Jorge and Espiche. Explore the roadsides and matos for orchids (masses of Pyramidal orchids and several kinds of bee-orchids), Portuguese Squill and other attractive wildflowers. Little is known about the butterflies in this area, but the habitat and location are promising.

C – Whales and seabird watching from Sagres

   The ocean near Cape St. Vincent is one of those special places where whales, dolphins and seabirds concentrate. With patience, you may see some of it from the coast, but if you really want to see ocean life you have to go out at sea. There you will discover another world: mysterious pelagic birds that feed very close to your boat, groups of dolphins playing on the surface, perhaps a whale popping up close to you – all if you're lucky of course.

Several companies offer whalewatching trips from the harbour of Sagres. We enjoyed a trip with the marine biologists of Marilimitado (**www.marilimitado.com**, boat tours from € 40). These enthusiasts for sealife can tell all you want to know and how to see it. An educational briefing precedes the trip.

Common Dolphin is the most likely cetacean you may encounter, followed by Bottlenose Dolphin and Harbour Porpoise. Minke Whale shows up regularly between August and October. Much rarer are sightings of Risso´s and Striped Dolphins and Orcas. Loggerhead and Leatherback Turtles are other (distant) possibilities. There are sightings every year. The best period is between June and December, when the frequency of cetacean sightings is more than 80%. To increase your chances on success, choose a day with fine weather with little wind. You can check with the companies what is seen on the previous days. Seabirds can be numerous, especially in autumn. Cory´s Shearwater is abundant, followed by Great, Sooty and Balearic Shearwater. Gannet, Lesser Black-backed and Yellow-legged Gull are common as well, Wilson´s Storm-petrel and Sabine´s Gull are rare.

Cory's Shearwater is the most common shearwater species off the coast.

D – Cabo São Vicente on foot

   GPS: 37.046411, -8.976913. It is remarkable that almost everybody who visits São Vicente for the flora (or other reasons) visits the same area of cliffs between Sagres and Cabo São Vicente. Much wilder and not so much visited is the long and in places fairly strenuous walk along the western cliffs, from the cape up north to the *Praia do Telheiro* (about 3 kms) and back (either along the same path or via the minor road that runs further inland; see map on page 200). Along this route, you'll cross large areas of clifftop matos and dunes, both of which with the stunning vegetation for which Cabo São Vicente is famous.

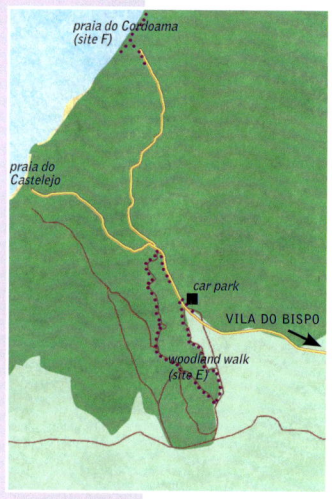

praia do Cordoama (site F)

praia do Castelejo

car park

VILA DO BISPO

woodland walk (site E)

E – The Vila do Bispo woodland

  GPS: 37.092029, -8.932391. A pretty, short and easy loop (1.5 hours) through the pinewoods west of Vila do Bispo offers an attractive counterweight to a visit to Cabo São Vicente. Instead of the busy cape area, with its fierce sunshine and constant wind, this walk is an oasis of peacefulness, shade and shelter. It lacks the dramatic scenery of the cape, but has an attractive landscape and very different flora instead. First and foremost, there is an outstanding population of the rare Two-leaved Gennaria Orchid (flowering Jan-March), which is confined to the southwest of Portugal, the Macaronesian islands and just a few other spots in the western Mediterranean. Furthermore, there are large numbers of Green-winged orchids (March-April) and a confusing variety (with hybrids) of tongue orchids, including Heart-flowered, Small-flowered and Common (April-May).

To get to the start of the walk, leave Vila do Bispo following the signs *praias*. About 1.5 km outside the village, there is a car park on the right. The loop starts some 50 metres further ahead on the left side of the road and is signposted *Trilho Ambiental*.

F – Praia do Cordoama

  GPS: 37.108894, -8.935873. This may just be the most scenic of the secluded beaches of the Costa Vicentina, although it's tricky to be certain as there are so many candidates for this title. Judge for yourself. The cliffs that tower above the rock-strewn beach are dark and gloomy, giving this area the rough feel of the Icelandic coast, but with a much more benign climate. This is the place for a lonely stroll along the beach beneath the cliffs.

To get here, follow the signs *praias* in Vila do Bispo and keep right, following the signs Praia de Cordoama. On the way, you pass the starting point of the previous site.

G – Estuary and dunes of Bordeira

White Storks breed on the sea cliffs at Cabo Sardão. (Opposite page)

  GPS: 37.192860, -8.902297. The southernmost of the rivers that has created a fine estuary on the Costa Vicente lies near the village of Carrapateira. On its southern shore, there is a huge dune complex with a splendid flora. On the north side, the interplay of sea and river has created a huge, desert-like sand-spit. Bee-eaters breed further upstream, near the main road.

To get there, Leave the village of Carrapateira in northern direction and at the last houses, go left, signposted *Bordeira*.

H – Cabo Sardão

GPS: 37.597640, -8.817052.

The Cabo Sardão is, like so many others on the rugged south-west coast, a beautiful spot with splendid views, seabirds and an attractive scrubland. In addition to this, it has something extra. On a small rocky islet, secluded from the wind by two promontories on the north and south, there are a number of stork nests on the cliffs. This unusual 'seabird' is joined by more familiar ones such as Shag and Yellow-legged Gull, which can be observed here at closer distance than elsewhere. There is also a small colony of Jackdaws (an uncommon bird here) and Thekla's Larks and Sardinian Warbler show themselves well in the coastal scrub. It is possible to start walks from here in the dunes (which lie on top of the cliffs).

To get there, follow the signs *Cabo Sardão* from the N120 that at the north end of the town of São Teotónio.

TOURIST INFORMATION & OBSERVATION TIPS

Travel

Travelling to southern Portugal

There are currently three practical ways to get to southern Portugal: by plane, bus or car. Lisbon was also served by a night train from Madrid, called Trenhotel Lusitania, but this service was terminated during the Covid pandemic and since when it seems to be defunct. However, it may be worth checking rail connections following promised EU funding. There are cheap and fairly fast buses from Madrid to Lisbon, though – see **www.omio.com** or **www.flixbus.com**. There are also daily flights that connect Lisbon and Faro to most European airports, all of which have the disadvantage of more excessively contributing to climate change, which is already greatly impacting southern Portugal. Drivers from the UK can reduce their driving time by taking a ferry to northern Spain.

The drive to southern Portugal from northern Europe takes a long time (over 20 hours driving time from the Channel ports and 8 hours for those arriving from the UK via Santander ferry). Once arriving in Portugal, it is worth using the toll roads to Lisbon or the Algarve. They are quiet, well-maintained and much faster than taking the backroads. The fastest route is to drive first to Madrid and take the A-5 to Mérida (in Extremadura). There, you have three options. The first is to go directly to Portugal by the toll road near Badajóz. From here, you can either explore the Lisbon – Setúbal area or enter the Alentejo. The next option is to drive south to Zafra, take there the small Ex-101 and enter Portugal at Barrancos (route 9) in the Alentejo. Finally, you can head south to Sevilla and enter the Algarve on the A22 which is conveniently close to Castro Marim (route 13).

Travelling in southern Portugal

The car is by far the easiest means of transport in Portugal. Driving the motorways is easy, comfortable and progress is fast – the backroads however, are the exact opposite – they are long and winding, although the state of repair is generally good.

Traffic is light overall, except in the Lisbon area and the main routes in the Algarve during the tourist season. The towns just south of Lisbon, on the banks of the Tejo are all suburbs from which people commute into Lisbon. In this area traffic is busy and sometimes a bit chaotic. So, if you plan to head into Lisbon, do as many other locals do and take a bus or train from the suburbs.

Toll roads

Toll roads in Portugal are a little complicated because there are two systems. Some roads will have the familiar toll booths where you get a ticket and pay, either by cash or credit card, as you leave the motorway. Others have an electronic toll system, which is activated by a box in your rental car. When you pass an electronic toll sensor, you will hear a soft bleep from the box to inform you are being charged. The rental company will probably offer you a system by which these charges are directly debited from your credit card. This saves a lot of hassle. If you don't choose this option, you must pay at a post office. However (and here's the rub), there is an administrative delay of 2 days before the charge is processed so that you can then pay the amount due at the post office. Hence you will incur an extra charge (plus a hefty service fine) from your rental company if you use these roads in the last two days of the hire period. If you bring your own car, which doesn't have the box installed, you are not charged at all. Toll costs are similar to those in Spain and France – in 2024, the drive from Badajóz to Lisbon was € 17.85. You can calculate your toll costs at **www.tollguru.com/ toll-calculator-portugal**

Southern Portugal by bus and train

Portugal has good public transport system, that, if you don't mind taking your time, will give you a good start in exploring the country's natural areas. However, it can't match driving a car for speed and convenience.

The railroad system (**www.cp.pt**) will take you to the most important towns (Lisbon, Setúbal, Beja, Faro, Lagos, etc), but you'll need the bus to get you deeper into the countryside. The national bus service is RENEX which serves all the major towns (check **www.rede-expressos.pt**). There is also a fine network of local bus networks in the Algarve (**www.eva-bus.com**), the Alentejo, (**www.rodalentejo.pt**) and in the Setúbal area (**www.tsuldotejo.pt**).

Cycling in southern Portugal

Cycling in Portugal has its challenges, but also its rewards. The interior of the Algarve and Alentejo is beautiful and quiet (away from the easily avoided N-roads), but towns and facilities are few and far between, requiring careful planning. Also, be aware that shade is sparse. The landscape is hilly but not at all too challenging, just enough to remain pleasant. The roads are generally good for cycling. Don't expect any facilities for cyclists, but as traffic is sparse, that shouldn't be a problem.

The Lisbon-Setúbal area and the coastal Algarve is radically different. Here are no facilities for cyclists either, but because traffic is busy and in places a little chaotic, it requires extra care. The upside is that there is plenty of accommodation. In all regions, winter, spring and autumn are the most pleasant, as temperatures are less challenging and traffic is less chaotic (except around Lisbon, where it is always busy).

Ferries

There are ferries across the Tejo from Lisbon and Sado near Setúbal. The Setúbal – Tróia service is by Atlantic Ferries (**www.atlanticferries.pt**). You don't need to book online. Just go to the port and queue up. In our experience, it is not busy, except, sometimes, at weekends and on holidays.

There is also a ferry from Lisbon to Cacilhas, just north of Costa Caparica (which is connected by bus) and you can make a trip from Lisbon to Montijo (site D – Montijo harbour, see page 137). For more information, see **www.transtejo.pt**.

Ferry trips are comfortable and often offer good birdwatching and, in season, chances on seeing dolphins.

Planning your trip

When to go

Southern Portugal is of interest throughout the year, although the summer season, when it is exceedingly hot and wildlife is shy, is the least rewarding.

Winter is the rainy season, but even then rainy spells usually last no more than a few days between prolonged periods of mild and sunny weather. The warm Gulf Stream has a major influence on the climate of southern Portugal, making its winters among the mildest in the whole of mainland Europe. November to February is a great season for birding. The wetlands on the coast are chock-a-block with wintering wildfowl that have fled the cold in northern Europe. The rice paddies are flooded, attracting thousands of waders and ibises. Since many of the Alentejo's birds are residents, the interior of our region is attractive in winter too (although not as good as spring). Late autumn to early spring is the best period for finding amphibians as well. These moisture-loving creatures spend the hot months hidden in the soil, but are active in the cooler, wetter months.

Due to the mild and stable climate, spring comes early, with narcissi, orchids and other bulbs starting to bloom in late February. The first reptiles also appear and early migrants (storks, Great Spotted Cuckoo, Swallows) are returning. March is a splendid month, with masses of wildflowers and orchids appearing everywhere. Spring butterflies like Spanish Festoon are on the wing. March is an important month for spring migrants, although April is still richer. For birds April and May, when all migrant birds arrive, are arguably the best months for bird-watching, although the rice paddies are drained, so there are fewer birds in the marshes.

From mid-May onwards, the countryside starts to turn brown as the wildflowers start to wither. Since there are no high mountains in the region, there is no prolonged period of blooming. From mid-May, a number of attractive dragonfly species appear in the rivers and late-arriving birds like White-rumped Swift and Rufous Bush Robin are best found in May and June. July and August are above all just hot and wildlife is in a summer slumber, although there are some attractive dragonflies and butterflies present. At the end of August it becomes more interesting, with seabirds and migratory waders appearing on the coast and marshes respectively. August and September are best for marine mammals as well. September is very enjoyable, with warm and stable weather and large numbers of migratory birds that peak early in October.

From November onwards, the winter birds arrive, completing the annual cycle.

Plan your trip and accommodation

It is impossible to cover the entire area from a single base. Ideally, to visit all the sites described in this book, you will need to stay in three or possibly four different places over a period of three weeks.

For sites in the Lisbon area, assuming you have a car, the capital, Setúbal or somewhere nearby makes a good base. For the Baixo Alentejo you'll need a different place to stay. On the Algarve the best solution is staying in two places, one in the south-east near Tavira and another on the west coast, say, around Aljezur.

If you, like most people, have less time to spend, you'll need to make some hard choices. Here are some helpful suggestions, including tips on accommodation:

Lisbon area: there is plenty of accommodation in Setúbal and Sesimbra, plus *casas rurales* in the Serra da Arrábida. Lisbon is easily visited by train and bus from there. Equally, it is easy to explore the area from your Lisbon Hotel, but be aware that, whilst a car makes a field trip vastly more effective, driving in and out of the city can be a nightmare.

Baixo Alentejo: Mértola is the most popular and attractive base to explore the Baixo Alentejo, but the sites in the north of the region are still a long way to drive. Castro Verde or Beja are good alternatives. There are lots of *turismo rural* options in the countryside.

Algarve and Costa Vicentina: this area is basically one long string of sites. You can visit them from one central point (which would be around Lagos), but to reach the spots at the extreme ends of the Algarve coast you'll have to travel quite a lot. If your schedule allows it, you're better off staying in two places. If birds are your main focus, you may want to skip the Costa Vicentina (the attractions of which lie largely in the scenery, flora and insects) and shift a bit further east, for example to Portimão or Faro. If you are looking for charming, rural hotels or B&Bs, forget the 'golden coast' of the southern Algarve (all uninspiring hotel towers and golf resorts), and consider the towns further inland or on the west coast, around Aljezur, from which the entire Costa Vicentina, Serra de Monchique and the south coast up to Portimão are within an hour's drive.

Convenient Travel and Safety Issues

Annoyances and hazards

Overall, southern Portugal is a safe and laid-back place. Both in terms of general safety and natural hazards there is little to fear. However, do keep the following in mind.

Theft: Although Portugal has a good name with respect to crime, mass tourism always attracts thieves, so be a little extra careful when visiting busy towns and the south coast. As far as possible, don't leave valuables in your car nor any items in plain view.

The sun: In many parts of southern Portugal shade is sparse. Dense woodland is scarce, trees are far between and *matos* too low to offer any protection from the sun. Make sure you dress appropriately, use sunglasses, a cap or hat and use plenty of sun screen. Take enough water with you if you go on a walk.

Bugs and dangerous animals: Apart from mosquitoes (in some years) on the coastal marshes, there are few annoyances to be expected from non-human lifeforms. The only snake with a venomous bite, the Lataste's Viper, is rare and shy, and its venom is not all that potent, so effectively, one could say that there are no dangerous snakes. Scorpions and the large Megarian Banded Centipede have painful stings and bites respectively, but you won't find them unless you actively go out to search for them.

Permits and restrictions

No permits are required to visit the routes in this book. All sites are free of charge, except the Ria Formosa natural park (route 14) and entrance to Sagres Fort (route 21), which have small entrance fees. Keep in mind that it is important to always respect private property signs.

Responsible Tourism

'Take nothing but photos, leave nothing but footprints' is the well-known phrase that summarizes the idea of responsible tourism. It goes without saying that, as a visitor to a nature reserve (or other sites mentioned in this guide), you have a responsibility to leave your surroundings and everything in it undisturbed. But it may be less than obvious what is and is not damaging in southern Portugal. So here are some points of which you should be particularly aware when visiting this area. First, be careful with fire. The summer drought combined with the wind makes the risk of forest fires very high in southern Portugal (especially where Eucalyptus aka "gasoline trees" are concerned). It is not just a campfire or carelessly thrown away cigarette butts that are a problem – glass bottles (or fragments) are just as dangerous. Be careful how you dispose of either.

Ecotourism code of conduct

We appeal to every naturalist, birdwatcher and nature photographer to abide by this code of conduct in the interests of birds, wildlife and their environment.

- Learn patterns of animal behaviour – know when not to interfere with an animal's life cycle.
- Acquaint yourself with the fragility of the ecosystem – stay on trails that are intended to lessen impact.
- When out in the field, use good judgement – treat the wildlife, plants and places as if you were their guest.
- Treat other observers and photographers courteously – ask before joining others already in an area.
- Keep distance to the birds to avoid stressing or exposing them to danger, exercise restraint and caution during observation, photography, sound recording or filming. Use appropriate lenses to photograph wild animals – if an animal shows stress, move back and use a longer lens.
- Keep well back from burrows, nests, colonies, roosts, display areas and important feeding sites. Do not handle birds, chicks or eggs unless for recognised research activities.
- Before advertising the presence of a rare species of plant or animal, evaluate the potential for disturbance, its surroundings and other people in the area, and proceed only if access can be controlled, disturbance minimized, and, where applicable, permission has been obtained from private land-owners. Unless officially publicised, the sites of rare nesting birds should be divulged only to the proper conservation authorities.
- Do not enter private property without the owner's explicit permission.
- Tactfully inform others if you observe them engaging in inappropriate or harmful behaviour – many people unknowingly endanger themselves and animals. If this doesn't help, report inappropriate behaviour to proper authorities.
- Be a role model – educate others by your actions; enhance their understanding.
- Support the protection of important bird habitat.

Also linked to the climate, is water consumption. The high water demand during the warm months is the reason that so many large reservoirs have been constructed and new ones are planned. So be conservative in your use of water (although don't stint in keeping yourself hydrated). It is your water consumption, added to that of all other tourists, that creates the demand that puts the ecologically devastating dam-building projects on the agenda. The greatest other water consumer, apart from agriculture, is the golf industry. Our preference here is simple; don't play golf. Instead, spend your money in more sustainable economic endeavours: ecotourism and the consumption of local produce. The production of cork, carob, honey and locally produced meat and cheese sustains the biodiverse landscape of southern

Portugal. Purchasing these products are a direct support to nature conservation. Indirectly, your presence and spending shows governments and local communities alike that the environment and its associated wildlife have an economic value in the form of sustainable green tourism, a pragmatic argument that usually carries more weight than appeals to beauty, a landscape's historical significance or the intrinsic value of nature. Local B&Bs or hotels in the countryside are a better (and much more enjoyable) choice than impersonal tourist apartments or hotel chains. When exploring the Algarve, consider the more pleasant option of staying in a rural B&B (mostly north of the motorway) rather than in the tourist resorts at the coast.

When out in the field, avoid damaging activities. Hiking, cycling, a canoe or a drive through the countryside are fine. Off-road quad 'adventures' as frequently advertised, are not. Especially in the Algarve, such trips often go to the few remaining wild sites and are potentially very damaging.

Hiking in southern Portugal

Hiking has been in vogue in southern Portugal only recently. However, unlike the north of the country, southern Portugal is not a great hiking region. It is too hot for much of the year and many areas in the interior and south coast have few hiking trails and are a bit too monotonous for pleasant walks.

The great exceptions are the *Rota Vicentina* and *Rota Algarviana* – two multiple-day and in places demanding, long distance trails. The *Rota Vicentina* follows the wild south-west coast. In several places along this route, there are shorter loops for full or half day treks. The *Rota Algarviana* crosses the Algarve hills from east to west. Both trails meet at Cabo São Vicente.

In several other places in the Algarve there are short walks, such as at Fonte de Benémola (route 16) and Rocha da Pena (route 17). The Serra de Monchique is also plugged as a hiking area with trails available in the tourist office of Monchique village, but much of this area is so thoroughly vandalised by Eucalyptus plantations that hiking is only recommended in the small areas around both peaks of the range (see route 18). The brochures of the Baixo Alentejo list a number of hiking trails in the area, but many of them either follow (linear) tracks or roads through open country, or are small trails that only seem to exist on paper. Positive exceptions are near Barrancos (route 9).

If you plan on hiking in southern Portugal, make sure you bring a GPS device or a fully charged phone with good maps on it, to prevent getting lost (or failing that a compass and good maps). Signposting is, in places, poor and trails, consequently, may not be easy to find. The mobile phone network does not cover all the little corners in the area, but is good overall. Furthermore, make sure to bring sufficient food and water and precautions against exposure to the sun (see page 221).

For further details, see **www.walkalgarve.com** (English) or **www.wandeleninportugal.info** (Dutch).

Additional information

Recommended reading

General tourist information: There are numerous guidebooks on the Algarve and on Portugal in general, which complement this guide in offering information on arts, culture, nightlife and, in some cases, history. For more practical information, we advise to check **www.visitportugal.com** and check out the regions portal for information on the Lisbon area, the Algarve and Alentejo respectively.

Wildflowers There are two sources we highly recommend: first, the *Wildflowers of the Algarve* by Chris Thorogood and Simon Hiscock (Kew Publishing; ISBN: 9781842464977) which is the most complete field guide for the region. Although it focusses on the Algarve, it is very useful for the Alentejo and Lisbon region too. The second is the Portuguese online flora at **www.flora-on.pt**, which is an excellent and complete flora of the whole of Portugal with excellent photographs, flowering periods and distribution maps – a gem of a website.

If it is orchids you are interested in, the *Finding Orchids in the Algarve* by Sue Parker (First Nature; ISBN: 9780956054487) is recommended too. It gives a complete overview of all orchid species, including good photographs and field characteristics, plus a number of sites where many orchids can be found.

Reptiles and Amphibians We recommend the new *Reptiles and Amphibians of Britain and Europe* by Jeroen Speybroek, Wouter Beukema et al. (Bloomsbury; ISBN-13: 9781408154595).

Mammals The standard field guide for European mammals is *Mammals of Europe, North Africa and the Middle East* by Stéphane Aulagnier et al (Helm; ISBN-13: 9781408113998) which adequately covers the region. This can be supplemented by *Tracks and Signs of the Animals and Birds of Britain and Europe* by Lars-Henrik Olsen (Princeton University Press; ISBN-13: 9780691157535).

Birds The definitive European field guide is *Collins Bird Guide* by Lars Svensson (Harper Collins; ISBN-13: 9780007268146). A peerless and comprehensive guide to the status and distribution of Spanish and Portuguese birds is *The Birds of the Iberian Peninsula* by Eduardo de Juana and Ernest Garcia (Bloomsbury Publishing; ISBN-13: 9781408124802). *Aves de Portugal* by Helder Costa et al (Lynx; ISBN-13: 9788496553804) is only available in Portuguese and only available second-hand. **www.avesdeportugal.info** is a website with a tremendous amount of information on birds and birdwatching sites in Portugal. It is maintained by local birders. Part of the site is in English. The website **www.visitportugalbirdwatching.com** also offers information on birdwatching sites, as does **www.vogelsportugal.nl** for Dutch readers. **www.spea.pt** is the website of the Portuguese BirdLife partner. For checklists and bar charts for many sites in the area check the hotspots map at **www.ebird.org/ ebird/hotspots**.

Several British and Dutch citizens have moved to the Algarve and started interesting blogs on the region with observation tips on birds, butterflies, orchids etc. Some also offer guided tours in their new homeland. Among them are the aforementioned **www.vogelsportugal.nl** (Dutch and English) and **www.algarvebirdman.com** (English).

Butterflies and dragonflies The standard guides for butterflies are *Butterflies of Europe* by Tristan Lafranchis (ISBN: 9782952162005; also available in Dutch) and *Collins Butterfly Guide* by Tolman & Lewington (Harper Collins; ISBN-13: 9780007279777) whilst for dragonflies we recommend *A Field Guide to the Dragonflies of Britain & Europe* by Dijkstra & Lewington (British Wildlife Publishing; ISBN-13: 9780953139941). Other insects are covered in the excellent *Photographic Guide to Insects of Southern Europe and the Mediterranean* by Paul D. Brock (Pub. NatureBureau; ISBN-13: 9781874357797).

Walking and naturalist guides Although there is very little information on walking in the Alentejo, you can find plenty about the trails in the Algarve and Costa Vicentina. The familiar Cicerone, Rother and Sunflower all have walking available in English, Dutch and/or German. A good online source of walks (and other information) in the Costa Vicentina is **www.rotavicentina.com**. The routes can be downloaded free of charge. Brochures on walks in the Serra de Monchique are freely available in the tourist info booth in the village of Monchique.

Apps The apps of **observation.org**, **naturgucker.de** and **eBird** (birds only) are great for posting your sightings and look for what others have found.

Maps

In Portugal, good maps are surprisingly hard to come by. It is best not to rely on getting them in the local petrol station, but to buy them beforehand in your own travel bookstore. For general use, the Michelin and Marco Polo maps of Portugal are good value. There is a very good and detailed walking map available on the entire *Parque Natural de Vicentina*, which you can order on **www.rotavicentina.com/quiosque**. Detailed maps can be obtained from the *Centro de Informação Geoespacial do Exército* **www.igeoe.pt** (also in English).

Nearby destinations worth visiting

If you wish to combine your visit to southern Portugal with other areas nearby, you have three options. First, heading east will bring you into Andalucía, where, only a stone's-throw from the Algarve, the marshes of Odiel and Coto Doñana await. These are among Europe's very best wetland areas, in many respects a more complex and more diverse extension of the coastal marshes of the Algarve. Beyond Sevilla, there are huge cork oak woodlands and karst mountains with excellent hiking options and a magnificent flora and fauna. All these areas are covered in the *Crossbill Guide to Western Andalucía*.

Secondly, you can opt to head to the northeast, where the Spanish region of Extremadura awaits. In terms of landscape, Extremadura is a continuation of the Baixo Alentejo, with huge areas of montado (in Spain called *dehesa*) and steppes, but Extremadura is generally wilder and has more rocky terrain and sierras. So if you got a taste for the wild in the Alentejo and want to see lots of eagles, vultures and other birds of prey, definitely consider heading to Extremadura (covered by the *Crossbill Guide to Extremadura*).

Your third option is to drive north to visit central and northern Portugal. Northern Portugal is much greener and mountainous than the south and is particularly inviting to hikers. The scenery is great, the villages and towns beautiful and the walking options are virtually endless. Moreover, the flora and butterfly fauna of northern Portugal is very attractive.

Food and drinks

Southern Portugal is an excellent region to taste some fine, typical and local rural dishes. Each area has its own specialities, but be aware that in the most touristy places, 'local food' is a term that is often without substance. On the coast, you are usually better off in small fishing communities visited by few tourists – enough to make it worthwhile to have a restaurant, but not so many that there's a race to the bottom to attract tourists with the lowest possible prices. We found great places at Sesimbra, Setúbal, Comporta, pretty much the whole southwest coast and at Alvor. In the interior, good, local food is available in many restaurants.

The *prato do dia* (dish of the day) is a cheap meal you can get around midday at any Portuguese restaurant. It is always a bargain – inexpensive, simple and usually good value. The best *pratos do dia* are found in non-touristy towns and villages where, at midday, the restaurants resemble canteens for local workforce. In tourist towns, restaurants often compete with one another with the *prato do dia*, in which excessively low prices also mean lower quality (and no regard to sustainable production).

When on the Portuguese coast, you should try some of the fish dishes. Fish and seafood form the culinary pride of the Portuguese. They are especially fond of their *bacalhau* (dried or salted cod). The technique of salt-based curing of cod goes back at least 500 years from when the Newfoundland cod fishery was discovered. The credit for this discovery is usually given to Basque fishermen (although the Scandinavians may also have a claim).

The cooks grill their fresh fish slowly which is the best way to do it. Grilled sardines you can eat everywhere and the same applies to *carapaus alimados* (poached horse mackerel). Octopus is another common dish often accompanied by bread or rice, or simply baked in the oven. Clams, oysters and cockles, freshly harvested by hand, are prepared on a griddle or in a frying pan. There are seafood festivals in Olhão and Faro.

In the Alentejo, savory meals, soups, stews (*ensopado* or *cozido*) and meat dishes (lamb – *borrego*; goat – *cabrito*) are on the menu. The most famous soup is the *açorda*. It is made with bread soaked in tasty broth with olive oil, garlic, coriander and a poached egg. The Alentejo has lots of cheeses (*queijo*) too, often straight out of the montado.

If you have a sweet tooth, try the *pastéis de nata*. These typically Portuguese cream pastries are sold everywhere, from the bakeries in Lisbon to the smallest cafés in remote villages. They are an excellent companion to your coffee (which, in Portugal is usually an excellent strong espresso). *Pasteis de nata* are said to be 'invented' in 1837, their production is based on a secret recipe of the Jeronimos Monastery in Belém (part of Lisbon), hence they are also called *pastéis de Belém*. After dinner, there are typical sweet desserts like *Tiborna* (a kind of cake) and *Bolo de mel* (honey cake), to name but a few.

With the exception of Port and Madeira, Portuguese wines have generally been regarded as the poor cousins to those of Spain. However, with greatly improved winemaking techniques and better trained staff, the quality of the wines is now being more highly regarded (see **www.winesofportugal.info**). Algarve has a 2000-year tradition of viticulture, its south facing hillsides, excellent soils and climate favour good wines. The major towns gave name to the region's four wine region denominations (DOC; *Denominação de Origem Controlada*): Lagos, Portimão, Lagoa and Tavira. Algarve red wines are generally regarded as superior to the whites. This has to do with the relatively high temperature which is not really suitable for white wines. Conditions are more challenging for viticulture in the Alentejo with its poor soils and hotter summers but producers manage to make quite good wines. *Trincadeira* is the oldest red grape variety of the Alentejo and commonly used for Port wine. The two DOCs Setúbal and Palmela are primarily the Muscat wines (sweet dessert wines).

And now to a digestive to end a fine dinner. In southern Portugal, the choice is easy: *Licor* (or *aguardente*) *de Medronho* – a strong spirit made from Strawberry Tree berries. Apart from the taste, the attraction is twofold – the Strawberry Tree is typical of the acidic soils of Portugal and since it isn't planted commercially, most *aguardentes* are made by local berry pickers and hardly sold in stores, except in some small villages. Try *Licor de Medronho* in and around Monchique, where it is easiest to find in restaurants or shops.

Observation tips

Finding orchids

In southern Portugal, orchids are an early spring delight. Some species (e.g. Two-leaved Gennaria, Giant and Fan-lipped Orchid) start to bloom as early as January, while on warm and exposed spots in the Algarve, the great swathes of orchids open their flower buds at the end of February. By late April, most species have finished blooming, although in the cooler spots they may linger until mid-May. Only a handful of species appear later, flowering in April and on until late May.

When it comes to finding orchids, it's all about the three L's: location, location, location. In that sense, it is not unlike the region's real estate. For most species of orchids, the preferred spots are roadsides and little-grazed, grassy *matos* on limestone soils. The *barrocal* in the Algarve, the Serra da Arrábida near Lisbon and a few isolated limestone outcrops in the Alentejo form the holy trinity of orchid sites in southern Portugal. Many of the top spots feature on routes and sites in this book.

Most of the orchids, both in number of species and of individuals, belong to the bee orchid genus, *Ophrys*. A scatter of thin, pale stems and small flowers are the typical image of these plants. However, for such beautifully patterned and coloured flowers, they are surprisingly hard to spot as they blend in perfectly against the background. A tip for the novice orchid hunter: scan the grassy spots and roadsides (especially the latter) for the bigger orchid species, like Naked-man and Pyramidal Orchids. They catch the eye immediately, and where these species are present, the Ophrys species are usually not far away. In the Algarve, the conspicuous big blue Portuguese Squills (p. 68) share the same habitat as many orchids and can also guide you to the right spots. Once on location, you'll notice that although most orchids share roughly the same habitat, they often prefer, like the proverbial birds-of-a-feather, to flock together. Make sure you walk around in the area a bit, or walk down the road to see what's further ahead. Often, you'll come across clumps of different species when you start rambling.

Not all orchids prefer the dry limestone grasslands. Open woodlands, both on limestone and acidic soils have their share of orchids too. In wet, grassy spots along rivers, look for tongue orchids and Champagne Orchid.

Pelagic boat trips – seabirds and whales

Southern Portugal is quite a good region for watching seabirds and cetaceans (whales and dolphins). It doesn't rank among the top sites in Europe, but trips, especially in late summer and early autumn, can be really rewarding.

The way to watch seabirds and cetaceans is by booking a seat on a guided trip – this is infinitely more convenient than scanning the ocean from the coast and views are much closer with greater opportunities for photography. The best areas are off the coast of Setúbal and Sagres, but only the latter is serviced by whalewatching trips. Don't forget to take precautions against getting burnt by the sun (cooling sea breezes can be deceptive) and preventative measures against seasickness.

Excursions depart from Tavira, Faro and Alhão **www.formosamar.com** and from Sagres **www.marilimitado.com**, the latter being the most rewarding as it is closest to the submarine canyons where most whales and dolphins occur. The latter company also offers trips especially dedicated to birdwatching. Each trip is preceded by an educational briefing. They are marine biologists that spend time and money on conservation. Prices range from € 35.00 to € 50.00 (adults, 2023) and trips take 2-3 hours.

If you visit the harbours of Portimão and Alvor, you will find out that several other companies organise pelagic boat tours.

Finding snakes, spiders, scorpions and the like

A good thing about snakes, spiders and scorpions is that if you do not want to see them, they remain hidden, but if you do, there are ways to find them. The best way is to head for a rocky scrubland and start turning the stones. Places with waste, like plywood or plastic are, although not pretty, ideal for reptiles to hide underneath.

When you start turning stones, you'll mostly find ants and their nests, but every now and then you will stumble upon a Scorpion, Wolf Spider (related to the tarantulas), snake, Megarian Banded Centipede or one of the more drought-resistant amphibians. If you are lucky you might even find a Worm Lizard.

Flat stones give the best hit rate. Lift them up on one side, turn them over and step back. Be aware that some animals can cause painful stings or bites.

Be also aware that turning over stones is very invasive for the animals that are hiding underneath them. Many of them worked hard to create a nest underground. Therefore, make sure that you do not disturb the subterranean life for too long and place the stone back exactly as you found it.

Some snakes are active at night. In the late hours of the day, they warm themselves on rocks and the pavement of small country roads. A drive or walk at dusk can reveal Ladder, False and Southern Smooth Snakes. In spring and summer, diurnal snakes and lizards use these places to warm up in the morning light.

Finding steppe birds

The majestic Great Bustard, the beautifully marked, yet highly cryptic sandgrouse, the wide-eyed Stone Curlews, gracefully soaring Montagu's Harriers... the steppe birds are a true highlight for every birdwatcher. Southern Portugal, above all the area around Castro Verde, is amongst Europe's best steppe regions – both for the birds and for those wishing to see them. However, with steppe birds it is not just about the where. The when and how are just as important. Here are a series of tips to maximise your success.

Before you head out, appreciate that steppe birds are under pressure. Take great care not to disturb them – see page 222 for the do's and don'ts of birdwatching.

Timing The most obvious tip we have for you is about timing. In order to maximise your chances, you need to rise early and be on the spot at sunrise. Steppe birds are well adapted to the heat – they simply stop moving around as soon as it gets too warm. Especially in summer, temperatures rise quickly and after a few hours, birds become inactive. What does become active is the air so what little activity birds do exhibit is obscured by the heat haze. The later hours of the day are again good.

Timing is not only about the moment in the day, but also the time of year. In winter, the above-mentioned midday inactivity does not apply. Great and Little Bustard, sandgrouse and other birds on the ground can be seen in winter time with the same ease in the morning as in the afternoon. The shorter days also mean that the birds must make the most out of limited opportunities to find food. Many steppe birds are resident, so they remain all year in the area. However, in winter, they flock together, which means that you need to move around more to spot them. But if you do, you'll hit the jackpot. We've seen groups of 40-50 Little Bustards, and flocks of hundreds of Calandra Larks.

Location The steppe is not uniform. Different species have their preferences for certain types of grasslands. The bustards, sandgrouse, Calandra Larks, Montagu's Harriers and Stone Curlews prefer level or slightly undulating terrain with not too many obstacles like rocks and bushes. In particular areas where cereal fields and grassy areas occur together, these birds are at home. The more bushy and stony steppes are preferred by Little Owls, both shrikes and Black-eared Wheatear. Areas with some rivers attract Bee-eaters. Wires and fences along the road should always be checked for Rollers, Bee-eaters, Great Spotted Cuckoos, Lesser Kestrels and other raptors, shrikes and of course the masses of Corn Buntings.

Bare soils and short-grass steppes, in particular near drinking pools are another hotspot, in particular for Short-toed Lark and Collared Pratincole. Black-bellied Sandgrouse has a particular liking for ploughed fields.

Strategy The best way to find steppe birds is to drive around and make regular stops. Do not wait until you see anything, just scan gentle slopes with your telescope and binoculars using, where possible, vantage points in the landscape, Once you've pulled over (always to the side of the road and visible for other drivers from both directions!) stay in the car and scan first. Then step out to look and listen, but remain close to the car. Make regular stops, get out of your car, wait, search, listen and go for another spot. A walk into the fields is usually not the best way to find the birds.

When scanning, look for unusual bumps or patches in the landscape. What appear to be clods of earth in a field, might be a group of sandgrouse. And always scan the poles and fences for perching birds.

With steppe birds, bird-*listening* is often as important as birdwatching as several species are more easily detected by call and song (check these on **www.xeno-canto.org**). Sandgrouse fly around (especially in the morning) and call frequently as they do. The calls are typical and carry far – as soon as you hear them, look for a pair or flock of fast-flying, plover-like birds. Stone Curlews normally sit still and are very hard to see, but its Curlew-like call can be heard from afar, especially when a soft rain starts. Learn the 'raspberry' courtship call of the Little Bustard, you can hear them in spring from the cereal fields where calling males stick their necks up like periscopes. Steppe birds are notoriously good at hiding and you will have to work to find them. You may be lucky and see all you want in just a few stops. But if you have an unlucky day, you may come away empty-handed after a dozen stops. Do not despair – just keep on going. Eventually, you'll get there.

Birdwatching list

Note that, until recently, Portugal was rather overlooked by ornithologists in favour of nearby Spain. A good number of species have also declined historically. As a consequence, the precise status of some scarce or rare birds (esp. migrants) may be understated as the coverage of the country has been patchy and episodic until recently. However, a growing interest in birds by the Portuguese themselves and a growing number of active ex-pats promises to clarify the situation.

The numbers between the brackets () refer to the routes on page 109 onwards.

Geese and ducks The only regularly occurring goose is the Grey-lag Goose. It winters in small numbers in the Tagus estuary (1) and irregularly in the eastern Algarve. Shelduck is a winter visitor in relatively small numbers (November – February) mainly on the Tagus (best 1, 3, 6, 7, 13, 14) but a few have bred since 2000 at Castro Marim. Mallard is the only duck with a wide distribution. Concentrations are found in the coastal wetlands and estuaries and rice fields. Gadwall mainly breeds in the eastern Algarve (13, 14, 15) plus a few inland sites (site A, page 158). In winter, numbers increase and Gadwall can also be seen at 1, 2 and 3. The Santo André lagoon (7) is the most important site for the Red-crested Pochard, with several hundreds wintering and a few breeding. Other regular sites are on routes 13 and 14. Pochard is a rare resident, with wintering birds at 1, 2, 3, 6, 7. Wigeon, Teal, Shoveler and Pintail are wintering species (Nov-Feb; 1, 2, 3, 6, 7, 13, 14, 15 and site A on page 158). Pochard, Ferruginous and Tufted Ducks occur in small numbers outside the breeding season. Garganey is seen mainly on passage in March. Small numbers of Common Scoter winter at sea as do Red-breasted Merganser, although most are found in the Sado Estuary (e.g. 6).

Pheasants and partridges Red-legged Partridge is common in all rural and agricultural areas, especially in the Alentejo (e.g. 8 – 11). Quail is common in cereal fields.

Divers and grebes All divers are extremely rare at sea in winter. Black-necked Grebe is a winter visitor in the Atlantic and the mouth of the estuaries. Little Grebe is a widespread resident in wetlands, also in small freshwater pools. Great Crested Grebe is a scarce breeding bird along reservoirs and lagoons. Their numbers increase in winter (e.g. 7 and at Salgados; site A on page 195).

Cormorants, shearwaters, storm-petrels and Gannet Seabirds are abundant on the Atlantic Ocean off southern Portugal especially in autumn and in winter. Passage of seabirds can be observed from Cape St. Vincent (21) and Cape Espichel (4). Gannet, Cory´s and Balearic Shearwater are possible pretty much all year but most abundant at the end of summer and in autumn. Great Cormorant is an increasingly common winter visitor. Shag breeds along coasts with rocks and cliffs and is present all year (4, 21, site H on page 214). Other seabirds are only regularly seen from pelagic boat trips.

Herons Little and Cattle Egret are the most abundant of the herons. Little Egret is fairly common in all kind of wetlands, the coastal saltwater estuaries, the inland freshwater wetlands and the along the rivers. Cattle Egrets are abundant in fields, where they take advantage of cattle that flush up insects. Groups of Grey Herons can be seen in good numbers in the Tejo and Sado estuaries (1, 2, 3, 4), in smaller numbers in the Algarve coastlands, while single birds are found along the rivers. Great White Egret is a wintering bird on the coast in small but increasing numbers. Purple Heron and Little Bittern breed and are mostly confined to reedbeds (15, Albufeira; E on page 137, and Salgados and Vilamoura; A and B on pages 195-196). Night and Squacco Herons are quite scarce (best 6).

Storks White Storks are very common and conspicuous throughout the region, often breeding in roadside trees, electricity pylons and of course in the villages. Remarkable is the off-shore colony on the stacks of Cabo Sardão (site H, page 214). Many birds stay all winter. Black Stork breed along the Guadiana river (11, less so 8, 9, B and E on pages 159-160), During autumn migration, their numbers increase and they'll visit other wetlands too.

Ibisses, Spoonbill and Flamingo Glossy Ibis can be seen in winter and spring by thousands in rice fields and by hundreds in other wetlands (2, 6, 7 site C on page 136, F on page 139, A on page 158). Spoonbill returned as a breeding species in the 1980s and is found in groups of up to several dozens in the estuaries and coastal wetlands (1, 2, 3, 6, 13, 14, 15 and inland, site A on page 158). Their numbers peak in the passage periods. Greater Flamingo does not breed, but is year-round present in the estuaries (1, 2, 3, 6, 13, 14, 15).

Vultures The Egyptian Vulture no longer breeds in the Guadiana basin, but birds appear during autumn migration (21). Many Griffon Vultures visit the Alentejo

(9, 10) throughout the year, with fewer numbers in the Algarve mountains (18, 21). The same goes for Black Vulture, only in smaller numbers.

Eagles and other broad-winged raptors Short-toed and Booted Eagle occur throughout during the breeding season, both in low numbers (e.g. 2, 3, 4, 8-12). Some Booted Eagles winter. Bonelli´s Eagle breeds in the Serra da Arrábida, Guadiana valley and in Monchique mountains and non-breeding birds disperse over a wider area (e.g. 4, 5, 9, 10, 11, 18). A small but increasing population of the Spanish Imperial Eagle breeds in the Guadiana valley and non-breeding birds are seen in a wider area (e.g. 9, 10, 18). Golden Eagle can be seen at the Guadiana near Barrancos (9, 10, 11 and 21). During migration and in winter the Osprey can be seen at estuaries and wetlands near the coast (e.g. 1, 2, 3, 6, 7, 13, 14, 15).

The Buzzard is a resident in low numbers but the Honey Buzzard appears only during migration. Black Kite breeds all over the region, but Red Kites are restricted to the Guadiana valley and near the Costa Vicentina (8-12, 21, 22). Their numbers greatly increase in winter. The Black-winged Kite is widespread in the Setúbal region and the Alentejo (1, 2, 3, 6, 8, 9, 10, 12). After the breeding season it also appears in the Algarve. Small numbers of Marsh Harrier breed in wetlands with reeds (e.g. 2, 3, 6, sites E (Albufeira) on page 137 and B (Vilamoura) on page 196). A few pairs of Hen Harrier may still breed (8, 9) and their numbers increase in winter when they may feed on the same fields as Marsh Harrier (10). Montagu´s Harrier can be seen on the steppes and cereal fields (e.g. 8, 10, 13, site A (Lagoa dos Patos) on page 158 and F (Azinhal) on page 161).

During winter and migration Goshawk and Sparrowhawk can be seen in wooded areas, but only very few breed.

Falcons The Lesser Kestrel is almost entirely restricted to the Castro Verde – Mértola area (10, E on page 160) where it is easy to see in spring/summer. After the breeding season it shows up in the Algarve and at Cape Espichel (e.g. 4, 21). Common Kestrel is a widely-distributed resident. The Merlin is a winter bird (e.g. 10), while the Hobby is mostly seen on migration (e.g. 21). Only a few pairs breed. Some Peregrine Falcons breed, more are seen in winter and during migration (e.g. 2, 10, 21, C on page 196). A few Eleonora´s Falcon are seen during spring (rare) and autumn (more regular) migration (e.g. 21).

Rails and coots Water Rail is mainly found in coastal marshes and the Tagus estuary. Crakes are very rare (e.g. site E (Albufeira on page 137), A (Salgados on page 195). Moorhen is locally common. Purple Gallinule is recovering and resident in reeds (6, 7, 15 and site E on page 137 and site A on page 195). Common Coot is common, with high numbers in winter (e.g. 7). Long absent, a handful of Crested Coot have been recorded in recent years (e.g. 2; Tagus estuary).

Common Crane and bustards Cranes are common winter birds in the eastern Alentejo (8, 9). Small numbers may turn up elsewhere. Little and Great Bustard are best seen on 10, and site F and G on pages 161-162. Little Bustard is more widespread than Great, with low numbers in steppe-like habitats. It is more numerous in winter.

Waders Black-winged Stilt has a wide distribution (1, 2, 3, 6, 7, 13, 14, 15,19, 20, 22). Avocet is scarcer as a breeding bird (1, 13), but is present all year round and in many coastal wetlands.

Stone Curlew is a bird of fields and steppes (10, site F on page 161), and some coastal lands (e.g. 13). Collared Pratincole breeds on only a few sites (10, 13, site C on page 136 and site A on page 158), but during spring migration, it is seen on more places. Little Ringed Plover breeds near rivers and small wetlands (e.g. 11, 18). Kentish Plover is a resident of coastal marshes while Ringed Plover arrives in the same areas on passage and during winter (1, 2, 3, 6, 7, 13, 14, 15, 19, 20, 22). Groups of Golden Plovers winter on fields in the interior (8, 10). Grey Plover is a passage and wintering bird of all coastal marshes. Lapwing is also a bird that spends the winter on fields and steppes (e.g. 10).

The estuaries (1, 2, 3, 6, 7, 13, 14, 15, 19, 20) are home to numerous waders. Birds that are present in large numbers on migration with many staying for winter include Sanderling, Little Stint, Dunlin, Ruff, Black-tailed Godwit, Bar-tailed Godwit, Whimbrel, Curlew, Turnstone, Common Sandpiper (also in the interior), Green Sandpiper and Redshank (a handful breed). Oystercatcher, Greenshank, Spotted Redshank, Wood Sandpiper and Purple Sandpiper occur in much smaller numbers. Curlew Sandpiper only occur as migrants as do Temminck´s Stint (albeit in much smaller numbers) and Dotterel (often with Golden Plovers).

Common Snipe is common during migration and in winter along rivers and brooks; the precise status of Jack Snipe is unknown. Woodcock winters and is heavily hunted.

Gulls, terns and skuas Yellow-legged Gull is common year-round along the entire coast. Lesser Black-backed Gull breeds sporadically but is abundant in winter. Black-headed Gull is common at the coast and inland lakes in winter. The Audouin's Gull (13, 14) is scarce, mainly occurring after the breeding season (although two small colonies have been established on the Algarve coast since 2001). Mediterranean Gull is common in autumn, winter and spring (1, 2, 3, 7, 13, 14, 15, 19, 20). Slender-billed Gull was, until recently, a rarity but in recent years modest flocks have appeared in autumn (13, 14). Kittiwake periodically occurs in large numbers after storms. Other gulls are scarce or vagrants, usually off the coast. The four species of skuas are rare in winter off the coast. Great Skua is the most abundant.

Terns Sandwich Tern is common at the coast in winter and during migration (6, 13-15, 19, 20). Common Tern breeds sporadically in very small numbers, but is common during migration (1, 3). Caspian Tern is found at the coast during migration and in winter (1, 13, 15, 19, 20). Gull-billed Tern has bred, but is usually only seen on migration (e.g. A Lagao dos Patos page 158). Little Tern has several breeding colonies (1, 7, 13) and migrants show up in spring and autumn. Whiskered Tern is largely a scarce migrant but a few breed on the Tagus (1, 2). Black Terns are also scarce migrants (they have bred in the Algarve).

Auks Razorbill (regular) and Puffin (scarce) are winter birds at sea.

Sandgrouse Black-bellied Sandgrouse is declining and limited to the Alentejo, especially Moura (8) and Castro Verde (10) and sites F and G on page 162.

Pigeons and doves Wood Pigeon is an uncommon breeding bird in wooded areas, with large flocks arriving from the north for winter. Stock Dove is a thinly spread winter visitor. Collared Dove is common around towns and villages. Turtle Dove breeds in low numbers in riverine forest, in the hills and in the mountains (12, 18, 22, 23). Feral Pigeon/Rock Dove can be seen almost everywhere with seemingly wild Rock Doves found on the rocky coasts of the Algarve.

Cuckoos Common Cuckoo is widely distributed. The Great Spotted Cuckoo occurs in steppes, cork and holm Oak montados and other half open areas (e.g. 3, 8, 10, 11 and site F on page 139). It is quite common at Castro Verde (10).

Owls Barn Owl and Little Owl are common in places with old trees, barns and deserted buildings, especially in the Alentejo (8-11). The soft call of the Scops Owl can be heard in woodlands and from trees in villages (e.g. Mértola). Tawny Owl breeds in the forests. Long-eared Owl is a very scarce resident, while Short-eared Owl is a winter visitor in low numbers (1, 2, 6, 13-15 and site C on page 136). Eagle Owl is also uncommon, with few pairs breeding on cliffs and rocks in open areas (mainly along the Spanish border and the south-west).

Woodpeckers The call of the Iberian Green and Great Spotted Woodpeckers is commonly heard from wooded areas, above all riverine forest. Lesser Spotted Woodpecker is scarce in oak montados, most numerous just east of the Sado bay. Wryneck breeds in open woodland in the Algarve and on the Vicentina coast, some birds stay the winter and others can be found on migration.

Nightjars Red-necked Nightjar has a wide distribution and is most abundant in the Algarve (e.g. 2, 4, 5, 6 7, 12, 13, 18, 20). European Nightjar is a migrant; a few breed (1).

Swifts Common and Pallid Swift are common, the first is the most abundant overall, but in the Algarve and on the Vicentina coast it is reversed. Alpine Swift only breeds in sea cliffs of the Algarve and Vicentina coasts (D, E Algarve, 21 and D Vicentina). The rare White-rumped Swift can be found in the Alentejo (9, 12, sites D and E on page 160).

Roller, bee-eater, hoopoe and kingfisher Roller has a very restricted breeding range in traditional agricultural lands (10). Bee-eater is frequent and widespread (e.g. 2, 8, 9, 10, 12, 18, 22). Hoopoe is common in farmlands and fields with old trees and orchards. Many stay in winter. Kingfishers live around rivers and freshwater lakes. Their number increases in winter (e.g. 15, 18, 21, 22 and at Albufeira (site E on page 137), Lagoa dos Patos (A on page 158) and the Algarve coast (A and B on page 195-196)).

Larks Calandra and Thekla's Larks are frequent in extensive agricultural fields and in pastures, especially in the eastern Alentejo (e.g. 8, 10, 12). The Crested Lark inhabits more intensive agricultural fields, often close to roads, and is more widespread than the Thekla's Lark (e.g. 8, 9, 11, 12, 13, 21). Short-toed Lark, a summer visitor, is widespread on dry farmland but only common in the Castro Verde steppes and the Sagres Peninsula (10, 21, site F on page 161). Lesser Short-toed Lark is restricted to some salt marshes in the Algarve (13, 20). Woodlark is a widespread bird in montados and dunes with trees. Skylark is a common winter bird in agricultural areas and pastures. It also breeds in the Tejo estuary (1, 2).

Swallows and Martins Swallow and House Martin are common and widespread, a few of the former winter. Red-rumped Swallow is widely distributed too (e.g. 2, 8, 9, 11, 12, 13), and common during autumn migration, with high concentrations on fresh water lakes (e.g. site E on page 137, site A on page 158 and site A on page 195). Sand Martin is mostly seen on passage. It breeds locally (2, 3). Crag Martin breeds on cliffs and rocks (4, 8, 9, 11, 13, 16, site E (Mértola) on page 160) and many stay for winter.

Pipits and Wagtails Tawny Pipit is widespread, breeding in low densities in dunes and open fields (10, 21, 22, 23). Meadow Pipit is an abundant winter visitor of pastures and fields, and Water Pipit winters in marshes and on rice fields. Tree Pipit is a common migrant. Rock Pipit is a rare winter visitor to the coast. Yellow Wagtails of the Iberian *iberae* race breed in low numbers in wetlands along the coast (e.g. 13, site C on page 136), while other races are seen on migration (e.g. 6, 19). Grey Wagtail breeds along rivers (11, 13, 18, site E on page 160) and winters also on other wetlands. White Wagtail is scarce in agricultural areas.

Wren, Accentors, robins and 'chats' Wren is widespread, with low densities breeding in dense underbrush. Dunnock is a widespread winter visitor (best 18) but Alpine Accentor is very local in winter (best 18, 21). Rufous Bush Chat is a scarce breeder in the eastern Alentejo and Algarve (12, 13 site G on page 162). Robin is a scarce breeding bird in Algarve (18). Nightingale is an abundant breeder and passage migrant. Bluethroat is fairly common in winter (6, 15, 19 20, site C on page 136 and site D on page 137). Black Redstart is a scarce breeding bird on rock cliffs at the coast (best 21); numbers increase in winter. Redstart is mostly a bird on passage, but some breed in the Algarve woods (18). Stonechat is a common resident and Whinchat a migrant; both prefer half open areas with scattered shrubs. Wheatear can be very abundant during migration (8, 9, 10, 12, Mina São Domingo and Mértola (both on page 160). Black-eared Wheatear breeds in dry, rocky and open grounds (e.g. 8, 10, 12, 18 and sites A, D, E on pages 158-160).

Thrushes Blue Rock Thrush breeds on dry rocks hills (9, 11, 17, 18, 21, site D and E on page 160). Ring Ouzel is a scarce migrant. Blackbird is common in woodlands. Song Thrush is a common winter visitor and Fieldfare and Redwing are scarce winter visitors. Mistle Thrush is a scarce resident of old oak woodlands.

Warblers Cetti´s Warbler (e.g. 2, 6, 7, 15, 18) and Zitting Cisticola (e.g. 2, 23) are common in any damp areas, the first preferring bushes and the latter grasslands. Reedbed species are Savi´s Warbler (rare, 7), Reed Warbler (scarce) and Great Reed Warbler (6, 7, sites A and B on pages 195-196). Western Olivaceous Warbler is a very rare breeding bird (perhaps 12), while Melodious Warbler is common, particularly in riverine vegetation (2, 8, 10, 13). Sardinian Warbler is common in all scrubland types. Dartford Warbler prefers low scrub (6, 7, 12, 13). Western Subalpine Warbler is common in half open lands with oaks and in higher areas (best 11, site B and E on pages 159-160), while the Spectacled Warbler is a rare bird in salt marshes in the Algarve (13, 14) but more frequent on the Sagres Peninsula (21) and in some inland areas (11). Western Orphean Warbler is rare (9). The odd Whitethroat breeds at Monchique (18) in the Algarve mountains and the Blackcap has a wide distribution in dense, damp woodlands. It is abundant in winter. Other warblers pass through on migration.

Only a few Western Bonelli´s Warbler breed (4, 9, site F on page 139), others are seen during migration. Willow Warbler is common on passage and Chiffchaff on passage and in winter. Iberian Chiffchaff breeds in woodlands in the Algarve mountains, Serra da Arrábida and along the western Alentejo (1, 2, 3, 4, 5, 18, 22, 23). Firecrest breeds at Monchique (18) and is an uncommon winter bird.

Flycatchers Pied Flycatcher can be surprisingly abundant during migration. Spotted Flycather is a widespread but scarce resident and can be abundant during passage.

Shrikes Woodchat Shrike is common in half open lands with scrubs and Iberian Grey Shrike is fairly common, especially near cereal fields and steppes, but also in open montados and pinewoods (e.g. 3, 8, 10, 11).

Crows Jay is widespread in forested areas (e.g 17, 18). Azure-winged Magpie (2, 3, 4, 8, 9, 10, 11, 14, 15, 18, 20) is a common resident and one of the star birds of the region. Common Magpie is more restricted to the west. Jackdaw is scarce and Red-billed Chough breeds at São Vicente (21). Raven is a scarce bird in the area (11). Carrion Crow is widespread, but scarce in the Algarve.

Tits, Nuthatch and treecreepers Long-tailed, Crested, Blue and Great Tit are common. Coal Tit breeds only and in low numbers near Setúbal and near the Spanish border. Penduline Tit is very scarce on coastal marshes in winter (e.g. 2, 3, 15). Nuthatch and Short-toed Treecreeper are widespread.

Starlings and orioles Golden Oriole is regular in riverine forests (8, 10, 12, 16, 18, 22, 23 and near Mértola (site B and E on page 159-160)). Spotless Starling is a common resident, while the (Common) Starling occurs in winter in variable numbers.

Sparrows Tree Sparrow is widespread but scarce. House Sparrow is common everywhere. Spanish Sparrow has increased recently, and can be found in the eastern Alentejo and Algarve (8, 9, 10, 12 and sites D and E on pages 159-160). Rock Sparrow is more widespread (8, 12), but uncommon and largely absent from the southern Algarve.

Finches Chaffinch, Serin, Greenfinch, Goldfinch and Linnet are all common and widespread in open woodland and farmland. In winter, low numbers of Brambling and Siskin appear. Hawfinch is a scarce resident in oak forests and more widespread in winter (Site F on page 139, site A on page 158 and site E on page 160). Crossbill sporadically appears in winter as does Bullfinch.

Buntings Cirl Bunting lives in open woods and riverine forests (3, 4, 9, 11, 17, 18 and Albufeira; site E on page 137). Rock Bunting is resident in rocky terrain with herbal vegetation (4, 9, 11, 13, 17, 18 and along the Guadiana (sites B and E on pages 159-160)). Corn Bunting is abundant in cereal fields and steppes. Reed Bunting winters in reedbeds (7, 15, and freshwater lagoons on site E on page 137 and A and B on pages 195-196). Ortolan Bunting is a scarce migrant.

Exotics The list of exotics of southern Portugal is long. No less than 55 species have been recorded, but only few species have established populations. Among these are Crested Myna which lives in the Lisboa-Setúbal area (e.g. 4, site B on page 135), Common Waxbill (2, 3, 6, 15, 18, 23 and site B on page 196) and Black-headed Weaver (2, 6, 15, site A on page 195) are found in wet and bushy habitats. Confusingly, a few Village Weavers, sometimes also called Black-headed Weaver, have also been reported in reedbeds. Yellow-crowned Bishop (2, 3) is seen in coastal wetlands and Chestnut Munia is mainly found at the Ria de Aveiro (but many have been retrapped for the cagebird trade). Remarkably, a small population of Pin-tailed Whydah, a brood parasite (like Cuckoo), has persisted for some years at Ria de Aveiro by using Common Waxbill as a host. Red Avadavat is established around Elvas (Alentejo) and the Barroca marshes near Lisbon but has also been reported elsewhere. Rose-ringed Parakeets are well established in Lisbon. Monk Parakeet is less common but breeding has been reported from Lisbon and Faro.

ACKNOWLEDGEMENTS

Over the years, the Crossbill Guides Foundation has gathered a large group of naturalists, some of them authors themselves, who have supported us by gathering information, proof-reading, offering photos and so on. Without them, this book good not have been made.

We thank the Bert Snijder and his family, local resident and bird guide for his support, information and excellent photographs that he provided for this guide. Ivo Rodrigues for taking us out and sharing his butterfly and orchid sites in the Alentejo with us. Another thank you for Constant Swinkels, who helped us greatly with assembling the route maps. The Crossbill Guides veterans Kim Lotterman, John Cantelo, Gino Smeulders and Albert Vliegenthart have enriched this guide greatly by checking and complementing the flora, birds, geology and insect chapters respectively. In addition, Kim took upon himself the precise work of creating the species list, while Albert wrote for us the 'other invertebrates'. John meticulously checked all the routes and the bird and historical information and Brian Clews edited the manuscript before going to print. Thanks for all your hard work.

Furthermore, we wish to thank our illustrator Hortst Wolter and all the photographers whose collective work makes you want to see all of southern Portugal's splendour for yourself. Thank you Bert and Eline Snijder, Mark Zekhuis and Bart Vastenhouw, the Saxifraga foundation, Albert Vliegenthart, Wil Luiijf, Rob Mooser, Jörg Mager, Luc Hoogenstein, Kim Lotterman, Cor Fikkert, Frank Jouandoudet, Jan Sohler, Carlos Sanz and Bouke ten Cate.

Finally, we thank of course our own families, in particular Kees' Pilar Uriarte and Dirk's Oscar Lourens, for your continuous support, both at home and in the field. And of course for making the production of this book such a pleasurable experience. For our 2024 reprint we checked and updated the routes. Some of these checks we did ourselves, but for others we are greatly thankful to Berndnaut Smilde and Annegret Kellner, who walked some of the routes and checked some sites in the Algarve.

Dirk Hilbers and Kees Woutersen
February 2024

PICTURE AND ILLUSTRATION CREDITS

In the references that follow, the numbers refer to the pages and the letters to the position on the page (t=top, c=centre, b=bottom, with l and r indicating left and right).

Crossbill Guides / Cate, Boute ten: 174
Crossbill Guides / Hilbers, Dirk: 4 (2nd and 4th from above), 5 (all), 10, 13, 17, 22 (t+b), 23, 28 (t+b), 29, 30 (t+b), 33, 34, 35, 39 (b), 41, 42, 43, 44 (b), 46, 49 (b), 50 (t+b), 51, 52, 54, 60 (t+b), 63, 64, 65 (t), 66, 68 (t, c, b), 69, 70, 71 (t+b), 72 (t, c, b), 81, 84 (t), 96, 100 (t+b), 104 (b), 106, 119, 120 (b), 121, 123 (t+b), 124 (t+b), 125, 127 (t, c, b), 129, 130, 133 (t), 134 (t, c, b), 146 (t+b), 147 (t+b), 149, 153 (t+b), 155 (t, c, b), 157 (t+b), 160 (b), 163, 165, 166 (t + b), 167 (b), 173, 175 (t, c, b), 177 (b), 177 (t+b), 179 (t+b), 181 (t+b), 183 (t, c, b), 185, 187, 188, 197, 198, 201 (t, c, b), 202 (t+b), 203, 204 (t+b), 207 (t, c, b), 208, 210 (t+c), 211 (t+b), 212 (t+b), 213, 215, 216
Crossbill Guides / Lotterman, Kim: 65 (b), 67 (l+r), 93, 138 (l)
Crossbill Guides / Swinkels, Constant: 210 (b)
Crossbill Guides / Vliegenthart, Albert: 101, 102, 103, 105 (t+b), 120 (t+c), 156, 161, 167 (t), 211 (c)
Crossbill Guides / Woutersen, Kees: 4 (3rd from above), 15, 24, 26, 32, 40, 49 (t), 56, 75, 76, 92, 110, 111 (b), 115 (b), 131, 135, 143, 169, 186, 190 (t), 191, 193, 195, 196
Fikkert, Cor: 36 (t), 87, 111 (t+c), 133 (b), 136, 138 (r), 170, 190 (b)
Hoogenstein, Luc: 112
Jouandoudet, Franck: 74
Mager, Jörg: 39 (t), 77 (b), 82 (b), 83, 85, 88, 115 (t), 144 (t), 148, 151
Mooser, Rob: 116
Luiijf, Wil: 94
Sanz, Carlos: 98, 171
Saxifraga / Kruit, Rik: 78
Saxifraga / Vastenhouw, Bart: 194, 205
Saxifraga / Zekhuis, Mark: 27
Sohler, Jan: 84 (b)
Unknown artist: 48
Uriarte, Pilar: 25
Vogels Portugal / Snijder, Bert (www.birdwatchingalentejo.com): 4 (t), 36 (b), 37, 44 (t), 58, 79, 80, 82 (t), 86, 89, 90 (2nd and 4th from top), 91, 114, 144 (b), 152, 159, 160 (t), 178, 210 (t)
Vlinders Portugal / Snijder, Eline (www.vlindersportugal.nl): 99, 104 (t), 140

Commons.wikimedia.org / Charlesjsharp – Sharp Photography, CC BY-SA 4.0: 90 (3rd from top); https://commons.wikimedia.org/w/index.php?curid=53930240
Commons.wikimedia.org / Photo by Laitche – BY-SA 4.0: 90 (t)
https://commons.wikimedia.org/w/index.php?curid=42188975

All illustrations by Crossbill Guides / Wolter, Horst

The following list comprises all species mentioned in this guidebook and gives their scientific, German and Dutch names. It is not a complete checklist of the species of Southern Portugal. Some names have an asterisk (*) behind them, indicating an unofficial name. See page 7 for more details.

Flora

English	Scientific	German	Dutch
Alder	Alnus glutinosa	Schwarz-Erle	Zwarte els
Alkanet, Chalk*	Anchusa calcarea	Kalk-Ochsenzunge*	Kalkossentong*
Alkanet, Large Blue	Anchusa azurea	Italienische Ochsenzunge	Italiaanse ossentong
Allseeds, Stichwort-leaved*	Polycarpon alsinifolium	Miereblättriges Nagelkraut*	Muurbladig kransmuur*
Almond	Prunus dulcis	Mandelbaum	Amandelboom
Anemone, Palmate	Anemone palmata	Iberische Frühlings-Anemone	Mediterrane gele anemoon*
Ash, Narrow-leaved	Fraxinus angustifolia	Schmalblättrige Esche	Smalbladige es
Asphodel, White	Asphodelus albus	Weisser Affodill	Witte affodil
Bartsia, Southern Red	Parentucellia latifolia	Breitblättrige Bartsie	Kleinbloemige ogentroost*
Bartsia, Trixago	Bartsia trixago	Bunte Bellardie	Bellardia
Bartsia, Yellow	Parentucellia viscosa	Klebrige Parentucellie	Kleverige ogentroost
Bellevalia	Bellevalia hackelii	Hackel´s Bellevalie	Algarvedruifjes*
Bellflower, Lusitanian Spreading*	Campanula lusitanica	Lusitanische Wiesen-Glockenblume*	Iberisch weideklokje*
Bellflower, Rampion	Campanula rapunculus	Rapunzel-Glockenblume	Rapunzelklokje
Bindweed, Sea	Convolvulus soldanella	Strandwinde	Zeewinde
Bird's-nest, Violet	Limodorum abortivum	Violetter Dingel	Paarse aspergeorchis
Birthwort, Andalusian*	Aristolochia baetica	Baetische Pfeifenwinde*	Baetische Pijpbloem*
Bluebell, Brown	Dipcadi serotinum	Schweifblatt	Bruine hyacint*
Broomrape, Stinking	Orobanche foetida	Stinkende Sommerwurz	Stinkende bremraap
Bucklar-mustard, Saint Vincent*	Biscutella vicentina	St. Vicent-Brillenschötchen*	Sint Vincent Brilkruid*
Candytuft, Dune	Iberis procumbens	Düne Schleifenblume	Duinscheefbloem*
Capeflower	Arctotheca calendula	Kaplöwenzahn	Zonnengoudsbloem*
Cardoon	Cynara cardunculus	Artischocke, Kardone	Wilde artisjok, Kardoen
Carrot, Sea	Daucus halophilus	Meeres-Möhre*	Zeepeen*
Catchfly, Nice	Silene nicaeensis	Nizza-Leimkraut	Nice-silene*
Catchfly, Pink	Silene colorata	Farbiges Leimkraut	Kleurige silene*
Catchfly, Rothmaler's*	Silene rothmaleri	Algarve-Leimkraut*	Algarve silene*
Catchfly, Seaside*	Silene littorea	Strand-Leimkraut	Strandsilene
Catchfly, Small-flowered	Silene gallica	Französisches Lichtnelke	Franse silene
Centaury, Sea	Centaurium maritimum	Gelbes Tausendguldenkraut	Geel duizendguldenkruid
Cistanche, Yellow	Cistanche phelypaea	Gelbe Cistanche	Cistanche
Cistus, Grey-leaved	Cistus albidus	Weissliche Zistrose	Viltige cistusroos*
Cistus, Gum	Cistus ladanifer	Lackzistrose	Kleverige cistusroos*

Cistus, Narrow-leaved	Cistus monspeliensis	Montpellier-Zistrose	Montpellier cistusroos
Cistus, Poplar-leaved	Cistus populifolius	Pappelblättrige Zistrose	Populierbladige cistusroos*
Cistus, Sage-leaved	Cistus salvifolius	Salbeiblättrige Zistrose	Saliebladige cistusroos
Cistus, Saint Vincent*	Cistus palhinhae	Gefurchte Lack-Zistrose	Saint Vincent cistusroos*
Cistus, Wrinkle-leaved	Cistus crispus	Krause Zistrose	Gekroesde cistusroos
Cottonweed	Otanthus maritimus	Strand-Filzblume	Katoenkruid*
Cowl, Friar's	Arisarum vulgare	Gemeiner Krummstab	Gekapperde kalfsvoet
Crow's-foot, Water	Ranunculus spp.	Wasserhahnenfuss	Waterranonkel
Crowberry, Portuguese	Corema album	Weisse Krähenbeere*	Parelhei*
Crucianella, Coastal	Crucianella maritima	Strand-Kreuzblatt	Kustwalstro*
Cudweed, Pygmy	Filago pygmaea	Zwerg-Edelweiss	Dwergedelweiss*
Daffodil, Cadiz	Narcissus gaditanus	Cadiz-Jonquille	Cadiznarcis*
Daffodil, Hoop-petticoat	Narcissus bulbocodium	Reifrocknarzisse	Hoepelroknarcis
Daffodil, Sea	Pancratium maritimum	Strandlilie	Zeenarcis
Edelweiss, Steppe*	Paronychia capitata	Kopfige Mauermiere	Ronde steppe-edelweis
Eucalyptus	Eucalyptus sp.	Eucalyptus	Eucalyptus
Fern, Royal	Osmunda regalis	Königsfarn	Koningsvaren
Fig	Ficus carica	Feige	Vijg
Fig, Hottentot	Carpobrotus edulis	Gelbe Hottentottenfeige	Hottentotvijg
Figwort, Shrubby	Scrophularia frutescens	Strauch-Braunwurz	Struikhelmkruid*
Fritillary, Spanish	Fritillaria lusitanica	Portugiesische Schachblume	Iberische kievitsbloem
Galactitis	Galactitis tomentosum	Milchfleckdistel	Galactites*
Galingale, Dune	Cyperus capitatus	Dünen-Zypergras	Duincypergras*
Garlic, Rosy	Allium roseum	Rosen-Lauch	Roze look
Garlic, Spring	Allium subvillosum	Zottiger Lauch	Harig look*
Gennaria, Two-leaved	Gennaria diphylla	Zweiblättriger Grünstendel	Tweehartenorchis
Germander, Saint Vincent*	Teucrium vicentinum	Kap Vicente Gamander	St. Vincent gamander
Gladiole, Italian	Gladiolus italicus	Saat Siegwurz	Italiaanse gladiool
Gladiole, Wild	Gladiolus communis	Gewöhnliche Siegwurz	Gewone gladiool
Glasswort	Salicornia & Arthrocnemum	Queller und Gliedermelde	Zeekraal
Goldcoin	Pallenis maritima	Küsten-Sternauge	Dukaatbloem
Gorse, Dense-flowered	Ulex densus	Portugiesischer Stechginster*	Portugese gaspeldoor
Grape-hyacinth	Muscari neglectum	Weinbergs-Traubenhyazinthe	Troshyacint
Grass, Marram	Ammophila arenaria	Strandhafer	Helm
Greenweed, Spiny	Genista hirsuta	Behaarter Ginster	Behaarde brem*
Gromwell, Creeping	Lithodora prostrata	Niederliegender Steinsame	Liggend parelzaad*
Gromwell, Scrambling	Lithodora diffusa	Blauer Steinsame	Kruipend parelzaad*
Heath, Umbel-flowered	Erica umbellata	Schirmheide*	Schermdophei*
Heather	Calluna vulgaris	Heidekraut	Struikhei
Hedge-nettle, White	Prasium majus	Grosser Klippenziest	Klipnetel*
Helleborine, Portuguese	Epipactis lusitanica	Portugiesische Ständelwurz	Portugese wespenorchis*
Helleborine, Tremols	Epipactis tremolsii	Tremols-Stendelwurz*	Tremols' wespenorchi
Holly, Sea	Eryngium maritimum	Stranddistel	Blauwe zeedistel

Honeysuckle, Etruscan	*Lonicera etrusca*	Toskanisches Geissblatt	Toscaanse kamperfoelie*
Hyacinth, Tassel	*Muscari comosum*	Schopfige Traubenhyazinthe	Kuifhyacint
Iris, Spanish	*Iris xiphium*	Spanische Schwertlilie	Spaanse lis
Iris, Yellow	*Iris pseudacorus*	Sumpf-Schwertlilie	Gele lis
Jerusalem-sage, Iberian	*Phlomis lychnitis*	Filziges Brandkraut	Viltbrandkruid*
Jerusalem-sage, Purple	*Phlomis purpurea*	Purpurrotes Brandkraut	Paars brandkruid*
Juniper, Phoenician	*Juniperus phoenicea*	Phönizischer Wacholder	Phoenicische jeneverbes
Knapweed, Round-headed	*Centaurea sphaerocephala*	Kugelkopf- Flockenblume	Stekelkopcentaurie*
Lady's-tresses, Summer	*Spiranthes aestivalis*	Sommer-Drehwurz	Zomerschroeforchis
Lavender, French	*Lavandula stoechas*	Schopflavendel	Kuiflavendel
Lavender, Green	*Lavandula viridis*	Grüner Lavendel	Groene lavendel
Limoniastrum	*Limoniastrum monopetalum*	Strauch-Strandflieder	Struiklamsoor*
Lords-and-Ladies	*Arum maculatum*	Gefleckter Aronstab	Gevlekte aronskelk
Lupin, Narrow-leaved	*Lupinus angustifolius*	Schmallblättrige Lupine	Blauwe lupine
Lupin, Yellow	*Lupinus luteus*	Gelbe Lupine	Gele lupine
Mallow, Tree	*Lavatera arborea*	Baum-Lavatere	Boomkaasjeskruid
Marigold, Corn	*Glebionis segetum*	Saat-Wucherblume	Gele ganzenbloem
Marigold, Marsh	*Caltha palustris*	Sumpf-Dotterblume	Dotterbloem
Mezereon, Mediterranean	*Daphne gnidium*	Herbst-Seidelbast	Herfstpeperboompje*
Milkvetch, Lusitanian	*Erophaca baetica*	Lusitanischer Tragant	Reuzenhokjespeul*
Myrtle	*Myrtus communis*	Myrte	Mirte
Narcissus, Autumn	*Narcissus serotinus*	Spätblühende Narzisse	Herfstnarcis*
Nut, Barbary	*Moraea sisyrinchium*	Mittags-Schwertlilie	Barbarijse lis*
Oak, Algerian	*Quercus canariensis*	Kanarische Eiche	Canarische eik*
Oak, Cork	*Quercus suber*	Korkeiche	Kurkeik
Oak, Holm	*Quercus (ilex) rotundifolia*	Steineiche	Steeneik
Oak, Kermes	*Quercus coccifera*	Kermes-Eiche	Hulsteik
Oak, Portuguese	*Quercus faginea*	Portugiesische Eiche	Portugese eik
Oleander, Wild	*Nerium oleander*	Oleander	Oleander
Olive, Wild	*Olea europea*	Ölbaum	Wilde olijfboom
Orache, Shrubby	*Atriplex halimus*	Strauch-Melde	Struikmelde
Orchid, (Common) Tongue	*Serapias lingua*	Einschwieliger Zugenstendel	Gewone tongorchis
Orchid, Bee	*Ophrys apifera*	Bienen-Ragwurz	Bijenorchis
Orchid, Black Spider	*Ophrys (sphegodes ssp.) atrata*	Schwarze Ragwurz	Zwarte spinnenophrys
Orchid, Bumblebee	*Ophrys bombyliflora*	Drohnen-Ragwurz	Weidehommelorchis
Orchid, Champagne	*Anacamptis champagneuxii*	Dreiknolliges Knabenkraut	Blesharlekijn
Orchid, Fan-lipped	*Anacamptis collina*	Hügel-Knabenkraut	Heuvelorchis
Orchid, Giant	*Himantoglossum robertianum*	Roberts Mastorchis	Hyacinthorchis
Orchid, Green-winged	*Orchis morio*	Kleines Knabenkraut	Harlekijn
Orchid, Heart-flowered Tongue	*Serapias cordigera*	Herzförmiger Zungenstendel	Brede tongorchis
Orchid, Long-lipped Tongue	*Serapias vomeracea*	Pflugschar Zungenstendel	Lange tongorchis
Orchid, Lusitanian Mirror	*Ophrys (speculum ssp.) lusitanica*	Iberische Spiegel-Ragwurz	Iberische spiegelorchis*
Orchid, Man	*Orchis anthropophora*	Ohnsporn	Poppenorchis
Orchid, Mirror	*Ophrys speculum*	Spiegel-Ragwurz	Spiegelorchis

SPECIES LIST & TRANSLATION

Orchid, Naked-man	Orchis italica	Italienisches Knabenkraut	Italiaanse orchis
Orchid, Painted	Anacamptis (morio ssp.) picta	Lockerblutiges Kleines Knabenkraut	Slanke harlekijn
Orchid, Pink Butterfly	Anacamptis papilionacea	Schmetterlings-Knabenkraut	Vlinderorchis
Orchid, Pyramidal	Anacamptis pyramidalis	Hundswurz	Hondskruid
Orchid, Sawfly	Ophrys tenthredinifera	Wespen-Ragwurz	Wolzweverorchis
Orchid, Sharp-lipped Tongue	Serapias strictiflora	Gespreizter Zungenstendel	Scherpe tongorchis*
Orchid, Small-flowered Tongue	Serapias parviflora	Kleinblütiger Zungenstendel	Kleine tongorchis
Orchid, Sombre Bee	Ophrys fusca	Braune Ragwurz	Bruine orchis
Orchid, Southern Early Purple*	Orchis olbiensis	Hyères-Knabenkraut	Kleine mannetjesorchis
Orchid, Spanish Omega	Ophrys dyris	Marokkanische Ragwurz	Dyris orchis*
Orchid, Woodcock	Ophrys scolopax	Schnepfen-Ragwurz	Snippenorchis
Orchid, Yellow Bee	Ophrys lutea	Gelbe Ragwurz	Gele orchis
Peony, Western	Paeonia broteri	Westliche Pfingstrose*	Westelijke pioenroos*
Periwinkle, Great	Vinca major	Grosses Immergrün	Grote maagdenpalm
Pimpernel, Shrubby	Anagallis monelli	Leinblättriger Gauchheil	Struikguichelheil*
Pine, Umbrella	Pinus pinea	Pinie	Parasolden
Plant, Italian Curry	Helichrysum italicum	Italienische Strohblume	Kerrieplant
Purslane, Sea	Atriplex portulacoides	Portulak-Salzmelde	Gewone zoutmelde
Quillwort, Mediterranean*	Isoetes histrix	Land-Brachsenkraut	Landbiesvaren*
Restharrow, Branched*	Ononis ramosissima	Vielästige Hauhechel	Vertakt stalkruid*
Restharrow, Yellow	Ononis natrix	Gelbe Hauhechel	Geel stalkruid
Rockrose, Spotted	Tuberaria guttata	Geflecktes Sonnenröschen	Gevlekt zonneroosje
Rockrose, Yellow	Halimium calycinum	Küsten- Zistrose	Smalbladig struik-zonneroosje*
Rockrose, Yellow Scrub	Halimium halimifolium	Gelbe Zistrose	Geel struikzonneroosje
Rosemary	Rosmarinus officinalis	Rosmarin	Rozemarijn
Sand-crocus, (Large-flowered)	Romulea bulbocodium	Grossblütiger Scheinkrokus	Grootbloemige schijnkrokus*
Saxifrage, Meadow	Saxifraga granulata	Knöllchen-Steinbrech	Knolsteenbreek
Seablite	Suaeda maritima	Strand-Sode	Klein schorrenkruid
Sea-lavender, Common	Limonium vulgare	Gewöhnlicher Strandflieder	Lamsoor
Snapdragon	Antirrhinum majus	Garten-Löwenmaul	Grote leeuwenbek
Snowflake, Autumn	Leucojum autumnale	Herbst-Knotenblume	Herfstklokje
Snowflake, Three-leaved	Leucojum trichophyllum	Dreiblat-Knotenblume*	Driebladig sneeuwklok
Sorrel, Cape	Oxalis pes-caprae	Nickender Sauerklee	Knikkende klaverzurin
Spurge, Monchique	Euphorbia monchiquensis	Monchique-Wolfsmilch*	Monchique wolfsmelk
Spurge, Sea	Euphorbia paralias	Strand-Wolfsmilch	Zeewolfsmelk
Squill, Autumn	Scilla autumnalis	Herbst-Blaustern	Herfststerhyacint
Squill, One-leaved	Scilla monophyllos	Einblättriger Blaustern	Eenbladige sterhyacin
Squill, Portuguese	Scilla peruviana	Peru-Blaustern	Portugese sterhyacint
Squill, Saint Vincent's	Hyacinthoides (mauritanica) vicentina	Kap Vicente Hasenglöckchen*	St. Vincent hyacint*
Squill, Sea	Drimia maritima	Meerzwiebel	Zeeui
Stock, Sea	Malcolmia littorea	Strand-Malcolmie	Zeeviolier
Stonecrop, Mossy	Crassula tillaea	Moosblümchen	Mosbloempje

English	Scientific	German	Dutch
Stonecrop, Pale	Sedum sediforme	Felsen-Fetthenne	Rotsvetkruid*
Sundew, Portuguese	Drosophyllum lusitanicum	Taublatt	Portugese zonnendauw
Tamarisk	Tamarix sp.	Tamarisk	Tamarisk
Thistle, Golden	Scolymus hispanicus	Spanische Golddistel	Spaanse gouddistel
Thrift, Rouyan's	Armeria rouyana	Rouyan's Grasnelke*	Rouyan's Engels gras*
Thrift, Spiny	Armeria pungens	Stechende Grasnelke	Stekend Engels gras*
Thyme, Camphor	Thymus camphoratus	Kampfer-Thymian	Kamfertijm
Toadflax, Algarve	Linaria algarviana	Algarve Leinkraut	Algarve leeuwenbek*
Toadflax, Ballast*	Linaria spartea	Ruten-Leinkraut	IJle vlasbek*
Toadflax, Ficalho	Linaria ficalhoana	Ficalho-Leinkraut*	Ficalho leeuwenbek*
Toadflax, Malling	Chaenorhinum origanifolium	Majoranblättriger Orant	Marjoleinbekje
Tolpis	Tolpis barbata	Christusauge	Tolpis
Tree, Blue Gum	Eucalyptus globulus	Blauer Eukalyptus	Blauwe gomboom
Tree, Carob	Ceratonia siliqua	Johannisbrotbaum	Johannesbroodboom
Tree, Strawberry	Arbutus unedo	Erdbeerbaum	Aardbeiboom
Tulip, Wild	Tulipa australis	Südliche Tulpe	Zuidelijke tulp
Violet, Shrubby	Viola arborescens	Holz-Veilchen*	Houtviooltje*
Viper's-bugloss, Purple	Echium plantagineum	Wegerichblättriger Natterkopf	Weegbreeslangenkruid
Weld, Spade-leaved	Sesamoides spathulifolia	Spatelblättrige Sternfrücht	Spatelschijnreseda*
Willow, Mediterranean	Salix pedicellata	Mittelmeerweide*	Mediterrane wilg*

Mammals

English	Scientific	German	Dutch
Badger	Meles meles	Dachs	Das
Barbastelle	Barbastella barbastellus	Mopsfledermaus	Mopsvleermuis
Bat, Brown Long-eared	Plecotus auritus	Braunes Langohr	Gewone grootoorvleermuis
Bat, Daubenton's	Myotis daubentonii	Wasserfledermaus	Watervleermuis
Bat, European Free-tailed	Tadarida teniotis	Bulldoggfledermaus	Bulvleermuis
Bat, Geoffroy's	Myotis emarginatus	Wimperfledermaus	Ingekorven vleermuis
Bat, Greater Horse-shoe	Rhinolophus ferrumequinum	Grosse Hufeisennase	Grote hoefijzerneus
Bat, Greater Mouse-eared	Myotis myotis	Grosses Mausohr	Vale vleermuis
Bat, Grey Long-eared	Plecotus austriacus	Graues Langohr	Grijze grootoorvleermuis
Bat, Lesser Horse-shoe	Rhinolophus hipposideros	Kleine Hufeisennase	Kleine hoefijzerneus
Bat, Lesser Mouse-eared	Myotis blythii	Kleines Mausohr	Kleine vale vleermuis
Bat, Mediterranean Horse-shoe	Rhinolophus euryale	Mittelmeerhufeisennase	Paarse hoefijzerneus
Bat, Mehely's Horse-shoe	Rhinolophus mehelyi	Mehely-Hufeisennase	Mehely's hoefijzerneus
Bat, Natterer's	Myotis nattereri	Fransenfledermaus	Franjestaart
Bat, Schreiber's	Miniopteris schreibersii	Langflügelfledermaus	Schreibers' vleermuis
Bat, Serotine	Eptesicus serotinus	Breitflügelfledermaus	Laatvlieger
Boar, Wild	Sus scrofa	Wildschwein	Wild zwijn
Deer, Fallow	Damus damus	Dammhirsch	Damhert
Deer, Red	Cervus elaphus	Rothirsch	Edelhert
Deer, Roe	Capreolus capreolus	Reh	Ree
Dolphin, Bottlenose	Tursiops truncatus	Grosstümmler	Tuimelaar
Dolphin, Common	Delphinus delphis	Delphin	Gewone dolfijn

English	Scientific	German	Dutch
Dolphin, Risso´s	*Grampus griseus*	Rundkopfdelfin	Gramper, Grijze dolfijn
Dolphin, Striped	*Stenella coeruleoalba*	Streifendelfin	Gestreepte dolfijn
Dormouse, Garden	*Eliomys quercinus*	Gartenschläfer	Eikelmuis
Fox, Red	*Vulpes vulpes*	Rotfuchs	Vos
Genet	*Genetta genetta*	Ginsterkatze	Genetkat
Hare, Iberian	*Lepus granatensis*	Iberische Hase	Iberische haas
Hedgehog, Common	*Erinaceus europeus*	Braunbustigel	Egel
Lynx, Iberian	*Lynx pardinus*	Pardelluchs	Pardellynx, Iberische lynx
Marten, Beech	*Martes foina*	Steinmarder	Steenmarter
Mole, Iberian	*Talpa occidentalis*	Iberischer Maulwurf	Iberische blinde mol
Mongoose, Egyptian	*Herpestes ichneumon*	Ichneumon	Mangoeste
Mouse, Western House	*Mus musculus domesticus*	Westliche Hausmaus	Westelijke huismuis
Mouse, Wood	*Apodemus sylvaticus*	Waldmaus	Bosmuis
Noctule, Lesser	*Nyctalus leisleri*	Kleinabendsegler	Bosvleermuis
Orca	*Orcinus orca*	Schwertwal	Orca
Otter	*Lutra lutra*	Fischotter	Otter
Pipistrelle, Common	*Pipistrellus pipistrellus*	Zwergfledermaus	Gewone dwergvleermu
Pipistrelle, Kuhl´s	*Pipistrellus kuhlii*	Weissrandfledermaus	Kuhl's dwergvleermuis
Pipistrelle, Soprano	*Pipistrellus pygmaeus*	Mückenfledermaus	Kleine dwergvleermuis
Polecat, European	*Mustela putorius*	Waldiltis	Bunzing
Porpoise, Harbour	*Phocoena phocoena*	Schweinswal	Bruinvis
Rabbit	*Oryctolagus cuniculus*	Wildkaninchen	Konijn
Shrew, Etruscan (Pygmy)	*Suncus etruscus*	Etruskerspitzmaus	Wimperspitsmuis
Shrew, Greater White-toothed	*Crocidura russula*	Hausspitzmaus	Huisspitsmuis
Shrew, Iberian	*Sorex granarius*	Iberische Waldspitzmaus	Iberische bosspitsmuis
Vole, Cabrera´s	*Microtus cabrerae*	Cabrera-Wühlmaus	Cabrerawoelmuis
Vole, Lusitanian Pine	*Microtus lusitanicus*	Iberische Kleinwühlmaus	Baskische woelmuis
Vole, Mediterranean Pine	*Microtus duodecimcostatus*	Mittelmeer-Kleinwühlmaus	Provençaalse woelmuis
Vole, Southwestern Water	*Arvicola sapidus*	Westschermaus	West-Europese woelra
Weasel	*Mustela nivalis*	Mauswiesel	Wezel
Whale, False Killer	*Pseudorca crassidens*	Kleiner Schwertwal	Zwarte zwaardwalvis
Whale, Long-finned Pilot	*Globicephala melas*	Grindwal	Griend
Whale, Minke	*Balaenoptera acutorostrata*	Zwergwal	Dwergvinvis
Wildcat	*Felis silvestris*	Wildkatze	Wilde kat

Birds

English	Scientific	German	Dutch
Accentor, Alpine	*Prunella collaris*	Alpenbraunelle	Alpenheggemus
Avadavat, Red	*Amandava amandava*	Tigerfink	Tijgervink
Avocet	*Recurvirostra avosetta*	Säbelschnäbler	Kluut
Bee-eater	*Merops apiaster*	Bienenfresser	Bijeneter
Bishop, Yellow-crowned	*Euplectes afer*	Tahaweber	Napoleonwever
Bittern, Little	*Ixobrychus minutus*	Zwergdommel	Woudaapje
Blackbird	*Turdus merula*	Amsel	Merel
Blackcap	*Sylvia atricapilla*	Mönchsgrasmücke	Zwartkop
Bluethroat	*Luscinia svecica*	Blaukehlchen	Blauwborst
Brambling	*Fringilla montifringilla*	Bergfink	Keep
Bullfinch	*Pyrrhula pyrrhula*	Gimpel	Goudvink

Bunting, Cirl	*Emberiza cirlus*	Zaunammer	Cirlgors
Bunting, Corn	*Miliaria calandra*	Grauammer	Grauwe gors
Bunting, Ortolan	*Emberiza hortulana*	Ortolan	Ortolaan
Bunting, Reed	*Emberiza schoeniclus*	Rohrammer	Rietgors
Bunting, Rock	*Emberiza cia*	Zippammer	Grijze gors
Bustard, Great	*Otis tarda*	Grosstrappe	Grote trap
Bustard, Little	*Tetrax tetrax*	Zwergtrappe	Kleine trap
Buzzard	*Buteo buteo*	Mäusebussard	Buizerd
Buzzard, Honey	*Pernis apivorus*	Wespenbussard	Wespendief
Chaffinch	*Fringilla coelebs*	Buchfink	Vink
Chat, Rufous Bush	*Erythropygia galactotes*	Heckensänger	Rosse waaierstaart
Chiffchaff, (Common)	*Phylloscopus collybita*	Zilpzalp	Tjiftjaf
Chiffchaff, Iberian	*Phylloscopus ibericus*	Iberischer Zilpzalp	Iberische tjiftjaf
Chough, Red-billed	*Pyrrhocorax pyrrhocorax*	Alpenkrähe	Alpenkraai
Cisticola, Zitting	*Cisticola juncidis*	Cistensänger	Graszanger
Coot, Common	*Fulica atra*	Blässhuhn	Meerkoet
Coot, Crested	*Fulica cristata*	Kammblässhuhn	Knobbelmeerkoet
Cormorant, Great	*Phalacrocorax carbo*	Kormoran	Aalscholver
Crakes	*Rallidae*	Rallen	Rallen
Crane	*Grus grus*	Kranich	Kraanvogel
Crow, Carrion	*Corvus corone*	Aaskrähe	Zwarte kraai
Cuckoo, Common	*Cuculus canorus*	Kuckuck	Koekoek
Cuckoo, Great Spotted	*Clamator glandarius*	Häherkuckuck	Kuifkoekoek
Curlew	*Numenius arquata*	Grosser Brachvogel	Wulp
Curlew, Stone	*Burhinus oedicnemus*	Triel	Griel
Diver, Great Northern	*Gavia immer*	Eistaucher	IJsduiker
Diver, Red-throated	*Gavia stellata*	Sterntaucher	Roodkeelduiker
Dotterel	*Charadrius morinellus*	Mornellregenpfeifer	Morinelplevier
Dove, Collared	*Streptopelia decaocto*	Türkentaube	Turkse tortel
Dove, Stock	*Columba oenas*	Hohltaube	Holenduif
Dove, Turtle	*Streptopelia turtur*	Turteltaube	Tortelduif
Duck, Ferruginous	*Aythya nyroca*	Moorente	Witoogeend
Duck, Tufted	*Aythya fuligula*	Reiherente	Kuifeend
Dunlin	*Calidris alpina*	Alpenstrandläufer	Bonte strandloper
Dunnock	*Prunella modularis*	Heckenbraunelle	Heggenmus
Eagle, Bonelli´s	*Hieraaetus fasciatus*	Habichtsadler	Havikarend
Eagle, Booted	*Hieraaetus pennatus*	Zwergadler	Dwergarend
Eagle, Golden	*Aquila chrysaetos*	Steinadler	Steenarend
Eagle, Short-toed	*Circaetus gallicus*	Schlangenadler	Slangenarend
Eagle, Spanish Imperial	*Aquila adalberti*	Spanischer Kaiseradler	Spaanse keizerarend
Egret, Cattle	*Bubulcus ibis*	Kuhreiher	Koereiger
Egret, Great White	*Ardea alba*	Silberreiher	Grote zilverreiger
Egret, Little	*Egretta garzetta*	Seidenreiher	Kleine zilverreiger
Falcon, Eleonora´s	*Falco eleonorae*	Eleonorenfalke	Eleonora's valk
Falcon, Peregrine	*Falco peregrinus*	Wanderfalke	Slechtvalk
Fieldfare	*Turdus pilaris*	Wacholderdrossel	Kramsvogel
Firecrest	*Regulus ignicapillus*	Sommergoldhähnchen	Vuurgoudhaantje
Flamingo, (Greater)	*Phoenicopterus roseus*	Flamingo	Europese flamingo
Flycatcher, Pied	*Ficedula hypoleuca*	Trauerschnäpper	Bonte vliegenvanger
Flycatcher, Spotted	*Muscicapa striata*	Grauschnäpper	Grauwe vliegenvanger

SPECIES LIST & TRANSLATION

Gadwall	*Anas strepera*	Schnatterente	Krakeend
Gallinule, Purple	*Porphyrio porphyrio*	Purpurhuhn	Purperkoet
Gannet	*Morus bassanus*	Basstölpel	Jan-van-gent
Garganey	*Anas querquedula*	Knäkente	Zomertaling
Godwit, Bar-tailed	*Limosa lapponica*	Pfuhlschnepfe	Rosse grutto
Godwit, Black-tailed	*Limosa limosa*	Uferschnepfe	Grutto
Goldfinch	*Carduelis carduelis*	Distelfink	Putter
Goose, Greylag	*Anser anser*	Graugans	Grauwe gans
Goshawk	*Accipiter gentilis*	Habicht	Havik
Grebe, Black-necked	*Podiceps nigricollis*	Schwarzhalstaucher	Geoorde fuut
Grebe, Great Crested	*Podiceps cristatus*	Haubentaucher	Fuut
Grebe, Little	*Tachybaptus ruficollis*	Zwergtaucher	Dodaars
Greenfinch	*Carduelis chloris*	Grünling	Groenling
Greenshank	*Tringa nebularia*	Grünschenkel	Groenpootruiter
Gull, Audouin's	*Ichthyaetus audouinii*	Korallenmöwe	Adouins meeuw
Gull, Black-headed	*Larus ridibundus*	Lachmöwe	Kokmeeuw
Gull, Great Black-backed	*Larus marinus*	Mantelmöwe	Grote mantelmeeuw
Gull, Lesser Black-backed	*Larus graellsii*	Heringsmöwe	Kleine mantelmeeuw
Gull, Mediterranean	*Ichthyaetus melanocephalus*	Schwarzkopfmöwe	Zwartkopmeeuw
Gull, Ring-billed	*Larus delawarensis*	Ringschnabelmöwe	Ringsnavelmeeuw
Gull, Sabine's	*Xema sabini*	Schwalbenmöwe	Vorkstaartmeeuw
Gull, Yellow-legged	*Larus michahellis*	Weisskopfmöve	Geelpootmeeuw
Harrier, Hen	*Circus cyaneus*	Kornweihe	Blauwe kiekendief
Harrier, Marsh	*Circus aeruginosus*	Rohrweihe	Bruine kiekendief
Harrier, Montagu's	*Circus pygargus*	Wiesenweihe	Grauwe kiekendief
Hawfinch	*Coccothraustes coccothraustes*	Kernbeisser	Appelvink
Heron, Grey	*Ardea cinerea*	Graureiher	Blauwe reiger
Heron, Night	*Nycticorax nycticorax*	Nachtreiher	Kwak
Heron, Purple	*Ardea purpurea*	Purpurreiher	Purperreiger
Heron, Squacco	*Ardeola ralloides*	Rallenreiher	Ralreiger
Hobby	*Falco subbuteo*	Baumfalke	Boomvalk
Hoopoe	*Upupa epops*	Wiedehopf	Hop
Ibis, Glossy	*Plegadis falcinellus*	Braunsichler	Zwarte ibis
Jackdaw	*Corvus monedula*	Dohle	Kauw
Jay	*Garrulus glandarius*	Eichelhäher	Gaai
Kestrel, Common	*Falco tinnunculus*	Turmfalke	Torenvalk
Kestrel, Lesser	*Falco naumanni*	Rötelfalke	Kleine torenvalk
Kingfisher	*Alcedo atthis*	Eisvogel	IJsvogel
Kite, Black	*Milvus migrans*	Schwarzmilan	Zwarte wouw
Kite, Black-winged	*Elanus caeruleus*	Gleitaar	Grijze wouw
Kite, Red	*Milvus milvus*	Rotmilan	Rode wouw
Knot	*Calidris canutus*	Knutt	Kanoet
Lapwing	*Vanellus vanellus*	Kiebitz	Kievit
Lark, Calandra	*Melanocorypha calandra*	Kalanderlerche	Kalanderleeuwerik
Lark, Crested	*Galerida cristata*	Haubenlerche	Kuifleeuwerik
Lark, Lesser Short-toed	*Calandrella rufescens*	Stummellerche	Kleine kortteenleeuweril
Lark, Short-toed	*Calandrella brachydactyla*	Kurzzehenlerche	Kortteenleeuwerik
Lark, Thekla's	*Galerida theklae*	Theklalerche	Theklaleeuwerik
Linnet	*Carduelis cannabina*	Bluthänfling	Kneu

Magpie, Azure-winged	*Cyanopica cyana*	Blauelster	Blauwe ekster
Magpie, Common	*Pica pica*	Elster	Ekster
Mallard	*Anas platyrhynchos*	Stockente	Wilde eend
Martin, Crag	*Ptyonoprogne rupestris*	Felsenschwalbe	Rotszwaluw
Martin, House	*Delichon urbicum*	Mehlschwalbe	Huiszwaluw
Martin, Sand	*Riparia riparia*	Uferschwalbe	Oeverzwaluw
Merganser, Red-breasted	*Mergus serrator*	Mittelsäger	Middelste zaagbek
Merlin	*Falco columbarius*	Merlin	Smelleken
Moorhen	*Gallinula chloropus*	Teichhuhn	Waterhoen
Munia, Black-headed	See: Munia, Tricoloured		
Munia, Scaly-breasted	*Lonchura punctulata*	Muskatamadine	Muskaatvink
Munia, Tricoloured	*Lonchura malacca*	Schwarzbauchnonne	Driekleurennon
Myna, Crested	*Acridotheres cristatellus*	Haubenmaina	Kuifmaina
Nightingale	*Luscinia megarhynchos*	Nachtigal	Nachtegaal
Nightjar, European	*Caprimulgus europaeus*	Ziegenmelker	Nachtzwaluw
Nightjar, Red-necked	*Caprimulgus ruficollis*	Rothals-Ziegenmelker	Moorse nachtzwaluw
Nuthatch	*Sitta europaea*	Kleiber	Boomklever
Oriole, Golden	*Oriolus oriolus*	Pirol	Wielewaal
Osprey	*Pandion haliaetus*	Fischadler	Visarend
Ouzel, Ring	*Turdus torquatus*	Ringdrossel	Beflijster
Owl, Barn	*Tyto alba*	Schleiereule	Kerkuil
Owl, Eagle	*Bubo bubo*	Uhu	Oehoe
Owl, Little	*Athene noctua*	Steinkauz	Steenuil
Owl, Long-eared Owl	*Asio otus*	Waldohreule	Ransuil
Owl, Scops	*Otus scops*	Zwergohreule	Dwergooruil
Owl, Short-eared Owl	*Asio flammeus*	Sumpfohreule	Velduil
Owl, Tawny	*Strix aluco*	Waldkauz	Bosuil
Oystercatcher	*Haematopus ostralegus*	Austernfischer	Scholekster
Parakeet, Ring-necked	*Psittacula krameri*	Halsbandsittich	Halsbandparkiet
Partridge, Red-legged	*Alectoris rufa*	Rothuhn	Rode patrijs
Peregrine	See: Falcon, Peregrine		
Pigeon, Feral	*Columba livia f. domestica*	Stadttaube	Stadsduif
Pigeon, Wood	*Columba palumbus*	Ringeltaube	Houtduif
Pintail	*Anas acuta*	Spiessente	Pijlstaart
Pipit, Meadow	*Anthus pratensis*	Wiesenpieper	Graspieper
Pipit, Red-throated	*Anthus cervinus*	Rotkehlpieper	Roodkeelpieper
Pipit, Rock	*Anthus petrosus*	Strandpieper	Oeverpieper
Pipit, Tawny	*Anthus campestris*	Brachpieper	Duinpieper
Pipit, Tree	*Anthus trivialis*	Baumpieper	Boompieper
Pipit, Water	*Anthus spinoletta*	Bergpieper	Waterpieper
Plover, Golden	*Pluvialis apricaria*	Goldregenpfeifer	Goudplevier
Plover, Grey	*Pluvialis squatarola*	Kiebitzregenpfeifer	Zilverplevier
Plover, Kentish	*Charadrius alexandrinus*	Seeregenpfeifer	Strandplevier
Plover, Little Ringed	*Charadrius dubius*	Flussregenpfeifer	Kleine plevier
Plover, Ringed	*Charadrius hiaticula*	Sandregenpfeifer	Bontbekplevier
Pochard	*Aythya ferina*	Tafelente	Tafeleend
Pochard, Red-crested	*Netta rufina*	Kolbenente	Krooneend
Pratincole, Collared	*Glareola pratincola*	Rotflügel-Brachschwalbe	Vorkstaartplevier
Puffin	*Fratercula arctica*	Papageitaucher	Papegaaiduiker
Quail	*Coturnix coturnix*	Wachtel	Kwartel

Rail, Water	*Rallus aquaticus*	Wasserralle	Waterral
Raven	*Corvus corax*	Kolkrabe	Raaf
Razorbill	*Alca torda*	Tordalk	Alk
Redshank	*Tringa totanus*	Rotschenkel	Tureluur
Redshank, Spotted	*Tringa erythropus*	Dunkler Wasserläufer	Zwarte ruiter
Redstart	*Phoenicurus phoenicurus*	Gartenrotschwanz	Gekraagde roodstaart
Redstart, Black	*Phoenicurus ochruros*	Hausrotschwanz	Zwarte roodstaart
Redwing	*Turdus iliacus*	Rotdrossel	Koperwiek
Robin	*Erithacus rubecula*	Rotkehlchen	Roodborst
Roller	*Coracias garrulus*	Blauracke	Scharrelaar
Ruff	*Philomachus pugnax*	Kampfläufer	Kemphaan
Sanderling	*Calidris alba*	Sanderling	Drieteenstrandloper
Sandgrouse, Black-bellied	*Pterocles orientalis*	Sandflughuhn	Zwartbuikzandhoen
Sandgrouse, Pin-tailed	*Pterocles alchata*	Spiessflughuhn	Witbuikzandhoen
Sandpiper, Common	*Actitis hypoleucos*	Flussuferläufer	Oeverloper
Sandpiper, Curlew	*Calidris feruginea*	Sichelstrandläufer	Krombekstrandloper
Sandpiper, Green	*Tringa ochropus*	Waldwasserläufer	Witgat
Sandpiper, Purple	*Calidris maritima*	Meerstrandläufer	Paarse strandloper
Sandpiper, Wood	*Tringa glareola*	Bruchwasserläufer	Bosruiter
Scaup	*Aythya marila*	Bergente	Topper
Scoter, Common	*Melanitta nigra*	Trauerente	Zwarte zee-eend
Serin	*Serinus serinus*	Girlitz	Europese kanarie
Shag	*Phalacrocorax aristotelis*	Krähenscharbe	Kuifaalscholver
Shearwater, Balearic	*Puffinus mauretanicus*	Balearensturmtaucher	Vale pijlstormvogel
Shearwater, Cory´s (Scopoli's)	*Calonectris borealis*	Kanarensturmtaucher	Kuhls pijlstormvogel
Shearwater, Great	*Puffinus gravis*	Grosser Sturmtaucher	Grote pijlstormvogel
Shearwater, Scopoli's	*Calonectris diomedea*	Gelbschnabelsturmtaucher	Scopoli's pijlstormvo
Shearwater, Sooty	*Puffinus griseus*	Dunkler Sturmtaucher	Grauwe pijlstormvoge
Shelduck	*Tadorna tadorna*	Brandgans	Bergeend
Shoveler	*Anas clypeata*	Löffelente	Slobeend
Shrike, Iberian Grey	*Lanius meridionalis*	Südlicher Raubwürger	Zuidelijke klapekster
Shrike, Woodchat	*Lanius senator*	Rotkopfwürger	Roodkopklauwier
Siskin	*Carduelis spinus*	Erlenzeisig	Sijs
Skua, Arctic	*Stercorarius parasiticus*	Schmarotzerraubmöwe	Kleine Jager
Skua, Great	*Stercorarius skua*	Skua	Grote jager
Skylark	*Alauda arvensis*	Feldlerche	Veldleeuwerik
Snipe, Common	*Gallinago gallinago*	Bekassine	Watersnip
Sparrow, House	*Passer domesticus*	Haussperling	Huismus
Sparrow, Rock	*Petronia petronia*	Steinsperling	Rotsmus
Sparrow, Spanish	*Passer hispaniolensis*	Weidensperling	Spaanse mus
Sparrow, Tree	*Passer montanus*	Feldsperling	Ringmus
Sparrowhawk	*Accipiter nisus*	Sperber	Sperwer
Spoonbill	*Platalea leucorodia*	Löffler	Lepelaar
Starling, Common	*Sturnus vulgaris*	Star	Spreeuw
Starling, Spotless	*Sturnus unicolor*	Einfarbstar	Zwarte spreeuw
Stilt, Black-winged	*Himantopus himantopus*	Stelzenläufer	Steltkluut
Stint, Little	*Calidris minuta*	Zwergstrandläufer	Kleine strandloper
Stint, Temminck´s	*Calidris temminckii*	Temminckstrandläufer	Temmincks strandlop
Stonechat	*Saxicola torquata*	Schwarzkehlchen	Roodborsttapuit

English	Scientific	German	Dutch
Stork, Black	*Ciconia nigra*	Schwarzstorch	Zwarte ooievaar
Stork, White	*Ciconia ciconia*	Weissstorch	Ooievaar
Storm-petrel, Wilson´s	*Oceanites oceanicus*	Buntfuss-Sturmschwalbe	Wilsons stormvogeltje
Swallow, (Barn)	*Hirundo rustica*	Rauchschwalbe	Boerenzwaluw
Swallow, Red-rumped	*Cecropsis daurica*	Rötelschwalbe	Roodstuitzwaluw
Swift, Alpine	*Tachymarptis melba*	Alpensegler	Alpengierzwaluw
Swift, Common	*Apus apus*	Mauersegler	Gierzwaluw
Swift, Pallid	*Apus pallidus*	Fahlsegler	Vale gierzwaluw
Swift, White-rumped	*Apus caffer*	Kaffernsegler	Kaffergierzwaluw
Teal	*Anas crecca*	Krickente	Wintertaling
Tern, Black	*Chlidonias niger*	Trauerseeschwalbe	Zwarte stern
Tern, Caspian	*Hydroprogne caspia*	Raubseeschwalbe	Reuzenstern
Tern, Common	*Sterna hirundo*	Flussseeschwalbe	Visdief
Tern, Gull-billed	*Gelochelidon nilotica*	Lachseeschwalbe	Lachstern
Tern, Little	*Sterna albifrons*	Zwergseeschwalbe	Dwergstern
Tern, Sandwich	*Thalasseus sandvicensis*	Brandseeschwalbe	Grote stern
Tern, Whiskered	*Chlidonias hybrida*	Weissbart-Seeschwalbe	Witwangstern
Thrush, Blue Rock	*Monticola solitarius*	Blaumerle	Blauwe rotslijster
Thrush, Mistle	*Turdus viscivorus*	Misteldrossel	Grote lijster
Thrush, Song	*Turdus philomelos*	Singdrossel	Zanglijster
Tit, Blue	*Cyanistes caeruleus*	Blaumeise	Pimpelmees
Tit, Coal	*Periparus ater*	Tannenmeise	Zwarte mees
Tit, Crested	*Lophophanes cristatus*	Haubenmeise	Kuifmees
Tit, Great	*Parus major*	Kohlmeise	Koolmees
Tit, Long-tailed	*Aegithalos caudatus*	Schwanzmeise	Staartmees
Tit, Penduline	*Remiz pendulinus*	Beutelmeise	Buidelmees
Treecreeper, Short-toed	*Certhia brachydactyla*	Gartenbaumläufer	Boomkruiper
Turnstone	*Arenaria interpres*	Steinwälzer	Steenloper
Vulture, Black	*Aegypius monachus*	Mönchsgeier	Monniksgier
Vulture, Egyptian	*Neophron percnopterus*	Schmutzgeier	Aasgier
Vulture, Griffon	*Gyps fulvus*	Gänsegeier	Vale gier
Wagtail, (Iberian) Yellow	*Motacilla flava iberiae*	Iberische Schafstelze	Iberische kwikstaart
Wagtail, Grey	*Motacilla cinerea*	Gebirgsstelze	Grote gele kwikstaart
Wagtail, Pied	*Motacilla alba yarrellii*	Trauerbachstelze	Rouwkwikstaart
Wagtail, White	*Motacilla alba*	Bachstelze	Witte kwikstaart
Warbler, Cetti´s	*Cettia cetti*	Seidensänger	Cetti's zanger
Warbler, Dartford	*Sylvia undata*	Provencegrasmücke	Provençaalse grasmus
Warbler, Great Reed	*Acrocephalus arundinaceus*	Drosselrohrsänger	Grote karekiet
Warbler, Melodious	*Hippolais polyglotta*	Orpheusspötter	Orpheusspotvogel
Warbler, Reed	*Acrocephalus scirpaceus*	Teichrohrsänger	Kleine karekiet
Warbler, Sardinian	*Sylvia melanocephala*	Samtkopf-Grasmücke	Kleine zwartkop
Warbler, Savi´s	*Locustella luscinioides*	Rohrschwirl	Snor
Warbler, Spectacled	*Sylvia conspicillata*	Brillengrasmücke	Brilgrasmus
Warbler, Western Bonelli´s	*Phylloscopus bonelli*	Berglaubsänger	Bergfluiter
Warbler, Western Olivaceous	*Iduna opaca*	Isabellspötter	Westelijke vale spotvogel
Warbler, Western Orphean	*Sylvia hortensis*	Orpheusgrasmücke	Westelijke Orpheusgrasmus
Warbler, Western Subalpine	*Sylvia cantillans*	Weissbart-Grasmücke	Westelijke Baardgrasmus
Warbler, Willow	*Phylloscopus trochilus*	Fitis	Fitis
Waxbill, Common	*Estrilda astrild*	Wellenastrild	Sint-Helenafazantje
Weaver, Black-headed	*Ploceus melanocephalus*	Schwarzkopfweber	Zwartkopwever

Wheatear, (Common)	*Oenanthe oenanthe*	Steinschmätzer	Tapuit
Wheatear, Black	*Oenanthe leucura*	Trauersteinschmätzer	Zwarte tapuit
Wheatear, Black-eared	*Oenanthe hispanica*	Mittelmeer-Steinschmätzer	Blonde tapuit
Whimbrel	*Numenius phaeopus*	Regenbrachvogel	Regenwulp
Whinchat	*Saxicola rubetra*	Braunkehlchen	Paapje
Whitethroat	*Sylvia communis*	Dorngrasmücke	Grasmus
Wigeon	*Anas penelope*	Pfeifente	Smient
Woodlark	*Lullula arborea*	Heidelerche	Boomleeuwerik
Woodpecker, Great Spotted	*Dendrocopos major*	Buntspecht	Grote bonte specht
Woodpecker, Iberian Green	*Picus sharpei*	Iberischer Grünspecht	Iberische groene spec
Woodpecker, Lesser Spotted	*Dendrocopos minor*	Kleinspecht	Kleine bonte specht
Wren	*Troglodytes troglodytes*	Zaunkönig	Winterkoning
Wryneck	*Jynx torquilla*	Wendehals	Draaihals

Reptiles and Amphibians

English	Scientific	German	Dutch
Chameleon, European	*Chamaeleo chamaeleon*	Chamäleon	Gewone kameleon
Frog, Common Parsley	*Pelodytes punctatus*	Westlicher Schlammtaucher	Groengestipte kikker
Frog, Common Tree	*Hyla arborea*	Europäischer Laubfrosch	Boomkikker
Frog, Iberian Painted	*Discoglossus galganoi*	Iberischer Scheibenzüngler	Iberische schijftong-kikker
Frog, Iberian Parsley	*Pelodytes ibericus*	Iberischer Schlammtaucher	Iberische groengesti kikker
Frog, Iberian Water	*Pelophylax/Rana perezi*	Iberischer Wasserfrosch	Iberische groene kikk
Frog, Stripeless Tree	*Hyla meridionalis*	Mittelmeer-Laubfrosch	Mediterrane boomki
Gecko, Moorish	*Tarentola mauritanica*	Maurischer Gecko	Muurgekko
Gecko, Mediterranean House	see Turkish Gecko		
Gecko, Turkish	*Hemidactylus turcicus*	Europäischer Halbfinger	Europese tjiktjak
Lizard, Carbonell's Wall	*Podarcis carbonelli*	Carbonell-Mauereidechse	Zuidwest-Iberische muurhagedis
Lizard, Iberian Wall	*Podarcis hispanica*	Spanische Mauereidechse	Spaanse muurhaged
Lizard, Maria's Worm	*Blanus mariae*	Südwestiberische Netzwühle	Zuidwest-Iberische wormhagedis
Lizard, Ocellated	*Timon lepidus*	Perleidechse	Parelhagedis
Lizard, Schreiber's Green	*Lacerta schreiberi*	Iberische Smaragdeidechse	Iberische smaragd-hagedis
Lizard, Spiny-footed	*Acanthodactylus erythrurus*	Europäischer Fransenfinger	Franjeteenhagedis
Newt, Bosca's	*Lissotriton boscai*	Spanischer Wassermolch	Iberische water-salamander
Newt, Iberian Ribbed	*Pleurodeles waltl*	Spanischer Rippenmolch	Ribbensalamander
Newt, Southern Marbled	*Triturus pygmaeus*	Zwergmarmormolch	Dwergmarmer-salamander
Olm	*Proteus anguinus*	Grottenolm	Olm
Psammodromus, Large	*Psammodromus algirus*	Algrischer Sandläufer	Algerijnse zandloper
Psammodromus, Spanish	*Psammodromus hispanicus*	Spanischer Sandläufer	Spaanse zandloper
Salamander, Fire	*Salamandra salamandra*	Feuersalamander	Vuursalamander
Skink, Bedriaga's	*Chalcides bedriagai*	Iberischer Walzenskink	Iberische skink

English	Scientific	German	Dutch
Slider, Red-eared	Trachemys scripta	Rotwangenschildkröte	Roodwangschildpad
Snake, False Smooth	Macroprotodon cucullatus	Kapuzennatter	Mutsslang
Snake, Grass	Natrix natrix	Ringelnatter	Ringslang
Snake, Horseshoe Whip	Coluber hippocrepis	Hufeisennatter	Hoefijzerslang
Snake, Ladder	Elaphe scalaris	Treppennatter	Trapslang
Snake, Montpellier	Malpolon monspessulanus	Eidechsennatter	Hagedisslang
Snake, Southern Smooth	Coronella girondica	Girondische Glattnatter	Girondische gladde slang
Snake, Viperine	Natrix maura	Vipernatter	Adderringslang
Spadefoot, Western	Pelobates cultripes	Messerfuss	Iberische knoflookpad
Terrapin, European Pond	Emys orbicularis	Europäische Sumpfschildkröte	Europese moerasschildpad
Terrapin, Spanish	Mauremys leprosa	Spanische Wasserschildkröte	Moorse beekschildpad
Toad, Common	Bufo bufo	Erdkröte	Gewone pad
Toad, Iberian Midwife	Alytes cisternasii	Iberische Geburtshelferkröte	Iberische vroedmeester-pad
Toad, Natterjack	Bufo/Epidalea calamita	Kreuzkröte	Rugstreeppad
Toad, Spiny	Bufo spinosus	Mittelmeer-Erdkröte	Westelijke gewone pad
Turtle, Leatherback	Dermochelys coriacea	Lederschildkröte	Lederschildpad
Turtle, Loggerhead	Caretta caretta	Unechte Karettschildkröte	Dikkopschildpad
Viper, Lataste´s	Vipera latasti	Stülpnasenotter	Wipneusadder

Invertebrates

English	Scientific	German	Dutch
Blue, Adonis	Polyommatus bellargus	Himmelblauer Bläuling	Adonisblauwtje
Blue, African Grass	Zizeeria knysna	Amethist- Bläuling*	Amethistblauwtje
Blue, Baton	Pseudophilotes baton	Graublauer Bläuling	Klein tijmblauwtje
Blue, Black-eyed	Glaucopsyche melanops	Schwarz-Auge Blauling*	Spaans bloemenblauwtje
Blue, False Baton	Pseudophilotes abencerragus	Morischer Quendel-Bläuling	Moors tijmblauwtje
Blue, Lang's Short-tailed	Leptotes pirithous	Kleiner Wander-Bläuling	Klein tijgerblauwtje
Blue, Little	Cupido minimus	Zwerg-Bläuling	Dwergblauwtje
Blue, Lorquin's	Cupido lorquinii	Morischer Zwerg-Bläuling	Moors dwergblauwtje
Blue, Panoptes	Pseudophilotes panoptes	Panoptes-Bläuling	Spaans tijmblauwtje
Blue, Short-tailed	Cupido argiades	Kurzschwänziger Bläuling	Staartblauwtje
Blue-eye	Erythromma lindenii	Pokaljungfer	Kanaaljuffer
Bluet, Common	Enallagma cyathigerum	Gemeine Becherjungfer	Watersnuffel
Bluetail, Iberian	Ischnura graellsii	Spanische Pechlibelle	Iberische grasjuffer
Bronze, Geranium	Cacyreus marshalli	Pelargonien-Bläuling	Geraniumblauwtje
Cascader, Ringed	Zygonyx torridus	Wasserfall-Kreuzer	Watervallibel
Centipede, Megarian Banded	Scolopendra cingulata	Riesenläufer/ Gürtelskolopender	Scolopendra*
Chaser, Broad-bodied	Libellula depressa	Plattbauch	Platbuik
Chaser, Four-spotted	Libellula quadrimaculata	Vierfleck	Viervlek
Clam, Palourde	Ruditapes decussatus	Grosse Teppichmuschel	Geruite tapijtschelp
Cleopatra	Gonepteryx cleopatra	Mittelmeer-Zitronenfalter	Cleopatra
Clubtail, Pronged	Gomphus graslinii	Französische Keiljungfer	Gevorkte rombout
Clubtail, Western	Gomphus pulchellus	Westliche Keiljungfer	Plasrombout

Crab, Fiddler	*Uca tangeri*	Westafrikanische Winkerkrabbe	West-Afrikaanse wenkkrab
Cruiser, Splendid	*Macromia splendens*	Europäischer Flussherrscher	Prachtlibel
Damselfly, Small Red	*Ceriagrion tenellum*	Scharlachlibelle	Koraaljuffer
Darter, Red-veined	*Sympetrum fonscolombii*	Frühe Heidelibelle	Zwervende heidelibel
Demoiselle, Copper	*Calopteryx haemorrhoidalis*	Bronzene Prachtlibelle	Koperen beekjuffer
Demoiselle, Western	*Calopteryx xanthostoma*	Südwestliche Prachtlibelle	Iberische beekjuffer
Dropwing, Violet	*Trithemis annulata*	Violetter Sonnenzeiger	Purperlibel
Emerald, Orange-spotted	*Oxygastra curtisii*	Gekielte Smaragdlibelle	Bronslibel
Emperor, Blue	*Anax imperator*	Grosse Königslibelle	Grote keizerlibel
Emperor, Lesser	*Anax parthenope*	Kleine Königslibelle	Zuidelijke keizerlibel
Emperor, Vagrant	*Anax ephippiger*	Schabrackenlibelle	Zadellibel
Featherleg, Orange	*Platycnemis acutipennis*	Orangerote Federlibelle	Oranje breedscheenju...
Featherleg, White	*Platycnemis latipes*	Weisse Federlibelle	Witte breedscheenjuf
Festoon, Spanish	*Zerinthia rumina*	Spanischer Osterluzeifalter	Spaanse pijpbloem-vlinder
Fritillary, Aetherie	*Melitaea aetherie*	Aetherie-Scheckenfalter	Moorse parelmoer-vlinder
Fritillary, High Brown	*Argynnis adippe*	Feuriger Perlmutterfalter	Bosrandparelmoer-vlinder
Fritillary, Knapweed	*Melitaea phoebe*	Flockenblumen-Scheckenfalter	Knoopkruidparelmoe vlinder
Fritillary, Marsh	*Euphydryas aurinia*	Skabiosen-Scheckenfalter	Moerasparelmoervlir
Fritillary, Provencal	*Melitaea deione*	Leinkraut-Scheckenfalter	Spaanse parelmoer-vlinder
Fritillary, Spanish	*Euphydryas desfontainii*	Spanische Scheckenfalter	Mozaïekparelmoer-vlinder
Fritillary, Spotted	*Melitaea didyma*	Roter Scheckenfalter	Tweekleurige parelmoervlinder
Gatekeeper, Spanish	*Pyronia bathseba*	Spanischer Ochsenauge	Spaans oranje zando...
Goldenring, Common	*Cordulegaster boltonii*	Zweigestreifte Quelljungfer	Gewone bronlibel
Grayling, Striped	*Pseudotergumia fidia*	Streifen-Samtfalter*	Gestreepte heivlinder
Grayling, Tree	*Hipparchia statilinus*	Eisenfarbiger Samtfalter	Kleine heivlinder
Groundling, Northern Banded	*Brachythemis impartita*	Treuer Kurzpfeil	Noordelijke bandgrondlibel
Hairstreak, Blue-spot	*Satyrium spini*	Kreuzdorn-Zipfelfalter	Wegedoornpage
Hairstreak, Chapman's Green	*Callophrys avis*	Erdbeerbaum Zipfelfalter*	Aardbeiboomgroentj...
Hairstreak, False Ilex	*Satyrium esculi*	Südlicher Eichen-Zipfelfalter	Spaanse eikenpage
Hairstreak, Ilex	*Satyrium ilicis*	Brauner Eichen-Zipfelfalter	Bruine eikenpage
Hairstreak, Provencial	*Tomares ballus*	Ballusbläuling	Groene klaverpage
Heath, Small	*Coenonympha pamphilus*	Kleines Wiesenvögelchen	Hooibeestje
Hooktail, Green	*Paragomphus genei*	Afrikanische Sandjungfer	Groene haaklibel
Monarch	*Danaus plexippus*	Monarchfalter	Monarchvlinder
Orangetip, Moroccan	*Anthocharis belia*	Marokkanischer Aurorafalter	Geel oranjetipje

English	Scientific	German	Dutch
Oyster, Portuguese	Crassostrea angulata	Portugiesische Auster	Portugese oester
Pasha, Two-tailed	Charaxes jasius	Erdbeerbaumfalter	Aardbeiboomvlinder
Pennant, Black	Selysiothemis nigra	Teufelchen	Zwarte korenbout
Percher, Black	Diplacodes lefebvrii	Glänzender Schwarzpfeil	Moriaantje
Pincertail, Large	Onychogomphus uncatus	Grosse Zangenlibelle	Grote tanglibel
Pincertail, Small	Onychogomphus forcipatus	Kleine Zangenlibelle	Kleine tanglibel
Scarlet, Broad	Crocothemis erythraea	Feuerlibelle	Vuurlibel
Skimmer, Epaulet	Orthetrum chrysostigma	Rahmstreif-Blaupfeil	Epauletoeverlibel
Skimmer, Keeled	Orthetrum coerulescens	Kleiner Blaupfeil	Beekoeverlibel
Skimmer, Long	Orthetrum trinacria	Langer Blaupfeil	Lange oeverlibel
Skimmer, Yellow-veined	Orthetrum nitidinerve	Gelbader-Blaupfeil	Geeladeroeverlibel
Skipper, False Mallow	Carcharodus tripolinus	Südlicher Malven-Dickkopffalter*	Moors kaasjeskruid-dikkopje
Skipper, Mediterranean	Gegenes nostrodamus	Grosser Mittelmeer Dickkopffalter	Groot kustdikkopje
Skipper, Red-underwing	Spialia sertorius	Roter Würfel-Dickkopffalter	Kalkgraslanddikkopje
Skipper, Sage	Muschampia proto	Brandkraut-Dickkopffalter*	Klein brandkruid-dikkopje
Spectre, Western	Boyeria irene	Westliche Geisterlibelle	Schemerlibel
Spreadwing, Dark	Lestes macrostigma	Dunkle Binsenjungfer	Grote pantserjuffer
Spreadwing, Western Willow	Chalcolestes viridis	Gemeine Weidenjungfer	Houtpantserjuffer
Swallowtail	Papilio machaon	Schwalbenschwanz	Koninginnenpage
Swallowtail, Iberian Scarce	Iphiclides feisthamelii	Iberischer Segelfalter	Spaanse koningspage
Tortoiseshell, Large	Nymphalis polychloros	Grosser Fuchs	Grote vos
White, Green-striped	Euchloe belemia	Grüngestreifter Weissling	Gestreept marmerwitje
White, Iberian Marbled	Melanargia lachesis	Iberisches Schachbrett	Spaans dambordje
White, Portuguese Dappled	Euchloe tagis	Portugiesischer Gesprenkelter Weissling*	Klein marmerwitje
White, Spanish Marbled	Melanargia ines	Spanisches Schachbrett	Moors dambordje
White, Western Dappled	Euchloe crameri	Westlicher Gesprenkelter Weissling	Westelijk marmerwitje
White, Western Marbled	Melanargia occitanica	Westliches Schachbrett	Westelijk dambordje

Fish

English	Scientific	German	Dutch
Spanish minnowcarp	Anaecypris hispanica	Jarabugo*	Jarabugo*

CROSSBILL GUIDES
IF YOU WANT TO SEE MORE

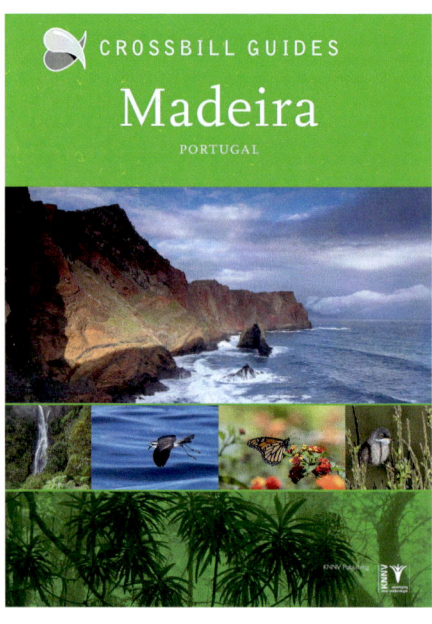

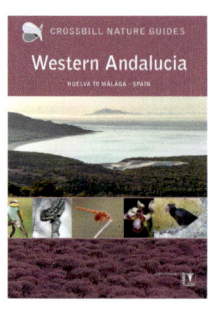

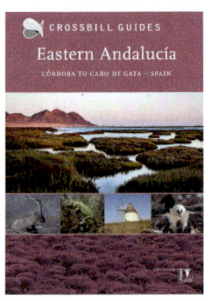

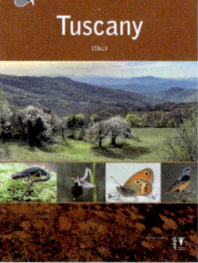

More titles are in preparation. Check our website for further details and updates.
WWW.CROSSBILLGUIDES.ORG